The
Postal Service
Guide to
U.S. Stamps

15TH EDITION

FULL COLOR

1989
STAMP VALUES

UNITED STATES
POSTAL SERVICE

United States Postal Service
Washington, D.C. 20260-6755
Item No. 0863

Explanation of Catalog Prices

The United States Postal Service sells only the commemoratives released during the past few years and current regular and special stamps and postal stationery.

Prices listed in this book are called "catalog prices" by stamp collectors. Collectors use catalog prices as guidelines when they are buying or trading stamps. It is important to remember the prices are simply guidelines to the stamp values. Stamp condition (see pp 12-13) is very important in determining the actual value of a stamp.

The catalog prices are given for unused (mint) stamps and used (cancelled) stamps, which have been hinged and are in Fine condition. Stamps in Superb condition that have never been hinged may cost more than the listed price. Stamps in less than Fine condition may cost less.

The prices for used stamps are based on a light cancellation; a heavy cancellation lessens a stamp's value. Cancelled stamps may be worth more than uncancelled stamps. This happens if the cancellation is of a special type or for a significant date. Therefore, it is important to study an envelope before removing a stamp and discarding its "cover."

Listed prices are estimates of how much you can expect to pay for a stamp from a dealer. If you sell the same stamp to a dealer, he may offer you much less than the catalog price. Dealers pay based on their interest in owning that stamp. If they already have a full supply, they will only buy more at a low price.

Prices in regular type for single unused and used stamps are taken from the *Scott 1989 Standard Postage Stamp Catalogue, Volume 1* © 1988, whose editors have based these values on the current stamp market. Prices quoted for unused and used stamps are for "Fine" condition, except where Fine is not available. If no value is assigned, market value is individually determined by condition of the stamp, scarcity and other factors.

Prices for Plate Blocks and First Day Covers are taken from *Scott's Specialized Catalogue of U.S. Stamps,* 1988 Edition, © 1987. The Scott numbering system for stamps is used in this book.

Prices for Souvenir Cards are taken from *Brookman Price Guide of U.S. First Day Covers, Souvenir Cards, USPS Panels and Pages,* published by Brookman Stamp Company. Prices for American Commemorative Panels are from The American Society of Philatelic Pages and Panels, an organization specializing in Commemorative Panels. Prices for Souvenir Pages are from Charles D. Simmons of Buena Park, California.

Table of Contents

Peer Into the Timeless Windows of a Great Nation's Soul

Each Commemorative Mint Set contains:
- All the U.S. commemorative stamps issued in a given year
- A beautifully illustrated folder
- Clear acetate mounts to protect, preserve and display stamps

Capture the spirit of America's past and present with Commemorative Mint Sets! The USPS issues stamps honoring historically important people, places, events and ideals. These commemorative stamps are assembled annually in mint sets that are popular with stamp collectors and the general public alike.

The Stories Behind the Stamps

Commemorative Mint Sets serve as educational tools, too. They provide informative details about each stamp and stamp subject as well as interesting biographical background on the designer.

Stamp collectors have known the pleasure of philately for years, and new enthusiasts are joining them regularly. Whether you are a veteran or a newcomer, the ongoing series of Commemorative Mint Sets will add to your collecting enjoyment. They are available at postal facilities that normally sell philatelic products.

1987 Commemorative Mint Set — Consists of all 41 commemorative issues from last year, including: colorful Christmas and Love stamps; a booklet pane of 10 Special Occasions stamps, Drafting of the Constitution and Locomotive booklet panes; and a randomly selected single stamp from the beautiful North American Wildlife pane of 50 commemoratives. ($12.95)

1988 Commemorative Mint Set — Contains all the new commemorative and special issues, including the Cats Quartet, Winter and Summer Olympics, Australia Bicentennial, Antarctic Explorers, Knute Rockne, New Sweden, 8 Statehood Bicentennial stamps, Classic Cars and Carousel Animals. ($14.50)

Once Upon a Time…

"Little Red Riding Hood," "The Sleeping Beauty," "Hansel and Gretel," "Old King Cole," "Little Miss Muffet": Fairy tales, legends and nursery rhymes were the first stories to make us cry and laugh as we sat on the edge of our parents' laps. Then we read about the adventures of Dick, Jane and Spot in school. Today we continue to excite our senses with mysterious movies, dramatic television programs, romantic novels and science-fiction stories. From Mother Goose and Dr. Seuss to Mark Twain and Stephen King, a good story is something we can all appreciate.

Postage stamps tell stories, too. "There is more behind stamps than just glue," emphasizes Gordon Morison, Assistant Postmaster General. "There are stories of high adventure and matchless courage, of war and hardship and political high drama." Yes, there is indeed more to a stamp than a picture—there is history.

Each one tells a true story, from famous individuals to important events, of interest to many people of all ages. In the United States alone there are more than 19 million stamp collectors.

While stamps are printed to move the mail, their stories detailing the American experience endure long after a letter is delivered. From early European explorers in the New World to men landing on the moon, the stories behind stamps have intrigued people for nearly 150 years. Because mail with U.S. stamps on it is delivered all over the world, people around the globe learn about celebrated Americans as well as historic and current events and contemporary social issues in the United States.

The first formal stamps appeared in England in May of 1840. America's first adhesive

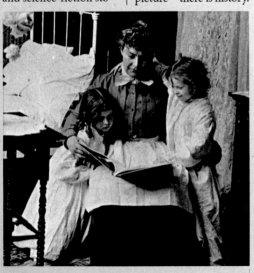

stamp was issued a year and a half later by City Despatch Post, a private carrier service in New York City run by Alexander Greig. Although valid only in New York, the delivery service was so successful that it was bought by the U.S. Post Office in six months. The first two *official* U.S. postage stamps, featuring Benjamin Franklin and George Washington, date back to July 1, 1847. Before long, these small, pictorial squares had become the world's window on America.

What Is Philately?

Collecting stamps is easier than pronouncing the technical word that describes it. **Philately** (fi-lat-el-lee) is the collecting and study of postage stamps and other postal materials. The name is derived from the Greek words *philos,* which means "loving," and *atelos,* which means "free of tax." In their most basic form, stamps are signs that the postal fees, or taxes, have been prepaid.

Stamp collectors are called **philatelists**. The key to enjoying philately is to save what you like best. **General collecting**—saving as many stamps as possible—is a good way to start. Many new collectors find it interesting to have a wide range of stamps. They are similar to beginning readers who want to experience all kinds of stories. To help build your stamp collection, check your mailbox daily for letters, postcards and packages with used stamps on them. Have your family and friends save envelopes they receive in the mail. And ask people who write you to use interesting stamps.

Longtime collectors often will help new philatelists by giving them some duplicates (extra stamps). Neighborhood businesses that get a lot of mail—banks, stores, travel agencies, utility companies—may be sources of stamps for you as well.

Topical collecting is another popular way to collect stamps because it lets people tailor their collections to their own interests. Simply choose one or two specific themes that really interest you—art and culture, science and technology, architecture, sports and transportation are just a few of the possibilities. If, for example, you love animals, there is a host of stamps issued within the past five years that can get your topical collection off to a great start. You could begin with the pane of 50 North American Wildlife stamps issued in 1987, then add blocks of four of horses (1985), dogs (1984) and cats (1988).

Whatever stamps you choose to collect, there are additional sources where you can obtain

INTRODUCTION TO COLLECTING STAMPS

Definitive

Commemorati[ve]

Special

Airmail

Booklet

Coil

them. Some stamp clubs meet at schools, YMCAs and community centers. If you are fortunate enough to have one of these institutions in your area, it may be a great place for stamps and philatelic advice. If you do not know of a stamp club in your area, the people at Linn's Club Center can help you locate clubs near your ZIP Code. Just write to them:

Linn's Club Center
P. O. Box 29
Sidney, OH 45365-0029

For information on the popular Benjamin Franklin Stamp Club program for children, read the accompanying article that begins on page 18.

Another good source for stamps is the classified ads in philatelic newspapers and magazines available at your library. (See page 25 for a listing of philatelic publications willing to send you a free copy.) After reviewing these periodicals, you may wish to subscribe.

Stamps are classified into several major categories according to their intended use:

• **Definitive** stamps are found on most mail in denominations ranging from 1¢ to $5. Their subjects traditionally are portraits of former presidents, statesmen, other prominent persons and national shrines. Printed in unlimited quantities for specific postal rates, definitives are available for several years.

• **Commemorative** stamps honor important people, events or special subjects of national appeal and significance. They usually are larger and more colorful than definitives. Printed in limited quantities, commemoratives are available only for two to three months at most post offices and for about one year by mail order from the Postal Service's Philatelic Sales Division.

• **Special** stamps include

issues that supplement the regular stamps, such as Christmas and Love stamps.

- **Airmail** stamps are used for sending mail overseas.
- **Booklet** stamps are issued in cardboard folders containing one or more panes of 3-20 stamps each. Each stamp will have one, two or three straight edges.
- **Coil** stamps are issued in rolls. Each one has two straight and two perforated edges.

Storing Your Valuables

Your stamps are just that—*your* stamps. You can do whatever you want with them. You can save entire envelopes and store them anywhere, from shoe boxes to special albums. Or you can try to peel the stamps off the envelopes. However, the proper way to remove stamps from envelopes is to soak them.

Stamps are delicate little pieces of paper, so be careful. Tear or cut off the upper righthand corner of the envelope, or **cover**. Place the stamp face down in a small pan of warm water. After a few minutes, the stamp will float off the paper and sink to the bottom. Allow a few more minutes for any remaining gum to dislodge from the stamp, then lift it out using **tongs**—a metal grasping device with flat ends, similar to tweezers—if you have a pair. (Although many collectors touch stamps with their fingers, it is better to handle them with tongs. Even if your hands are clean, oil from your skin can damage stamps.)

To keep a stamp from curling while it dries, put it between two paper towels and apply pressure with a heavy object, such as a book. Leave the stamp there

overnight, and it will be flat the next day. Stamps with new, "invisible" gum are trickier to dry because they tend to retain gum after soaking and stick fast to paper when drying. Dry these stamps face down with nothing touching the back side, and flatten them later if they curl. To learn more about soaking stamps, look for a detailed handbook on stamp collecting at your local library.

Just as you may store your favorite books or videotapes on a shelf so they do not get damaged or lost, you will want to protect your stamps. As they accumulate, it is a good idea to put them in some kind of order. You can attach your stamps to loose-leaf paper organized in a simple three-ring binder. Or, arrange them in a more formal album available in stores.

Some stamp albums feature specific catego-

ries with pictures of the stamps that are supposed to appear on each page. It is usually best to select an album with loose-leaf pages so you can add pages easily as your collection grows. A **stock book** is an album with plastic or paper pockets on each page; there are no pictures of stamps, so you can organize it *your* way.

It is best to use a small strip of thin plastic, gummed on one side, to put stamps in your album. Called a **hinge**, this strip is available either folded or unfolded. If you use a folded hinge, lightly moisten the short end and press it to the back of the stamp with the fold about ⅛″ from the top. Then hold the stamp (with your tongs) and lightly moisten the long end of the hinge. Place the stamp where you want it in the album and secure it by pressing down. Using your tongs, gently lift the stamp's corners to make sure none have stuck to the page. By using a hinge—instead of tape or glue—you can peel the stamp from the page, if you wish, without damaging it.

Collectors may use mounts instead of hinges to prevent air and dirt from damaging their stamps and to keep excess moisture from disturbing gum. A **mount** is a small, clear (usually plastic) sleeve into which an entire stamp is inserted. Mounts are more expensive than hinges, but

many collectors believe the extra protection is well worth the price. With your first "story" in place, you will be ready to add more to your storybook of stamps.

With used stamps and a few inexpensive accessories, such as a small album and a package of hinges, even collectors with a limited budget can have a great time. Remember to mention stamps, stamp albums and hinges to your friends and relatives before Christmas and your birthday!

Tools of the Trade

In addition to the tongs, hinges and mounts previously described, other equipment that can aid stamp collectors includes:

Glassine (glass-ene) **envelopes** are used to store and keep stamps that you have yet to add to your album. Glassine is a special thin paper that keeps grease and air from damaging stamps.

A **stamp catalog** is a handy reference with many illustrations that can help identify stamps; it also provides information such as values for used and unused stamps.

A **magnifying glass** helps examine stamps.

A **perforation gauge** measures the jagged cuts or little holes, called *perforations*, along the edges of stamps. Size and number of perforations are sometimes needed to identify stamps. "Perfs" make stamps easy to tear apart.

A **watermark tray** and **watermark fluid** are used to make more visible the designs or patterns (called *watermarks*) that are pressed into some stamp paper during its manufacture.

Stamp Condition

Like an old book, the value of a stamp depends largely on two factors: how rare it is and what condition it is in. You can get an idea of how rare a stamp is by the price listed for it in a catalog. Depending on its condition, however, a stamp may sell for more or less than the catalog price. A very rare stamp may be quite expensive even though it is in poor condition. At first, you'll probably be collecting stamps that are not very expensive, but you still should try to get them in the best condition you can find. Here are some things to look for when judging stamp condition:

Examine the front of the stamp. Are the colors bright or faded? Is the stamp dirty, stained or clean? Is the stamp torn? Torn stamps are not considered "collecti-ble." Is the design in the center of the paper, or is it a little crooked or

Light Cancel-Very Fine

Medium Cancel-Fine

Heavy Cancel

Superb

Very Fine

Fine

Good

off to the side? Are the edges in good condition, or are some of the perforations missing? A stamp with a light cancellation mark is in better condition than one with heavy marks across it. Now look at the back of the stamp. Is there a thin spot in the paper? It may have been caused by careless removal from an envelope or a hinge.

Stamp dealers put stamps into categories according to their condition. Look at the examples to see the differences in these categories. A stamp listed as **mint** is in the same condition as when purchased from the post office. An **unused** stamp has not been canceled but may not have any gum on it. Stamps in mint condition usually are more valuable than unused or used stamps.

Catalog prices listed in *The Postal Service Guide to U.S. Stamps* are for used and unused stamps in Fine condition that have been hinged. A stamp that has not been hinged and has excellent centering and color may cost more; a stamp in less than Fine condition that has been heavily canceled may be worth less than the catalog listing.

How Stories Become Stamps

In addition to being powerful devices for education and communication, stamps and their stories often function as a public service, stimulating people to take worthwhile action. Similar to other mass mediums, such as television, radio, magazines and newspapers, postage stamps bring important messages to a large audience.

One collector wrote to *Linn's Stamp News* in April 1987 with an idea for a 1992 stamp issuance commemorating the 500th anniversary of Christopher Columbus' discovery of America. In addition to honoring the nations founded in the discovered territory, the stamps could help develop "international goodwill…," the collector suggested. But who decides whether this seemingly noteworthy story will be told by stamps?

Like the idea described above, almost all subjects are suggested by the general public. The USPS's Citizens' Stamp Advisory Committee receives hundreds of suggestions every week, but just a few can be recommended because of the limited number of stamps issued each year. Established more than 30 years ago, the Committee meets six times a year. It consists of historians, artists, businesspeople, philatelists and others interested in American

history and culture. Keeping all postal customers in mind, they use a set of eligibility guidelines to aid in their difficult task. Once a recommended subject receives the "stamp of approval," a Committee design coordinator assists in selecting a professional artist to design the stamp. The Committee reviews preliminary artwork and may request changes before a final version is approved.

If you think a story should be told on a stamp, submit your idea at least 36 months before its logical date of issue. Send suggestions, along with helpful background information, to:

United States Postal Service
Citizens' Stamp
Advisory Committee
Room 5670
475 L'Enfant Plaza West, SW
Washington, D C
20260-6753

It is recommended that artwork not be submitted; unsolicited artwork is seldom used because stamp designing is an exacting task requiring extraordinary skill.

Other Postal Collectibles

Stories come in many forms—novels, short stories, poems, movies— and so do stamps. In addition to their regular form, stamp designs are printed or embossed (made with a raised design) directly on envelopes, postal cards and aerogrammes. Available at post offices, these **postal stationery** products are particularly popular among more serious collectors.

Stamped envelopes are made in several sizes and styles, including the window type. First issued in 1853, more than 600 million stamped envelopes now are printed every year.

Postal cards are made of a heavier paper

than envelopes. Plain 1835 and simple, one-color postal cards were first issued in 1873, and the first U.S. multicolored commemorative postal card came out in 1956. Several different postal cards are usually issued during a year and approximately 800 million are printed annually.

An **aerogramme** (air letter) is a flat sheet of paper that is a letter and an envelope all in one. It is specially stamped, marked for folding and already gummed. Meant for foreign airmail only, an aerogramme will carry your message anywhere in the world at a lower postage rate than regular airmail.

There are other philatelic items to collect, too, including:

Blocks of Four, used or unused, unseparated stamps that have two stamps above and two below.

Plate Blocks, which

rk Twain · 1910 · Halley's Comet · 1985

© USPS 1985

USA 36

me in with Halley's Comet
. It is coming again next
and I expect to go out with
it. It will be
the greatest dis-
appointment of
my life if I don't
go out with Hal-
ley's Comet. **99**

AEROGRAMME · VIA AIRMAIL · PAR AVION

② Second fold

③ Seal top flap last

Seal top flap last

25 USA

itted

America the Beautiful USA 15

USA 22
Abyssinian Cat, Himalayan Cat

USA 22
American Shorthair Cat, Persian Cat

USA 2
Siamese Cat, Exotic

Mai

Booklet Panes are panes with three or more of the same stamps. One or more panes of stamps are affixed inside a thin cardboard cover to form a booklet. Booklet pane collectors usually save entire panes.

First Day Covers (FDCs) are envelopes with new stamps on them that have been postmarked on the first day of sale at a city designated by the USPS.

Souvenir Cards are issued as keepsakes of stamp exhibitions. Although they cannot be used for postage, some souvenir cards are available canceled. Of special interest is the annual souvenir card for National Stamp Collecting Month each October that was first issued in 1981.

usually are four stamps from a corner of a pane with the printing plate number in the margin, or **selvage**, of the pane. The USPS began a new plate numbering system in 1981. Each color plate used first in stamp production is represented by a number 1 in the group of numbers in the margin. When a plate wears out and is replaced, a number 2 takes the place of the 1. The color of the number is the same as the color of the plate it represents.

Copyright Blocks, which feature the copyright symbol © followed by "United States Postal Service" or "USPS" and the year in the margin of each pane of stamps. The USPS began copyrighting new stamp designs in 1978.

A 111

Ordering First Day Covers

For each new postal stamp or stationery issue, the USPS selects one town or city related to the stamp's story as the site of the "first day" dedication ceremony. First day covers (FDCs) are envelopes with new stamps canceled with the "FIRST DAY OF ISSUE" date and city.

The quickest way to receive a first day cover is to buy the stamp yourself (new stamps usually go on sale the day after the first day of issue), attach it to your own cover and send it to the first day post office for cancellation. You may submit up to 50 envelopes per order. Write your address in the lower righthand corner of each first day envelope, at least ⅝" from the bottom; use a peel-off label if you prefer. Leave plenty of room for the stamp(s) and the cancellation. Fill each envelope with cardboard about the thickness of a postal card. You can tuck in the flap or seal it.

Put your first day envelope(s) inside another, larger envelope and mail it to "Customer-Affixed Envelopes" in care of the postmaster of the first day city. Your envelope(s) will be canceled and returned. First day envelopes may be mailed up to 30 days after the stamp's issue date.

Or, you can send an envelope addressed to yourself, but without a stamp attached. Put the self-addressed envelope(s) into another, larger envelope. Address this outside envelope to the name of the stamp, in care of the postmaster of the first day city. Send a check, bank draft or U.S. Postal money order (made out to the United States Postal Service) to pay for the stamp(s) that are to be put on your envelope(s). Do not send cash.

If a new stamp has a denomination less than the First-Class rate, add postage or payment to bring each first day envelope up to the First-Class rate. Do not send requests more than 60 days prior to the issue date. If you receive a damaged first day cover, return it to the first day city postmaster for a replacement.

Many stamp collectors also enjoy the variety of postmarks available. Some collect cancellations from every city or town in their respective counties or even states. Remember, a stamp collection is whatever you, personally, want to make it.

A Greeting to First-Time Collectors

Whatever your age, the USPS welcomes you to the fascinating world of stamps. We hope this introduction has provided you with the basics to get under way. You are about to write your own chapter in the history of American philately, and we're sure your experience will be unique, enjoyable and long-lasting. Stamp collecting is the most popular hobby in the world, and you are just beginning to realize the universal moral of its story: Nearly one in ten Americans collects stamps for one primary reason—for the fun of it!

For Young Beginners: Benjamin Franklin Stamp Clubs

The clubs' namesake, Benjamin Franklin, appeared on one of the first U.S. stamps ever issued, in July of 1847.

People of all ages can learn from stamps and the stories they tell. Statistics show, however, that most of America's 19 million stamp collectors were introduced to stamps before they were 16 years old, with the vast majority exposed to stamps before age 12. And where better for children to learn from stamps—and **about** stamps—than in school?

The United States Postal Service (USPS) currently supports some 30,000 Benjamin Franklin Stamp Clubs (BFSCs) in public and private elementary schools and libraries throughout the nation. And the number is growing!

Named after our first Postmaster General and leader in organizing the U.S. postal system, the Benjamin Franklin Stamp Club Program was established in 1974 to create an awareness of stamps and to demonstrate their educational and entertaining benefits to students in the fourth through seventh grades. Stamp collecting is an enjoyable experience that teaches important skills applicable to everyday life (for example, organization, appreciation of valuable objects, the value of money and how to manage money).

American educators agree that studying stamps is a great way to learn. Stamps have been used as teaching tools in

Stamps always draw a fascinated crowd at sessions of Cushing School's Ben Franklin Stamp Clubs.

schools for more than 100 years. In the February 1987 edition of its monthly newsletter, *Communicator*, the National Association of Elementary School Principals called stamp collecting "...a unique teaching tool.." The BFSC program, in its first 14 years of existence, has introduced more than seven million students and teachers to the fascination and pleasures of the hobby of philately.

BFSC Activities

A large number of students at the Cushing Elementary School in Scituate, Massachusetts certainly have learned many of the joys of stamp collecting through their participation in the BFSC Program. But it will take something spectacular to rival the excitement the youngsters experienced in May when they participated in a one-hour cable television broadcast of one of their club meetings.

The local Scituate cable company thought the activities of the Cushing Ben Franklin Stamp Clubs would be of community interest; so, it filmed a special meeting in which teachers and Postal Service coordinators announced the winners of the "Design a Stamp and Write a Letter" contest and the "Why I Like Stamp Collecting" essay contest. All winners were presented awards, and they read and displayed their entries on the air. Other activities featured on the TV program included students writing letters to friends and relatives, a game in which students identified places and events on stamps, and a Show-and-Tell session in which students explained how they are building their own stamp collections. The program was scheduled to be shown to the Scituate community

"I like stamp collecting because it is fun... and because stamps are very pretty."
— Annely Richardson
Cushing School
Scituate, MA

(a suburb of Boston) and made available to other elementary schools throughout southeastern Massachusetts.

The Cushing BFSC Program was started three years ago by Mrs. Joan Sheehan because she felt it would be an excellent teaching aid for such subjects as mathematics, English, reading, social studies, geography and science. Inspired by the success

Students listen to an essay on "Why I Like Stamp Collecting" during a televised BFSC meeting at Cushing School in Scituate, MA.

of that first club and the support material provided by the Postal Service, other teachers enrolled their classes, and Cushing Elementary now boasts the largest active program in the area.

The school's teachers, along with area Postal Service BFSC coordinators, have developed a vigorous schedule for the clubs. The students eagerly participate in numerous activities, including listening to guest speakers who teach them the Hows and Whys of stamp collecting.

The Postal Service BFSC materials enable the teachers to use stamps as educational aids. These materials are provided as a public service to all teachers and students. At the beginning of each school year, the Cushing School Clubs receive a Ben Franklin Organization Kit and copies of *Introduction to Stamp Collecting*, a reprint of selected sections of *The Postal Service Guide to U.S. Stamps*. Two BFSC newsletters, *Stamp fun* (for club members) and *Leader feature* (for teachers), are sent five times during the school year; they suggest activities, such as games, puzzles and class projects. In addition to the newsletters, there are films (on a loan basis from the Postal Service) and stamp activity guides available to club members and leaders.

Starting a BFSC

Teachers or administrators interested in starting clubs can call their local postmaster or, for more information on the BFSC Program, write to:

U.S. Postal Service
Ben Franklin
Stamp Club Program
Washington, DC
20260-6755

The Cushing School clubs are examples of how Ben Franklin Stamp Clubs can be fun and educational. Committed, enthusiastic teachers and an interested student body are big first steps in getting started. More than 900,000 BFSC members across the nation now share in the excitement of learning from stamps and their stories, and many of them will continue to enjoy stamps as they mature—because philately is the hobby of a lifetime!

The Ultimate
In Collecting Convenience

The U.S. Postal Service has established a Standing Order Service that automatically ships new stamps, stationery and philatelic products on a quarterly basis. It is the most convenient method for reserving the items you want in the format you prefer. In effect, you order once and *never* miss future issues of your favorite single, booklet or coil stamps; plate number blocks or strips; full panes; postal stationery and/or other products.

Subscribers receive mint-condition postal items of exceptional quality — the best of centering, color and image registration. If you are not completely satisfied, simply return the item within 30 days for a full refund or replacement.

All products are sold strictly at face value — there are no markups, extra fees or shipping and handling charges. All you need to do is make an advance deposit. You will be notified when further deposits are required. For additional details, send in the postage-paid request card following page 312 or write to:

USPS Guide
Standing Order Service
Philatelic Sales Division
United States Postal Service
Washington, D.C. 20265-9974

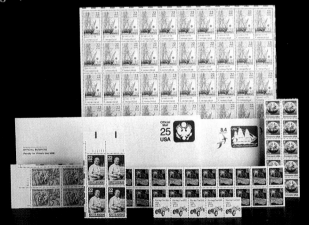

Stamp Collecting Words and Phrases

Accessories The tools used by stamp collectors, such as tongs, hinges, etc.

Adhesive A gummed stamp made to be attached to mail.

Aerophilately Branch of collecting airmail stamps and covers and their usage.

Album A book designed to hold stamps and covers.

Approvals Stamps sent by a dealer to a collector for examination. Approvals must either be bought or returned to the dealer within a specified time.

Auction A sale at which philatelic material is sold to the highest bidder.

Block An unseparated group of stamps, at least two stamps high and two stamps wide.

Booklet Pane A small sheet of stamps specially cut to be sold in booklets.

Bourse A marketplace, such as a stamp exhibition, where stamps are bought, sold or exchanged.

Cachet (ka-shay') A design on an envelope describing an event. Cachets appear on first day of issue, first flight and stamp exhibition covers, etc.

Cancellation A mark placed on a stamp by a postal authority to show that it has been used.

Centering The position of the design on a postage stamp. On perfectly centered stamps the design is exactly in the middle.

Coils Stamps issued in rolls (one stamp wide) for use in dispensers or vending machines.

Commemoratives Stamps that honor anniversaries, important people or special events.

Condition The state of a stamp in regard to such details as centering, color and gum.

Cover An envelope that has been sent through the mail.

Definitives Regular issues of postage stamps, usually sold over long periods of time.

Deltiology Postcard collecting.

Denomination The postage value appearing on a stamp, such as 5 cents.

Duplicates Extra copies of stamps that can be sold or traded. Duplicates should be examined carefully for color and perforation variations.

Error A stamp with something incorrect in its design or manufacture.

Face Value The monetary value or denomination of a stamp.

First Day Cover (FDC) An envelope with a new stamp and cancellation showing the date the stamp was issued.

Gum The coating of glue on the back of an unused stamp.

Hinges Small strips of gummed material used by collectors to affix stamps to album pages.

Imperforate Indicates stamps without perforations or separating holes. They usually are separated by scissors and collected in pairs.

Label Any stamp-like adhesive that is not a postage stamp.

Maximum Card A postcard that has an illustration, stamp and cancel with a common theme.

Miniature Sheet A single stamp or block of stamps with a margin on all sides bearing some special wording or design.

Mint Indicates a stamp in the same condition as when it was issued.

Overprint Additional printing on a stamp that was not part of the original design.

Pane A full "sheet" of stamps as sold by the Post Office. Four panes make up the original sheet of stamps as printed.

Perforations Lines of small holes or cuts between rows of stamps that make them easy to separate.

Philately The collection and study of postage stamps and other postal materials.

Plate Block (or **Plate Number Block**) A block of stamps with the margin attached that bears the plate number used in printing that sheet.

Postage Due A stamp issued to collect unpaid postage.

Postal Stationery Envelopes, postal cards and aerogrammes with stamp designs printed or embossed on them.

Postmark A mark put on envelopes or other mailing pieces showing the date and location of the post office where it was mailed.

Postmaster's Provisionals Stamps made by local postmasters before the government began issuing stamps.

Precancels Cancellations applied to stamps before the stamps were affixed to mail.

Reissue An official reprinting of a stamp that was no longer being printed.

Revenue Stamps Stamps not valid for postal use but issued for collecting taxes.

Selvage The unprinted paper around panes of stamps, sometimes called the margin.

Se-tenant An attached pair, strip or block of stamps that differ in design, value or surcharge.

Surcharge An overprint that changes the denomination of a stamp from its original face value.

Coils

Overprint

Precancel

Perforate

Imperforate

Tagging Chemically marking stamps so they can be "read" by mail-sorting machines.

Tied On Indicates a stamp whose postmark touches the envelope.

Tongs A tool, used to handle stamps, that resembles a tweezers with rounded or flattened tips.

Topicals Indicates a group of stamps with the same theme—space travel, for example.

Unused Indicates a stamp that has no cancellation or other sign of use.

Used A stamp that has been canceled.

Want List A list of philatelic material needed by a collector.

Watermark A design pressed into stamp paper during its manufacture.

Surcharge

The Bicentennial of the Constitution of the United States of America
1787-1987   USA 22

We the people of the United States, in order to form a more perfect Union...
Preamble, U.S. Constitution   USA 22

Establish justice, insure domestic tranquility, provide for the common defense, promote the general welfare...
Preamble, U.S. Constitution   USA 22

And secure the blessings of liberty to ourselves and our posterity...
Preamble, U.S. Constitution   USA 22

Do ordain and establish this Constitution for the United States of America.
Preamble, U.S. Constitution   USA 22

Se-tenant

Organizations, Publications and Resources

For Your Information...

Here's a list of philatelic resources that can increase your knowledge of stamps as well as your collecting enjoyment.

Organizations

American Air Mail Society
Stephen Reinhard
P.O. Box 110
Mineola, NY 11501
Specializes in all phases of aerophilately. Membership services include Advance Bulletin Service, Auction Service, free want ads, Sales Department, monthly journal, discounts on Society publications, translation service.

American First Day Cover Society
Mrs. Monte Eiserman
Dept. USG
14359 Chadbourne
Houston, TX 77079-8811
A full-service, not-for-profit, noncommercial society devoted exclusively to First Day Covers and First Day Cover collecting. Offers information on 300 current cachet producers, expertizing, foreign covers, translation service, color slide programs and archives covering First Day Covers.

American Philatelic Society
Keith A. Wagner
P.O. Box 8000
State College, PA 16803-8000
A full complement of services and resources for the philatelist. Membership offers: American Philatelic Research Library; expertizing service; estate advisory service; translation services; a stamp theft committee that functions as a clearing house for stamp theft information; sales service; and a monthly journal, *The American Philatelist*, sent to all members.

American Society for Philatelic Pages and Panels
Ron Walenciak
P.O. Box 64
Hillsdale, NJ 07642-0064
Focuses on souvenir pages and commemorative panels, with reports on news, varieties, errors, oddities and discoveries; free ads.

American Topical Association
Donald W. Smith
P.O. Box 630
Johnstown, PA 15907-0630
A service organization concentrating on the specialty of topical collecting. Offers handbooks on specific topics; an exhibition award; *Topical Time*, a bimonthly publication dealing with topical interest areas; a slide and film loan service; information, translation, biography and sales services; and an heirs' estate service.

Black American Philatelic Society
c/o Walt Robinson
9101 Taylor Street
Landover, MD 20785-2554
For collectors interested in the study of black Americans on postage stamps.

Booklet Collectors Club
Larry Rosenblum
1016 E. El Camino Real, #107
Sunnyvale, CA 94087-3759
Offers everything for the booklet collector, including *The Interleaf*, a journal.

Bureau Issues Association
834 Devonshire Way
Sunnyvale, CA 94087
Devoted to the study of U.S. stamps produced by the Bureau of Engraving and Printing.

Errors, Freaks and Oddities Collectors Club
John Hotchner
Box 1125
Falls Church, VA 22041-0125
Studies stamp production mistakes.

Junior Philatelists of America
Central Office
P.O. Box 701010
San Antonio, TX 78270-1010
Publishes a bimonthly newsletter, *The Philatelic Observer*, and offers auction, exchange, penpal and other services to young stamp collectors. Adult supporting membership and gift memberships are available. The Society also publishes various brochures on stamp collecting.

Mailer's Postmark Permit Club
Scott A. Shaulis
199 W. Sanner St.
Somerset, PA 15501-2213
Provides listings and information on mailers' precancel postmarks.

Maximum Card Study Club
Bill Kelleher
Box 375
Bedford, MA 01730-0375

Mobile Post Office Society
Andrew C. Koval
P.O. Box 502
Bedford Park, IL 60499
A nonprofit organization concentrating on transit markings and the history of postal transit routes. The Society is engaged in documenting and recording transit postal history by publishing books, catalogs and monographs, as well as a semimonthly journal.

Modern Postal History Society
Terence Hines
P.O. Box 258
Thornwood, NY 10594-0258

National Association of Precancel Collectors
Glenn V. Dye
5121 Park Blvd.
Wildwood, NJ 08260-0121
Publishes *Precancel Stamp Collector*, a monthly newsletter that contains information on precanceled stamps.

Perfins Club
Ralph W. Smith, Secretary
RR 1 Box 5645
Dryden, ME 04225
Send SASE for information.

Philatelic Foundation
270 Madison Avenue
New York, NY 10016-0656
A nonprofit organization known for its excellent expertization service. The Foundation's broad resources, including extensive reference collections, 5,000-volume library and Expert Committee, provide collectors with comprehensive consumer protection. It also publishes educational information. Slide and cassette programs are available on such subjects as the Pony Express, Provisionals, Confederate Postal History and special programs for beginning collectors.

Pictorial Cancellation Society
Robert Hedges
P.O. Box 306
Hancock, MD 21750
Studies and catalogues USPS pictorial cancellations.

Plate Block Collector Club
P.O. Box 937
Homestead, FL 33090-0937

Plate Number Society
9600 Colesville Road
Silver Spring, MD 20901-3144

Postal History Society
Diane Boehret
P.O. Box 61774
Virginia Beach, VA 23462
Devoted to the study of various aspects of the development of the mails and local, national and international postal systems; UPU treaties; and means of transporting mails.

Post Mark Collectors Club
Wilma Hinrichs
4200 SE Indianola Road
Des Moines, IA 50320-1555
Collects and preserves postmarks on U.S. and foreign letters.

Precancel Stamp Society
P.O. Box 160
Walkersville, MD 21793

Souvenir Card Collectors Society
Robin M. Ellis
P.O. Box 4155
Tulsa, OK 74159-4155
Provides member auctions, a quarterly journal and access to limited-edition souvenir cards.

United Postal Stationery Society
Mrs. Joann Thomas
Box 48
Redlands, CA 92373-0601

United States Possessions Philatelic Society
Geoffrey Brewster
141 Lyford Drive
Tiburon, CA 94920-1661
Nonprofit organization devoted to the collection and study of the postal history of Guam, Hawaii, U.S. Trust Territories, Puerto Rico, U.S. Administration of Cuba and the Philippines, D.W.I/ Virgin Islands, Ryukyu Islands and the Canal Zone. Quarterly journal. Annual dues: $10.

Universal Ship Cancellation Society
David Kent
P.O. Box 127
New Britain, CT 06050-0127
Specializes in naval ship cancellations.

Free Periodicals

The following publications will send you a free copy of their magazine or newspaper upon request:

American Stamp Dealers' Association
Joe Savarese
3 School Street
Glen Cove, NY 11542
Association of dealers engaged in every facet of philately, with 11 regional chapters nationwide. Sponsors national and local shows, seminars for member and nonmember dealers, credit information service, monthly newsletter and ASDA membership directory.

Council of Philatelic Organizations
P.O. Box COPO
State College, PA 16803-8340
A nonprofit organization comprised of more than 400 national, regional and local stamp clubs, organizations, societies and philatelic business firms. The objective of COPO is to promote and encourage the hobby of stamp collecting. Membership is open only to organizations; COPO uses a variety of methods to promote stamp collecting, including an ongoing publicity campaign, a quarterly newsletter and joint sponsorship (with the USPS) of National Stamp Collecting Month.

Linn's Stamp News
P.O. Box 29
Sidney, OH 45365-0029
The largest weekly stamp newspaper.

Mekeel's Weekly Stamp News
P.O. Box 1660
Portland, ME 04104-1660

The Minkus Stamp Journal
P.O. Box 1228
Fort Mill, SC 29715-1228
Quarterly. Articles of importance to collectors as well as complete listings of worldwide new issues.

The Philatelic Catalog
United States Postal Service
Washington, DC 20265-0001
Published bimonthly; includes every philatelic item offered by the USPS.

Stamp Collector
Box 10
Albany, OR 97321-0006
For beginning and advanced collectors of all ages.

Stamps Magazine
85 Canisteo St.
Hornell, NY 14843-1544
Published weekly for generalists since 1932.

Stamps Auction News
85 Canisteo Street
Hornell, NY 14843-1544

Stamp Collecting Made Easy
P.O. Box 29
Sidney, OH 45365-0029
A free, illustrated 96-page booklet.

Stamp Club Center
P.O. Box 29
Sidney, OH 45365-0029
Write for the name and address of the stamp club nearest your ZIP code.

Museums, Libraries and Displays

There is *no charge* to visit any of the following institutions. Please contact them before visiting because their hours may vary.

American Philatelic Research Library
100 Oakwood Ave.
State College, PA 16803-8000

Cardinal Spellman Philatelic Museum
235 Wellesley St.
Weston, MA 02193-1538
America's only fully accredited museum devoted to the display, collection and preservation of stamps and postal history. The museum contains three galleries of rare stamps, a philatelic library and a branch post office/philatelic counter.

The Collectors Club
22 East 35th St.
New York, NY 10016-3806
Regular services include a library and reading rooms, a publication and lectures on philatelic subjects. The group also honors a great American collector annually and actively supports national and international exhibitions.

Hall of Stamps
United States Postal Service
475 L'Enfant Plaza
Washington, DC 20260-0001
Located at USPS headquarters, this exhibit features more than $500,000 worth of rare U.S. stamps, a moon rock and letter canceled on the moon, original stamp design art, etc.

National Philatelic Collection
National Museum of American History
Third Floor
Smithsonian Institution
Washington, DC 20560

San Diego County Philatelic Library
4133 Poplar St.
San Diego, CA 92105-4541

Western Philatelic Library
Sunnyvale Public Library
665 West Olive Ave.
Sunnyvale, CA 94087

Western Postal History Museum
Box 40725
Tucson, AZ 85717-0725

Wineburgh Philatelic Research Library
University of Dallas
P.O. Box 830643
Richardson, TX 75083-0643

Literature

Basic Philately
Stamp Collector
Box 10
Albany, OR 97321-0006

Brookman Price Guide of U.S., U.N. & Canada Stamps
Arlene Dunn
Brookman Stamp Company
25 S. River Road
Box 429
Bedford, NH 03102-5457
Illustrated, 240-page, spiral-bound catalog.

Brookman Price Guide of U.S. First Day Covers, Souvenir Cards, USPS Panels & Pages
Arlene Dunn
Brookman Stamp Company
25 S. River Road
Box 429
Bedford, NH 03102-5457
Illustrated, 128-page, spiral-bound catalog.

Catalogue of United States Souvenir Cards
Washington Press
2 Vreeland Road
Florham Park, NJ 07932-1587

Compilation of U.S. Souvenir Cards
P.O. Box 4155
Tulsa, OK 74159-4155

First Day Cover Catalogue (U.S.-U.N)
Washington Press
2 Vreeland Road
Florham Park, NJ 07932-1587
Includes Presidential Inaugural covers.

Fleetwood's Standard First Day Cover Catalog
Fleetwood
Cheyenne, WY 82008-0001

Minkus US Specialized Catalog 1988
P.O. Box 1228
Fort Mill, SC 29715
A complete updated catalog of all U.S. and Possessions stamps, including a complete list of federal and state Duck stamps.

Noble Official Catalog of United States Bureau Precancels
P.O. Box 931
Winter Park, FL 32789-0931

Postage Stamp Identifier & Dictionary of Philatelic Terms
Washington Press
2 Vreeland Road
Florham Park, NJ 07932-1587

Precancel Stamp Society Catalogue of U.S. Bureau Precancels
P.O. Box 926
Framingham, MA 01701

Precancel Stamp Society Town and Type Catalogue of U.S. Local Precancels
P.O. Box 926
Framingham, MA 01701

Scott Stamp Monthly
P.O. Box 828
Sidney, OH 45365-0828

Scott Standard Postage Stamp Catalogue
Box 828
Sidney, OH 45365-8959

Scott Specialized Catalogue of United States Stamps
Box 828
Sidney, OH 45365-8959

Souvenir Pages Price List
Charles D. Simmons
P.O. Box 6238
Buena Park, CA 90622-6238
Please send self-addressed, stamped envelope to receive current listings.

Stamps of the World Catalogue
Stanley Gibbons Publications.
Available through dealers only.
All the stamps of the world from 1840 to date. Over 1,900 pages feature more than 200,000 stamps (47,900 illustrations) from over 200 issuing countries.

Standard Handbook of Stamp Collecting
Harper & Row
10 East 53rd St.
New York, NY 10022-5299

U.S. Postal Card Catalog
Box 48
Redlands, CA 92373-0601

Philatelic Centers

In addition to the more than 15,000 postal facilities authorized to sell philatelic products, the U.S. Postal Service also maintains more than 420 Philatelic Centers located in major population centers throughout the country.

These Philatelic Centers have been established to serve stamp collectors and make it convenient for them to acquire an extensive range of all current postage stamps, postal stationery and philatelic products issued by the Postal Service.

Centers listed are located at Main Post Offices unless otherwise indicated.

Alabama
351 North 24th Street
Birmingham, AL 35203

101 Holmes N.W.
Huntsville, AL 35804

250 St. Joseph
Mobile, AL 36601

Downtown Station
135 Catoma Street
Montgomery, AL 36104

1313 22nd Avenue
Tuscaloosa, AL 35401

Alaska
Downtown Station
3rd & C Streets
Anchorage, AK 99510

Downtown Station
315 Barnette Street
Fairbanks, AK 99707

Arizona
Osborn Station
3905 North 7th Avenue
Phoenix, AZ 85013

General Mail Facility
4949 East Van Buren
Phoenix, AZ 85026

1501 South Cherrybell
Tucson, AZ 85726

Arkansas
30 South 6th Street
Fort Smith, AR 72901

100 Reserve
Hot Springs National
Park, AR 71901

310 East Street
Jonesboro, AR 72401

600 West Capitol
Little Rock, AR 72201

724 West Walnut
Rogers, AR 72756

California
Holiday Station
1180 West Ball Road
Anaheim, CA 92802

Cerritos Branch
18122 Carmencita
Artesia, CA 90701

General Mail Facility
3400 Pegasus Drive
Bakersfield, CA 93380

2000 Allston Way
Berkeley, CA 94704

135 East Olive Street
Burbank, CA 91502

6330 Fountains Square Dr.
Citrus Heights, CA 95621

2121 Meridian Park Blvd.
Concord, CA 94520

2020 Fifth Street
Davis, CA 95616

8111 East Firestone
Downey, CA 90241

Cotten Station
3901 Walnut Drive
Eureka, CA 95501

1900 E Street
Fresno, CA 93706

313 East Broadway
Glendale, CA 91209

Hillcrest Station
303 East Hillcrest
Inglewood, CA 90311

5200 Clark Avenue
Lakewood, CA 90712

300 Long Beach Blvd.
Long Beach, CA 90801

300 N. Los Angeles St.
Los Angeles, CA 90012

Terminal Annex
900 North Alameda
Los Angeles, CA 90052

Village Station
11000 Wilshire Blvd.
Los Angeles, CA 90024

El Viejo Station
1125 "I" Street
Modesto, CA 95354

565 Hartnell Street
Monterey, CA 93940

Civic Center Annex
201 13th Street
Oakland, CA 94612

211 Brooks
Oceanside, CA 92054

1075 North Tustin
Orange, CA 92667

281 E. Colorado Blvd.
Pasadena, CA 91109

1647 Yuba Street
Redding, CA 96001

1201 North Catalina
Redondo Beach,
CA 90277

Downtown Station
3890 Orange Street
Riverside, CA 92501

2000 Royal Oaks Drive
Sacramento, CA 95813

Base Line Station
1164 North E Street
San Bernardino,
CA 92410

2535 Midway Drive
San Diego, CA 92199

7th & Mission Streets
San Francisco, CA 94188

1750 Meridian Drive
San Jose, CA 95101

40 Bellam Blvd.
San Rafael, CA 94901

Spurgeon Station
615 North Bush
Santa Ana, CA 92701

836 Anacapa Street
Santa Barbara,
CA 93102

120 W. Cypress Street
Santa Maria, CA 93454

730 Second Street
Santa Rosa, CA 95404

4245 West Lane
Stockton, CA 95208

15701 Sherman Way
Van Nuys, CA 91408

Channel Islands Station
675 E. Santa Clara St.
Ventura, CA 93001

396 South California St.
West Covina, CA 91790

Colorado
1905 15th Street
Boulder, CO 80302

201 East Pikes Peak
Colorado Springs,
CO 80901

1823 Stout Street
Denver, CO 80202

222 West Eighth Street
Durango, CO 81301

241 North 4th Street
Grand Junction,
CO 81501

5733 South Prince Street
Littleton, CO 80120

421 North Main Street
Pueblo, CO 81003

Connecticut
141 Weston Street
Hartford, CT 06101

Meridian & Waterbury Tpk.
Marion, CT 06444

11 Silver Street
Middletown, CT 06457

141 Church Street
New Haven, CT 06510

27 Masonic Street
New London, CT 06320

421 Atlantic Street
Stamford, CT 06904

Stratford Branch
3100 Main Street
Stratford, CT 06497

135 Grand Street
Waterbury, CT 06701

Delaware
55 The Plaza
Dover, DE 19801

Federal Station
110 East Main Street
Newark, DE 19711

11th & Market Streets
Wilmington, DE 19850

District of Columbia
National Capitol Station
North Capitol Street &
Massachusetts Avenue
Washington, DC 20002

Headsville Station
National Museum
of American History
Smithsonian Institution
14th & Constitution
Washington, DC 20560

USPS Headquarters
475 L'Enfant Plaza, SW
Washington, DC 20260

Pavilion Postique
Old Post Office Bldg.
1100 Pennsylvania, NW
Washington, DC 20004

Florida
824 Manatee Ave. West
Bradenton, FL 33506

100 South Belcher Road
Clearwater, FL 33515

Downtown Station
220 North Beach Street
Daytona Beach, FL 32015

1900 West Oakland Park
Fort Lauderdale, FL
33310

2655 North Airport Rd.
Fort Myers, FL 33906

401 S.E. 1st Avenue
Gainesville, FL 32601

1801 Polk Street
Hollywood, FL 33022

1110 Kings Road
Jacksonville, FL 32203

210 North Missouri Ave.
Lakeland, FL 33802

118 North Bay Drive
Largo, FL 33540

2200 NW 72nd Avenue
Miami, FL 33101

1200 Goodlette
Naples, FL 33940

400 Southwest First Ave.
Ocala, FL 32678

1335 Kingsley Avenue
Orange Park, FL 32073

46 East Robinson Street
Orlando, FL 32801

1400 West Jordan St.
Pensacola, FL 32501

99 King Street
St. Augustine, FL 32084

3135 First Avenue North
St. Petersburg, FL 33730

Open Air Postique
76 4th Street North
St. Petersburg, FL 33701

1661 Ringland Blvd.
Sarasota, FL 33578

2800 South Adams Street
Tallahassee, FL 32301

5201 Spruce Street
Tampa, FL 33630

801 Clematis Street
West Palm Beach, FL
33401

Georgia
115 Hancock Avenue
Athens, GA 30601

Downtown Station
101 Marietta Street
Atlanta, GA 30301

Perimeter Branch
4400 Ashford-
Dunwoody Road
Atlanta, GA 30346

Downtown Station
120-12th Street
Columbus, GA 31908

364 Green Street
Gainesville, GA 30501

451 College Street
Macon, GA 31201

2 North Fahm Street
Savannah, GA 31401

Hawaii
3600 Aolele Street
Honolulu, HI 96819

Idaho
770 South 13th Street
Boise, ID 83708

220 East 5th Street
Moscow, ID 83843

730 East Clark Street
Pocatello, ID 83201

Illinois
909 West Euclid Ave.
Arlington Heights, IL
60004

Moraine Valley Station
7401 100th Place
Bridgeview, IL 60455

1301 East Main Street
Carbondale, IL
62901

433 West Van Buren St.
Chicago, IL 60607

Loop Station
211 South Clark Street
Chicago, IL 60604

1000 East Oakton
Des Plaines, IL 60018

1101 Davis Street
Evanston, IL 60204

2350 Madison Avenue
Granite City, IL 62040

2000 McDonough St.
Joliet, IL 60436

901 Lake Street
Oak Park, IL 60301

123 Indianwood
Park Forest, IL 60466

5225 Harrison Ave.
Rockford, IL 61125

211-19th Street
Rock Island, IL 61201

Schaumburg Station
450 W. Schaumburg Rd.
Roselle, IL 60194

2105 E. Cook Street
Springfield, IL 62703

Edison Square Station
1520 Washington
Waukegan, IL 60085

Indiana
North Park Branch
4492-B 1st Avenue
Evansville, IN 47710

Fort Wayne Postal
Facility
1501 S. Clinton Street
Fort Wayne, IN 46802

5530 Sohl Street
Hammond, IN 46320

125 West Main Street
Indianapolis, IN 46206

2719 South Webster
Kokomo, IN 46901

3450 State Road 26, E.
Lafayette, IN 47901

424 South Michigan
South Bend, IN 46624

30 North 7th Street
Terre Haute, IN 47808

Iowa
615 6th Avenue, SE
Cedar Rapids, IA 52401

1165 Second Avenue
Des Moines, IA 50318

320 6th Street
Sioux City, IA 51101

Kansas
1021 Pacific
Kansas City, KS 66110

6029 Broadmoor
Shawnee Mission,
KS 66202

434 Kansas Avenue
Topeka, KS 66603

Downtown Station
401 North Market
Wichita, KS 67202

Kentucky
1088 Nadino Blvd.
Lexington, KY 40511

St. Mathews Station
4600 Shelbyville Road
Louisville, KY 40207

Louisiana
1715 Odom Street
Alexandria, LA 71301

750 Florida Street
Baton Rouge, LA 70821

1105 Moss Street
Lafayette, LA 70501

3301 17th Street
Metairie, LA 70002

501 Sterlington Road
Monroe, LA 71201

701 Loyola Avenue
New Orleans, LA 70113

Vieux Carre Station
1022 Iberville Street
New Orleans, LA 70112

2400 Texas Avenue
Shreveport, LA 71102

Maine
40 Western Avenue
Augusta, ME 04330

202 Harlow Street
Bangor, ME 04401

125 Forest Avenue
Portland, ME 04101

Maryland
900 E. Fayette Street
Baltimore, MD 21233

201 East Patrick Street
Frederick, MD 21701

6411 Baltimore Avenue
Riverdale, MD 20840

U.S. Route 50
& Naylor Road
Salisbury, MD 21801

Massachusetts
McCormick Station
Post Office &
Courthouse Bldg.
Boston, MA 02109

120 Commercial Street
Brockton, MA 02401

7 Bedford Street
Burlington, MA 01803

Center Station
100 Center Street
Chicopee, MA 01014

2 Government Center
Fall River, MA 02722

881 Main Street
Fitchburg, MA 01420

330 Cocituate Road
Framingham, MA 01701

385 Main Street
Hyannis, MA 02601

Post Office Square
Lowell, MA 01853

212 Fenn Street
Pittsfield, MA 01201

2 Margin Street
Salem, MA 01970

Main Street Station
1883 Main Street
Springfield, MA 01101

462 Washington Street
Woburn, MA 01888

4 East Central Street
Worcester, MA 01603

Michigan
2075 W. Stadium Blvd.
Ann Arbor, MI 48106

26200 Ford Road
Dearborn Heights,
MI 48127

1401 West Fort Street
Detroit, MI 48233

250 East Boulevard Dr.
Flint, MI 48502

225 Michigan Avenue
Grand Rapids, MI 49501

200 South Otsego
Jackson, MI 49201

General Mail Facility
4800 Collins Road
Lansing, MI 48924

735 West Huron Street
Pontiac, MI 48056

1300 Military Street
Port Huron, MI 48060

30550 Gratiot Street
Roseville, MI 48066

200 West 2nd Street
Royal Oak, MI 48068

1233 South Washington
Saginaw, MI 48605

6300 North Wayne Road
Westland, MI 48185

Minnesota
2800 West Michigan
Duluth, MN 55806

297 Baker Building
706 Second Avenue, S
Minneapolis, MN 55402

Downtown Station
102 South Broadway
Rochester, MN 55904

The Pioneer Postal
Emporium
133 Endicott Arcade
St. Paul, MN 55101

Mississippi
2421-13th Street
Gulfport, MS 39501

La Fleur Station
1501 Jacksonian Plaza
Jackson, MS 39211

500 West Miln Street
Tupelo, MS 38801

Missouri
920 Washington
Chillicothe, MO 64601

Columbia Mall Station
Columbia, MO 65203

315 Pershing Road
Kansas City, MO 64108

Northwest Plaza Station
500 Northwest Plaza
St. Ann, MO 63074

Pony Express Station
8th & Edmond
St. Joseph, MO 64503

Clayton Branch
7750 Maryland
St. Louis, MO 63105

H.S. Jewell Station
870 Boonville Avenue
Springfield, MO 65801

Montana
841 South 26th
Billings, MT 59101

215 First Ave., North
Great Falls, MT 59401

1100 West Kent
Missoula, MT 59801

Nebraska
204 W. South Front St.
Grand Island, NE 68801

700 R Street
Lincoln, NE 68501

300 East Third Street
North Platte, NE 69101

1124 Pacific
Omaha, NE 68108

Nevada
1001 Circus Circus Dr.
Las Vegas, NV 89114

200 Vassar Street
Reno, NV 89510

New Hampshire
15 Mount Forest Avenue
Berlin, NH 03570

50 South Main Street
Hanover, NH 03755

955 Goffs Falls Road
Manchester, NH 03103

80 Daniel Street
Portsmouth, NH 03801

New Jersey
1701 Pacific Avenue
Atlantic City, NJ 08401

Veterans Plaza
Bergenfield, NJ 07621

3 Miln Street
Cranford, NJ 07016

229 Main Street
Fort Lee, NJ 07024

Bellmawr Branch
Haag Ave. & Benigno
Gloucester, NJ 08031

Route 35 & Hazlet Ave.
Hazlet, NJ 07730

Borough Complex
East End & Van Sant Ave.
Island Heights, NJ 08732

160 Maplewood Avenue
Maplewood, NJ 07040

150 Ridgedale
Morristown, NJ 07960

Federal Square
Newark, NJ 07102

86 Bayard Street
New Brunswick,
NJ 08906

Nutley Branch
372 Franklin Avenue
Nutley, NJ 07110

194 Ward Street
Paterson, NJ 07510

171 Broad Street
Red Bank, NJ 07701

757 Broad Avenue
Ridgefield, NJ 07657

76 Huyler Street
South Hackensack,
NJ 07606

680 Highway 130
Trenton, NJ 08650

155 Clinton Road
West Caldwell,
NJ 07006

41 Greenwood Avenue
Wykoff, NJ 07481

New Mexico
1135 Broadway NE
Albuquerque,
NM 87101

200 E. Las Cruces Ave.
Las Cruces, NM 88001

415 N. Pennsylvania Ave.
Roswell, NM 88201

New York
General Mail Facility
30 Old Karner Road
Albany, NY 12212

Empire State Plaza
Station
Rockefeller Plaza N.E.
Albany, NY 12220

115 Henry Street
Binghampton,
NY 13902

Bronx General P.O.
149th Street &
Grand Concourse
Bronx, NY 10451

Parkchester Station
1449 West Avenue
Bronx, NY 10462

Riverdale Station
5951 Riverdale Avenue
Bronx, NY 10471

Throggs Neck Station
3630 East Tremont Ave.
Bronx, NY 10465

Wakefield Station
4165 White Plains Rd.
Bronx, NY 10466

Bayridge Station
5501 7th avenue
Brooklyn, NY 11220

Brooklyn General P.O.
271 Cadman Plaza East
Brooklyn, NY 11201

Greenpoint Station
66 Meserole Avenue
Brooklyn, NY 11222

Homecrest Station
2002 Avenue U
Brooklyn, NY 11229

Kensington Station
421 McDonald Avenue
Brooklyn, NY 11218

1200 William Street
Buffalo, NY 14240

1764 Route 9
Clifton Park, NY 12065

40 Main Street
Cooperstown, NY 13326

Downtown Station
255 Clemens Center Pkwy.
Elmira, NY 14901

1836 Mott Avenue
Far Rockaway, NY 11691

41-65 Main Street
Flushing, NY 11351

Ridgewood Station
869 Cypress Avenue
Flushing, NY 11385

Broadway & Maple St.
Glenham, NY 12527

16 Hudson Avenue
Glens Falls, NY 12801

185 West John Street
Hicksville, NY 11802

88-40 164th Street
Jamaica, NY 11431

Ansonia Station
1980 Broadway
New York, NY 10023

Bowling Green Station
25 Broadway
New York, NY 10004

Church Street Station
90 Church Street
New York, NY 10007

Empire State Station
350 Fifth Avenue
New York, NY 10001

F.D.R. Station
909 Third Avenue
New York, NY 10022

Grand Central Station
45th St. & Lexington
New York, NY 10017

Madison Square Station
149 East 23rd Street
New York, NY 10010

New York General P.O.
33rd and 8th Avenue
New York, NY 10001

Rockefeller Center
610 Fifth Avenue
New York, NY 10020

Times Square Station
340 West 42nd Street
New York, NY 10036

Main & Hunt Streets
Oneonta, NY 13820

Franklin & S. Main Sts.
Pearl River, NY 10965

10 Miller Street
Plattsburgh, NY 12901

55 Mansion Street
Poughkeepsie, NY 12601

1335 Jefferson Road
Rochester, NY 14692

250 Merrick Road
Rockville Centre,
NY 11570

29 Jay Street
Schenectady, NY 12305

25 Route 11
Smithtown, NY 11787

550 Manor Road
Staten Island, NY 10314

New Springville Station
2843 Richmond Ave.
Staten Island, NY 10314

5640 East Taft Road
Syracuse, NY 13220

10 Broad Street
Utica, NY 13503

100 Fisher Avenue
White Plains, NY 10602

78-81 Main Street
Yonkers, NY 10701

North Carolina
West Asheville Station
1300 Patton Avenue
Asheville, NC 28806

Eastway Station
3065 Eastway Drive
Charlotte, NC 28205

301 Green Street
Fayetteville, NC 28302

Four Seasons Station
Four Seasons Town Centre
High Point Road
Greensboro, NC 27427

310 New Bern Avenue
Raleigh, NC 27611

North Dakota
657 2nd Avenue North
Fargo, ND 58102

Ohio
675 Wolf Ledges Pkwy.
Akron, OH 44309

2650 N. Cleveland Ave.
Canton, OH 44701

Fountain Square Station
5th & Walnut Street
Cincinnati, OH 45202

301 W. Prospect Ave.
Cleveland, OH 44101

850 Twin Rivers Drive
Columbus, OH 43216

1111 East 5th Street
Dayton, OH 45401

105 Court Street
Hamilton, OH 45012

200 North Diamond St.
Mansfield, OH 44901

200 North 4th Street
Steubenville, OH 43952

435 S. St. Clair Street
Toledo, OH 43601

99 South Walnut Street
Youngstown, OH 44503

Oklahoma
101 East First
Edmond, OK 73034

115 West Broadway
Enid, OK 73701

102 South 5th
Lawton, OK 73501

525 West Okmulgee
Muskogee, OK 74401

129 West Gray
Norman, OK 73069

320 SW 5th Street
Oklahoma City,
OK 73125

333 West 4th
Tulsa, OK 74101

12 South 5th
Yukon, OK 73099

Oregon
520 Willamette Street
Eugene, OR 97401

751 N.W. Hoyt
Portland, OR 97208

1050 25th Street S.W.
Salem, OR 97301

Pennsylvania
442-456 Hamilton St.
Allentown, PA 18101

535 Wood Street
Bethlehem, PA 18016

115 Boylston Street
Bradford, PA 16701

229 Beaver Drive
Du Bois, PA 15801

Griswold Plaza
Erie, PA 16501

115 Buford Avenue
Gettysburg, PA 17325

238 S. Pennsylvania
Greensburg, PA 15601

10th and Markets Sts.
Harrisburg, PA 17105

West Avenue & Cedar Street
Jenkintown, PA 19046

111 Franklin Street
Johnstown, PA 15901

Downtown Station
48-50 W. Chestnut St.
Lancaster, PA 17603

980 Wheeler Way
Langhorne, PA 19047

Lehigh Valley Branch
Airport Rd. & Route 22
Lehigh Valley, PA 18001

Monroeville Mall Branch
348 Mall Circle Drive
Monroeville, PA 15146

1 W. Washington Street
Kennedy Square
New Castle, PA 16101

28 East Airy Street
Norristown, PA 19401

30th & Market Streets
Philadelphia, PA 19104

B. Free Franklin Station
316 Market Street
Philadelphia, PA 19106

Penn Center Station
2 Penn Center Plaza
Philadelphia, PA 19102

William Penn Annex
9th & Chestnut Streets
Philadelphia, PA 19107

Castle Shannon Branch
307 Castle Shannon Blvd.
Pittsburgh, PA 15234

McKnight Branch
McKnight & Seibert Rds.
Pittsburgh, PA 15237

Seventh Avenue
& Grant Street
Pittsburgh, PA 15219

59 North 5th Street
Reading, PA 19603

North Washington Ave.
& Linden St.
Scranton, PA 18503

237 South Frazer Street
State College, PA 16801

7th & Ann Streets
Stroudsburg, PA 18360

South & West Wayne Sts.
Wayne, PA 19087

300 South Main Street
Wilkes Barre, PA 18701

Center City Finance Station
240 West Third Street
Williamsport, PA 17703

200 S. George Street
York, PA 17405

Puerto Rico
General Post Office
18 Roosevelt Avenue
Hate Rey
San Juan, PR 00918

Plaza Las Americas
Station
San Juan, PR 00938

Rhode Island
24 Corliss Street
Providence, RI 02904

South Carolina
4290 Daley Avenue
Charleston, SC 29402

1601 Assembly Street
Columbia, SC 29201

600 West Washington
Greenville, SC 29602

South Dakota
500 East Boulevard
Rapid City, SD 57701

320 S. 2nd Avenue
Sioux Falls, SD 57101

Tennessee
General Mail Facility
6050 Shallowford Road
Chattanooga, TN 37401

Tom Murray Station
133 Tucker Street
Jackson, TN 38301

501 West Main Avenue
Knoxville, TN 37901

Colonial Finance Unit
4695 Southern Avenue
Memphis, TN 38124

Crosstown Finance Unit
1520 Union Avenue
Memphis, TN 38174

555 South Third
Memphis, TN 38101

901 Broadway
Nashville, TN 37202

Texas
2300 South Ross
Amarillo, TX 79105

300 East South Street
Arlington, TX 76010

Downtown Station
300 East 9th
Austin, TX 78701

General Mail Facility
8225 Cross Park Drive
Austin, TX 78710

300 Willow
Beaumont, TX 77704

1535 Los Ebanos
Brownsville, TX 78520

809 Nueces Bay
Corpus Christi, TX
78408

400 North Ervay Street
Dallas, TX 75221

5300 East Paisano Dr.
El Paso, TX 79910

251 West Lancaster
Fort Worth, TX 76101

401 Franklin Avenue
Houston, TX 77201

411 "L" Avenue
Lubbock, TX 79408

601 East Pecan
McAllen, TX 78501

100 East Wall
Midland, TX 79702

Downtown Station
615 East Houston
San Antonio, TX 78205

10410 Perrin Beitel Road
San Antonio, TX 78284

1411 Wunsche Loop
Spring, TX 77373

2211 North Robinson
Texarkana, TX 75501

221 West Ferguson
Tyler, TX 75702

800 Franklin
Waco, TX 76701

1000 Lamar Street
Wichita Falls, TX 76307

Utah
3680 Pacific Avenue
Ogden, UT 84401

95 West 100 South
Provo, UT 84601

1760 West 2100 South
Salt Lake City, UT 84119

Vermont
204 Main Street
Brattleboro, VT 05301

1 Elmwood Avenue
Burlington, VT 05401

151 West Street
Rutland, VT 05701

Virginia
111 Sixth Street
Bristol, VA 24201

1155 Seminole Trail
Charlottesville,
VA 22906

1425 Battlefield Blvd., N.
Chesapeake, VA 23320

700 Main Street
Danville, VA 24541

Merrifield Branch
8409 Lee Highway
Fairfax, VA 22116

809 Aberdeen Road
Hampton, VA 23670

300 Odd Fellows Road
Lynchburg, VA 24506

Tyson's Corner Branch
Tyson's Corner
Shopping Center
McLean VA 22103

Denbigh Station
14104 Warwick Blvd.
Newport News,
VA 23602

600 Granby Street
Norfolk, VA 23501

Thomas Corner Station
6274 East Virginia
Beach Boulevard
Norfolk, VA 23502

1801 Brook Road
Richmond, VA 23232

419 Rutherford Ave. NE
Roanoke, VA 24022

1430 North Augusta
Staunton, VA 24401

501 Viking Drive
Virginia Beach,
VA 23450

Washington
11 3rd Street N.W.
Auburn, WA 98002

Crossroads Station
15800 N.E. 8th
Bellevue, WA 98008

315 Prospect Street
Bellingham, WA 98225

3102 Hoyt
Everett, WA 98201

3500 West Court
Pasco, WA 99301

424 East 1st Street
Port Angeles, WA 98362

301 Union Street
Seattle, WA 98101

West 904 Riverside
Spokane, WA 99210

1102 A Street
Tacoma, WA 98402

205 West Washington
Yakima, WA 98903

West Virginia
301 North Street
Bluefield, WV 24701

Lee & Dickinson St.
Charleston, WV 25301

500 West Pike Street
Clarksburg, WV 26301

1000 Virginia Avenue, West
Huntington, WV 25704

217 King Street
Martinsburg, WV 25401

Wisconsin
325 East Walnut
Green Bay, WI 54301

3902 Milwaukee Street
Madison, WI 53707

345 West St. Paul Ave.
Milwaukee, WI 53203

235 Forrest Street
Wausau, WI 54401

Wyoming
150 East B Street
Casper, WY 82601

2120 Capitol Avenue
Cheyenne, WY 82001

FOREIGN CENTERS

Australia
Max Stern & Co.
Port Phillip Arcade
234 Flinders Street
Melbourne 3000

France
Theodore Champion
13 Rue Drouot
75009 Paris

**Federal Republic
of Germany**
Hermann W. Sieger
Venusberg 32-34
D-7073
Lorch/Wurttemberg

Netherlands
J.A. Visser
Post Office Box 184
3300 Ad Dordrecht

Sweden
Bo Follin
Frimarkshuset AB
S-793 01 Leksand

Switzerland
De Rosa International S.A.
Av Du Tribunal
Federal 34
CH-1005 Lausanne

Japan
Japan Philatelic Co., Ltd.
Post Office Box 2
Suginami-Minami
Tokyo 168-91

**PHILATELIC CENTERS
IN STAMP STORES**

Conejo Valley Stamp and Coin
2768 East Thousand Oaks Blvd.
Thousand Oaks, CA 91362

Fireside Stamp Company
302 Town & Country Village
Sunnyvale, CA 94086

United States Stamp Company
368 Bush Street
San Francisco, CA 94104

An Eternal Drive Down Main Street, U.S.A.

1928 Locomobile
1929 Pierce Arrow
1931 Cord
1932 Packard
1935 Duesenberg

The 1988 Classic Cars booklet stamps rolled into the nation's post offices in late August.

Cars symbolize the American lifestyle. Just as Detroit's nickname is Motown, we live in a virtual "Mocountry" where *Mo* stands for *motor*. During the 1890s, automobiles were such an oddity that they were shown in circuses. Today, less than 100 years later, nearly 10 million new cars are manufactured in the United States every year.

But there is something about old cars, in particular—from the 1920s, '30s and '40s—that fascinates Americans. Perhaps it's the nostalgia, those fond memories of eras gone by. Whatever the reason, auto appeal is strong—so strong, for example, that it attracts 150,000 people to a classic car convention held in the small town of Auburn, Indiana every Labor Day. They come to admire, touch and stare at the sleek lines of vintage automobiles.

And postage stamps are part of our automania. Millions of people will use the stamps from the Classic Cars booklet that was issued by the USPS on August 25, 1988. These classics— the 1928 Locomobile, the 1929 Pierce-Arrow, the 1931 Cord, the 1932 Packard and the 1935 Duesenberg—are not the first former kings of the road to be featured on postage stamps, and they won't be the last.

The first automobile illustrated on a U.S. postage stamp was a Columbia electric car. This vehicle was shown with the U.S. Capitol in the background on the 1901 Pan American Exposition Series stamp (#296).

When the 1901 stamp was issued, almost 40 percent of all automobiles sold were electric.

As the network of highways grew, however, the restrictions of the electric car proved to be a drawback. The battery, which weighed almost as much as the car itself, provided limited speed and range. Depending on the load, it had to be recharged every 35 miles—an operation that took nearly two hours!

Another short-lived form of personal transportation was the steam car. The Stanley twin brothers, Francis E. and Freelan O., built their Steamer (#2132) from 1896 until after World War I. Many people felt nervous riding behind a boiler of live steam, which lead to the development of the gasoline engine that is common today.

When the vehicles depicted on the new Classic Cars stamps were introduced to the public, they were greeted with mixed reactions ranging from wild acclaim to ridicule. They had one common denominator, however: They were built with care and precision that developed as a laboratory for the modern car. And each has earned its rightful place in the classic automotive world.

The Locomobile

The Locomobile started out as a steam car in the late 1800s. Although sales were satisfactory, the owners of the firm decided they had had enough of "teakettles on wheels" and sold the company in 1902 to the Stanley brothers. Their first gasoline vehicle came out of the Bridgeport, Connecticut plant in 1904. Its up-front motor was compared to the fine European cars of the period, and the Locomobile quickly became one of the country's top-quality products, with the slogan: "Easily the best-built car in America."

Auburn-Cord-Duesenberg Museum, Auburn, Indiana

Known for intricate details, the Locomobile, by its own claim, was "the best-built car in America" in the early 1900s.

The Locomobile, quite simply, was noted for its spectacular detail. The hardcover volume, *The Locomobile Book*, available in dealers' showrooms, exhibited the firm's pride in such statements as: "The rear seat cushion and back are provided with upholstery 10 inches thick...skillful distribution of weight and the perfect balance are two of the many reasons for its easy riding...the foot rest is a brass rod lightly knurled to prevent slipping...the four-speed transmission with its manganese bronze case and alloy steel shafts never gives trouble."

The more than 40 different models of the Pierce-Arrow had at least one thing in common: headlights in the fenders—the Pierce-Arrow signature.

The Pierce-Arrow

George N. Pierce founded the Pierce-Arrow Company in 1901 in Buffalo, New York. His first car was a one-cylinder motorette, but he added a novel feature—the gearshift on the steering column. In 1914, Pierce developed a new body design and put the headlamps in the fenders, the design trademark of all future Pierce-Arrows.

Studebaker Corporation bought the firm in 1928 and immediately added styling to the reputation for quality. The new Pierce-Arrows had greater horsepower (hp), a new transmission, three new chassis and four new wheelbases. More acceleration and the ability to climb hills in high gear were the featured advertising claims for the new models. Prices started at $2,685 and ranged to $10,000 for the custom models by Le Baron.

The Cord

Erret Lobban Cord never finished high school; he was too busy making money selling used Model-T Fords. After losing his money in several non-auto business ventures, Cord worked as a new car salesman selling Moon's "Victory" car and made as much as $30,000 per year at a time when the average skilled worker was happy to earn $2,000.

Auburn-Cord-Duesenberg Museum, Auburn, Indiana

In 1924 the Auburn Motor Company of Auburn, Indiana was insolvent, and the firm's owners gave Cord a free hand to reorganize the company. One year later the 1925 Auburn, with all new styling and a choice of six- or eight-cylinder engines, was a great success.

Not yet satisfied with his accomplishment, Cord acquired the Lycoming Aircraft Company in 1929 and introduced a new front-wheel-drive car bearing his name. The new Cord, with a Lycoming eight-cylinder engine, created a sensation in every Auburn show-room, in large part because of its low, sleek lines.

The Packard

James Ward Packard bought a Winton car in 1898 that continually broke down, causing him to express a low opinion of Winton's "Horseless." Winton replied, "If you're so smart, why don't you build a car yourself." Packard started building cars in Detroit, Michigan and remained a great name for many years after the Winton name disappeared from the auto showroom.

A huge sign was hung across the main street within the Packard plant that read simply, "Quality First." It was a constant reminder to all personnel that the principle aim of the firm was "the building of quality cars for a clientele of means and dis-tinction." By 1930, Packard achieved world-wide prominence and sold 28,177 units in one year. The car quickly became a favorite of kings and Arab potentates. And it is credited with contributing more than 1,000 innovations to the car manufacturing industry.

The 1932 Packard set a new standard for such innovations. The all new "Light Eight" model was easily distin-

The innovative Packard was one of the most popular cars in the 1930s. Models were available in a variety of color combinations, some with pinstriping and colored wheels!

guished by the broad forward sweep of the bottom portion of its V-shaped grill. The car had a silent synchromesh transmission, finger-control steering and shatterproof glass in every window, and every body was fully insulated. Ride-control shock absorbers, adjustable from the dashboard, were offered at no extra cost. In addition to all these new features, the new model was priced $500 less than any other Packard.

The company's big move came in 1935 when, in response to sluggish sales, it offered the famous Packard quality and design in a new 120 series at prices that began at only $995. For the next two years, the company pushed the Packard name at a reasonable price and reached an all-time high sales figure of 109,518 cars sold in 1937.

The Duesenberg

The Duesenberg, made at a plant in Indianapolis —not Germany—has the distinction of being the most admired American car of all time.

Frederick and August Duesenberg loved engines, and they spent their early years developing racing cars for Indy's 500-mile race. Under license for the Allies, they produced the 16-cylinder Bugatti aircraft during World War I. When the war ended they went back to making four-cylinder racing car engines. In 1920, a Duesenberg twin-engine took the world's land speed title at 156 miles per hour (mph). When the new engine powered the first and only American car ever to win the Grand Prix de France in 1921, the Duesenberg name was firmly established in connection with quality and high performance.

In 1926, Duesenberg, Inc. was formed, and the first Model "J" was

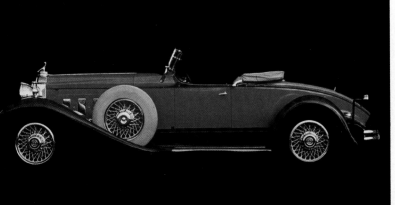

The Stock Market/Cindy Lewis 1984

shown to the public in December 1928. During the 1930s the Duesenbergs made no annual model change and only minor improvements on the instrument panel and the radiator shutters.

Duesenberg did not build the bodies for its cars; they were built to order by various high-class custom coach builders. The Duesenberg chassis ranged in price from $8,500 to $9,500, but the cost of a custom body ran anywhere from $5,000 to as much as $50,000 for the customer who wanted "the works."

The car was a speed-ster capable of generating more than 265 hp with its dual overhead camshaft engine. Even with a total weight of almost three tons, the Duesenberg reached 116 mph and was able to do 90 mph in second gear.

The dashboard, an engineer's delight, contained such "standard equipment" as a brake-pressure gauge with the ability to adjust the brakes from inside the car, a clock with a split-second hand and timer, oil pressure gauge, altimeter, ammeter, tachometer and compass, plus much more. It took a competent driver to learn the various switches and controls in the cab of a "Duesie."

The Duesenberg was the car selected by many of the socially elite of Hollywood. Although there were no production records kept, Duesenberg fans claim that less than 500 cars were built by the time the plant closed in 1937. A leading classic car enthusiast claims that it would cost at least $1 million to duplicate the Duesenberg today.

Preservation

There aren't many of these old cars around anymore, but several of the nation's museums exhibit automobiles of

Checklist of motor cars and trucks on U.S. postage stamps and stationery.

Scott No.	Value	Date of Issue	Description
296	4¢	May 1, 1901	Columbia Electric Auto
1007	3¢	March 4, 1952	American Automobile Assoc.
1025	3¢	October 27, 1953	Trucking Industry
1162	3¢	October 15, 1960	Wheels of Freedom
1286A	12¢	July 30, 1968	Henry Ford
1406	6¢	August 26, 1970	Woman Suffrage
1496 & 1498	8¢	April 30, 1973	Postal Service Employees
1572	10¢	September 3, 1975	Postal Service Bicentennial
1906	17¢	June 25, 1982	Detroit Electric Auto
2123	3.4¢	March 26, 1982	School Bus
2125	5.5¢	November 3, 1986	Star Route Truck
2129	8.5¢	January 24, 1987	Tow Truck
2131	11¢	April 18, 1985	Stutz Bearcat
2132	12¢	June 11, 1985	Stanley Steamer
2264	17.5¢	September 25, 1987	Racing Car
2381	25¢	August 25, 1988	Locomobile
2382	25¢	August 25, 1988	Pierce-Arrow
2383	25¢	August 25, 1988	Cord
2384	25¢	August 25, 1988	Packard
2385	25¢	August 25, 1988	Duesenberg
E14	20¢	April 11, 1925	Mail Truck Special Delivery
Q7	15¢	December 9, 1912	Mail Truck Parcel Post
U587	15¢	September 2, 1978	Auto Racing Postal Stationery

Gary Cooper and Mae West were two of many celebrities to drive Duesenbergs. Clark Gable once owned the car pictured here.

historic interest. And thousands of people make a hobby out of preserving and restoring fine cars of distinction. For example, the Classic Car Club of America has 4,500 members who own and keep running some 6,000 classic cars. But this number cannot compare with the millions of oldies that rolled off the printing press "assembly lines" in the form of Classic Cars postage stamps. Thanks to them, we all can enjoy classic cars from yesteryear as they travel the streets on America's mail.

UPU Congress Inspires Major USPS Philatelic Exhibition

For the first time in its history, the U.S. Postal Service will sponsor a stamp exhibition. And the show—WORLD STAMP EXPO '89™—promises to be a major extravaganza!

Running 14 days and spanning a three-week period from November 17 through December 3, 1989, the exhibition will be the world's longest stamp show. WORLD STAMP EXPO '89 is

being hosted in conjunction with the 20th Congress of the Universal Postal Union (UPU) at the Washington Convention Center in Washington, D.C.

Make a vacation out

of it! The exhibition will be open for three weekends and closed for a few days in between, enabling visitors to attend the wholesale stamp bourse and auctions *and* go sightseeing in the nation's capital.

WORLD STAMP EXPO '89 will have something for everyone—from priceless philatelic works of art for experienced philatelists to exhibits that reflect the pleasures of the world's No. 1 hobby to casual collectors and newcomers. It promises to be an

enjoyable, educational experience that attendees will remember for many years to come. You won't want to miss it!

The Show

The show will be divided into four segments: "Mail Delivery of the Past," "Mail Delivery of the Future," "Postal Stationery" and "Junior Fiesta," featuring an innovative learning center geared to novice collectors. Here are some activities that are scheduled:

A large section of the show will be devoted to postal administrations of the world. Each member nation of the UPU has been invited to use a special booth to sell that country's stamps and other philatelic items. This is the perfect chance to see the stamps of more than 150 nations in one location and decide if you want to collect the stamps of a foreign country.

There also will be many stamp dealers present from all parts of the world who will have stamps and envel-

Be a guest of the USPS! The Postal Service would like to treat you and a fellow stamp enthusiast to one day's admission at WORLD STAMP EXPO '89. *For information on how to get two free tickets (a $5 value), see the mail-in card following page 312.*

opes for sale. Stamps on display will range in value from a few cents to those that sell for tens of thousands of dollars.

There will be a series of slide shows, films and lectures on all aspects of stamp collecting. Experts can answer questions and show you how to start collecting, how to expand your collection and even how to sell duplicates or unwanted philatelic material. Presentations will focus on numerous types of collecting, from First Day Covers to topicals.

"Going, going... gone!" A series of auctions will be held by prominent firms that will offer rare and famous philatelic material for sale to the highest bidders. It can be rewarding to bid on items in your price range and fascinating to watch some collectors spend thousands of dollars with a nod or the flick of a finger.

The U.S. Postal Service will hold a number of First Day Ceremonies during the show. These events offer opportunities to buy the new stamps being issued, get First Day cancellations, obtain autographs of postal officials and stamp designers and receive special programs given to attendees.

In addition, WORLD STAMP EXPO '89 will have a different cancel for each day it is open. These pictorial cancels, to be postmarked on the new stamp issued for the show, are valued by collectors everywhere.

The UPU and You

WORLD STAMP EXPO '89 will overlap with the 20th meeting of the Universal Postal Congress, the main legislative body of the Universal Postal Union. Formed in Bern, Switzerland in 1874 to facili-

The logo for the international philatelic exhibition in 1989 features a stylized globe with a dove emerging from within the borders of a stamp.

WORLD STAMP EXPO '89™
United States Postal Service
Nov. 17 — Dec. 3, 1989
Washington Convention Center
Washington, DC

tate the exchange of mail between countries, the UPU remains confident about meeting its extraordinary challenge of delivering the world's mail. "Nothing," insists A.C. Botto de Barros, Director-General of the UPU, "stops [The Post] in its noble mission."

Today, international correspondence seems so simple. You can address a letter to any country in the world, affix an airmail stamp and drop it in any mailbox, assured of its delivery. It may be difficult to imagine that things were much more complicated, slow and expensive years ago. Imagine that the time is January 1870. Consider the story of one letter mailed from New York City to France during that period—and the tremendous bookkeeping headaches involved.

The cost of mailing a letter overseas was divided into four gen-eral categories, each demanding a fee for postage. First, there was the domestic rate of the country of origin. Then, there was sea postage to pay for the ship carrying the letter overseas. Next, a transit rate was assessed by each country through which the piece of mail traveled. Finally, the domestic rate of the country of destination was added to the grand total.

At that time the U.S. domestic rate for a letter weighing a half-ounce or less was two cents. The sea postage fee was an additional two cents. The post office clerk then looked up the departure dates of various ships bound for Europe that were authorized to carry mail and wrote the ship's name on the front of the letter.

With the letter finally on its way to Europe, its journey could take anywhere from four to eight months. The postage paid by the sender was only a small portion of the total costs.

The sea postage fee carried the letter to the closest British frontier. Britain would forward the letter to France under their mutual postal treaty. France, in turn, would collect postage due from the addressee. Eventually, France would credit Britain with a portion of the fee for forwarding the letter, and the United States would credit the owner of the ship two cents.

If the nations involved were angry at each other for any reason, mail would not be forwarded. Many countries frequently changed their rates, based on their rulers' whims. For countries like Turkey or China, there were as many as six alternate methods of mailing a letter, each with its own rate system. No wonder stamp collectors who study postal history often have a hard time figuring out the postage and postage due markings on old envelopes!

A New Postal Era

Reform was needed in the world's postal system, and it was an American who took the first practical step toward implementing an international postal agreement. In 1862, Montgomery Blair, Postmaster General of the United States, suggested that a conference be held to discuss ways to improve the international postal rate structure. A meeting took place in Paris on May 11, 1863, and the 15 postal administrations on hand drew up 31 articles as a basis for future conferences.

At the historic 1874 meeting in Bern, Switzerland, delegates from 22 countries decided on four main principles that are still valid today:

1. The postal service of the world should be regulated by a common treaty.

2. The right of transit by sea or land should be guaranteed by every country to every other country.

3. The country of origin should be responsible for the transmission of mail, and all the intermediate services should be paid for by fixed rates and according to periodic statistics.

4. Each country should keep all its postage collections on both paid and unpaid letters.

The UPU became a specialized agency of the United Nations in 1947. In addition to setting rules for the free flow of mail, it constantly strives to promote international cooperation in organizing and improving postal services. The UPU operates under an international agreement, called the Universal Postal Convention, that lists postal rates and uniform procedures for handling First-Class mail, including letters, postcards and small packets.

Under the convention, in principle, each country keeps the postage it collects on international mail, but each must repay other members for the cost of transporting mail across their borders.

The Universal Postal Congress usually meets every five years to review and amend the convention. The next meeting, in 1989, will mark only the second time the Congress has convened in the United States. It first met here more than 90 years ago (in 1897), when just 55 nations were represented by 102 delegates; next year's Congress will be attended by more than 1,000 delegates from 169 member countries.

Because WORLD STAMP EXPO '89 will coincide with this gathering, it is expected to be a showcase for the post offices of the world.

Organize Your Collection... Efficiently, Conveniently

Created in 1984 for new collectors, the Commemorative Stamp Club makes sure you get all the commemoratives issued in 1988 (an expected 35-40 stamps). The Club also includes definitive stamps as an option. Specially designed Commemorative Stamp Club Album pages include illustrations and space for two issues. They give information about the stamp subjects, including dates, places and interesting background.

Annual membership for the 1988 program costs just $19.95 and offers you these benefits:

- Advance announcements of every U.S. commemorative stamp
- Commemorative stamps mailed directly to you
- Automatic shipment of custom-printed album pages for current commemorative issues
- Clear acetate mounts to hold and protect the stamps
- A *free* one-year subscription to *The Philatelic Catalog,* a bimonthly publication with full-color illustrations of all stamps, stationery and other collectibles available through mail order
- A complimentary, gold-imprinted Commemorative Stamp Club Album ($3.95 value) for enrolling now
- Special offers for definitive stamps, album pages and annual commemorative sets issued in previous years.

How to Get Involved

A no-risk, money-back guarantee assures your satisfaction. If you discontinue your membership within 90 days, simply return the album pages and stamps with a label from one of your shipments, and we'll send you a complete refund; the album is yours to keep. For more detailed information, use the postage-paid request card following page 312 or write to:

USPS Guide
Commemorative Stamp Club
Philatelic Sales Division
United States Postal Service
Washington, D.C. 20265-9983

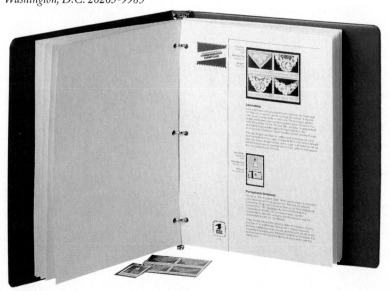

Significant Stamp Details

1¢ Franklin Types I-IV of 1851-56

5

Bust of **5**

Detail of **7, 20** Type II
Lower scrollwork incomplete
(lacks little balls and lower plume
ornaments).
Side ornaments are complete.

3¢ Washington Type I of 1851-56

10

Bust of **5**

Detail of **5, 18, 40** Type I
Has curved, unbroken lines
outside labels.
Scrollwork is substantially
complete at top, forms little
balls at bottom.

Detail of **5A** Type Ib
Lower scrollwork is incomplete,
the little balls are not so clear.

Bust of **5**

Detail of **8, 21** Type III
Outer lines broken in the middle.
Side ornaments are substantially
complete.

Detail of **8A, 22** Type IIIa
Outer lines broken top or
bottom but not both.

Detail of **10, 11, 25, 41** Type I
There is an outer frame line at
top and bottom.

5¢ Jefferson Type I of 1851-56

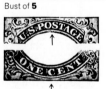

12

Bust of **5**

Detail of **6, 19** Type Ia
Same as Type I at bottom but
top ornaments and outer line
partly cut away.
Lower scrollwork is complete.

Bust of **5**

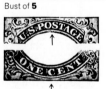

Detail of **9, 23** Type IV
Similar to Type II, but outer lines
recut top, bottom, or both.

Detail of **12, 27-29** Type I
There are projections on all four
sides.

10¢ Washington Types I-IV of 1855

15

Bust of **15**

Detail of **13, 31, 43** Type I
The "shells" at the lower corners are practically complete. The outer line below the label is very nearly complete. The outer lines are broken above the middle of the top label and the "X" in each upper corner.

Bust of **15**

Detail of **14, 32** Type II
The design is complete at the top. The outer line at the bottom is broken in the middle. The shells are partly cut away.

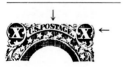

Detail of **15, 33** Type III
The outer lines are broken above the top label and the "X" numerals. The outer line at the bottom and the shells are partly cut away, as in Type II.

Bust of **15**

Detail of **16, 34** Type IV
The outer lines have been recut at top or bottom or both. Types I, II, III, and IV have complete ornaments at the sides of the stamps and three pearls at each outer edge of the bottom panel.

Bust of **5**

Detail of **24** Type V
Similar to Type III of 1851-56 but with side ornaments partly cut away.

Bust of **10**

Detail of **26** Type II
The outer frame line has been removed at top and bottom. The side frame lines were recut so as to be continuous from the top to the bottom of the plate.

Bust of **10**

Detail of **26a** Type IIa
The side frame lines extend only to the bottom of the stamp design.

Bust of **12**

Detail of **30-30A** Type II
The projections at top and bottom are partly cut away.

Bust of **15**

Detail of **35** Type V
(Two typical examples).
Side ornaments slightly cut away. Outer lines complete at top except over right "X". Outer lines complete at bottom and shells nearly so.

15¢ Columbus Landing Types I-III of 1869-75

118

Detail of **118** Type I
Picture unframed.

Detail of **119** Type II
Picture framed.

---

129 Type III. Same as Type I but without fringe of brown shading lines around central vignette.

Comparison of Issue of 1870-71: Printed by the National Bank Note Company. Issued without secret marks (134-141, 145-152, 187) and **Issues of 1873-80: Printed by the Continental and American Bank Note Companies.** Issued with secret marks (156-163, 167-174, 178, 180, 182-184, 186, 188-189, 192-199).

134   **135**   **136**   **137**

Detail of **134, 145**

Detail of **156, 167, 182, 192**
1¢. In the pearl at the left of the numeral "1" there is a small crescent.

Detail of **135, 146**

Detail of **157, 168, 178, 180, 183, 193**
2¢. Under the scroll at the left of "U.S." there is a small diagonal line. This mark seldom shows clearly.

Detail of **136, 147**

Detail of **158, 169, 184, 194**
3¢. The under part of the upper tail of the left ribbon is heavily shaded.

Detail of **137, 148**

Detail of **159, 170, 186, 195**
6¢. The first four vertical lines of the shading in the lower part of the left ribbon have been strengthened.

138   **139**   **140**   **141**

206   **207**

Detail of **206**
1¢. Upper vertical lines have been deepened, creating a solid effect in parts of background. Upper arabesques shaded.

Detail of **138, 149**

Detail of **160, 171, 196**
7¢. Two small semi-circles are drawn around the ends of the lines which outline the ball in the lower right hand corner.

Detail of **207**
3¢. Shading at sides of central oval is half its previous width. A short horizontal dash has been cut below the "TS" of "CENTS"

Detail of **139, 150, 187**

Detail of **161, 172, 188, 197**
10¢. There is a small semi-circle in the scroll at the right end of the upper label.

208   **209**

Detail of **140, 151**

Detail of **162, 173, 198**
12¢. The balls of the figure "2" are crescent-shaped.

Detail of **208**
6¢. Has three vertical lines instead of four between the edge of the panel and the outside of the stamp.

Detail of **141, 152**

Detail of **163, 174, 189, 199**
15¢. In the lower part of the triangle in the upper left corner, two lines have been made heavier, forming a "V". This mark can be found on some of the Continental and American (1879) printings, but not all stamps show it.

Detail of **209**
10¢. Has four vertical lines instead of five between left side of oval and edge of the shield. Horizontal lines in lower part of background strengthened.

2¢ Washington
Types I-III of 1894-1898

248

$1 Perry Types I-II of 1894

261

2¢ Washington Types I-VII
of 1912-21

406

Triangle of **248-250, 265**
Type I
Horizontal lines of uniform
thickness run across the triangle.

Triangle of **251, 266** Type II
Horizontal lines cross the
triangle, but are thinner within
than without.

Triangle of **252, 267, 279B-
279Be** Type III
The horizontal lines do not cross
the double frame lines of the
triangle.

Detail of **261, 276** Type I
The circles enclosing $1 are
broken.

Detail of **261A, 276A** Type II
The circles enclosing $1 are
complete.

10¢ Webster
Types I-II of 1898

282e

Detail of **282C** Type I
The tips of the foliate ornaments
do not impinge on the white
curved line below "TEN CENTS."

Detail of **283** Type II
The lips of the ornaments break
the curved line below the "E" of
"TEN" and the "T" of "CENTS."

Detail of **406-406a, 411, 413,
425-25e, 442, 444, 449,
453, 461, 463-63a, 482,
499-99f** Type I
One shading line in first curve of
ribbon above left "2" and one in
second curve of ribbon above
right "2". Toga button has only
a faint outline. Top line of toga
rope, from button to front of
the throat, is very faint. Shading
lines of face end in front of ear
with little or no joining to form
lock of hair.

Detail of **482a, 500** Type Ia
Similar to Type I but all lines are
stronger.

Detail of **454, 487, 491,
539** Type II
Shading lines in ribbons as in
Type I. Toga button, rope and
rope shading lines are heavy.
Shading lines of face at lock
of hair end in strong vertical
curved line.

Detail of **450, 455, 488, 492, 540, 546** Type III
Two lines of shading in curves of ribbons.

Detail of **526, 532** Type IV
Top line of toga rope is broken. Toga button shading lines form "DID". Line of color in left "2" is very thin and usually broken.

Detail of **527, 533** Type V
Top line of toga is complete. Toga button has five vertical shading lines. Line of color in left "2" is very thin and usually broken. Nose shading dots are as shown.

Detail of **528, 534** Type Va
Same as Type V except third row from bottom of nose shading dots has four dots instead of six. Overall height of design is 1/3 mm shorter than Type V.

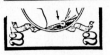

Detail of **528A, 534A** Type VI
Generally same as Type V except line of color in left "2" is very heavy.

Detail of **528B, 534B** Type VII
Line of color in left "2" is continuous, clearly defined and heavier than in Type V or Va but not as heavy as Type VI. An additional vertical row of dots has been added to upper lip. Numerous additional dots appear in hair at top of head.

3¢ Washington Types I-IV of 1908-19

Detail of **333, 345, 359, 376, 389, 394, 426, 445, 456, 464, 483, 493, 501-01b** Type I
Top line of toga rope is weak and rope shading lines are thin. Fifth line from left is missing. Line between lips is thin.

Detail of **484, 494, 502, 541** Type II
Top line of toga rope is strong and rope shading lines are heavy and complete. Line between lips is heavy.

Detail of **529** Type III
Top row of toga rope is strong but fifth shading line is missing as in Type I. Toga button center shading line consists of two dashes, central dot. "P", "O" of "POSTAGE" are separated by line of color.

Detail of **530, 535** Type IV
Toga rope shading lines are complete. Second, fourth toga button shading lines are broken in middle; third line is continuous, with dot in center. "P", "O" of "POSTAGE" are joined.

2¢ Washington Types I-II of 1923-29

Detail of **599, 634** Type I
No heavy hair lines at top center of head.

Detail of **599A, 634A** Type II
Three heavy hair lines at top center of head.

Commemorative and Definitive Stamps

1847-1875

1

2

3

4

5

11

12

15

17

30

37

38

39

	Issues of 1847, Printed by Rawdon, Wright, Hatch & Edson, Issues of 1847, Imperf., Unwmkd.	Un	U
1	5¢ Benjamin		
	Franklin, July 1	4,500.00	700.50
2	10¢ George		
	Washington,		
	July 1	18,500.00	2,000.00
	Issues of 1875, Reproductions of 1 & 2		
3	5¢ Franklin	1,100.00	—
4	10¢ Washington	1,500.00	—

Reproductions. The letters R, W, H. & E. at the bottom
of each stamp are less distinct on the reproductions
than on the originals.

5¢. On the original the left side of the white shirt frill
touches the oval on a level with the top of the "F" of
"Five." On the reproduction it touches the oval about
on a level with the top of the figure "5."

10¢. On the reproduction, line of coat at left points
to right of "X" and line of coat at right points to center
of "S" of CENTS. On the original, line of coat points to
"T" of TEN and between "T" and "S" of CENTS.

On the reproduction the eyes have a sleepy look, the
line of the mouth is straighter and in the curl of hair
near the left cheek is a strong black dot, while the
original has only a faint one.

	Issues of 1851-56, Printed by Toppan, Carpenter, Casilear & Co., Imperf.		
5	1¢ Franklin, type I	100,000.00	22,500.00
5A	1¢ Same, type Ib	9,500.00	3,750.00
	#6-9: Franklin (5)		
6	1¢ dark blue,		
	type Ia	16,000.00	5,500.00
7	1¢ blue, type II	450.00	85.00
8	1¢ blue, type III	5,250.00	1,450.00
8A	1¢ pale blue,		
	type IIIA	1,750.00	575.00
9	1¢ blue, type IV	300.00	75.00
10	3¢ orange brown Washington,		
	type I (11)	1,200.00	45.00
11	3¢ Washington, type I	130.00	7.00
12	5¢ Jefferson, type I	9,500.00	1,300.00
13	10¢ green Washington,		
	type I (15)	8,500.00	700.00
14	10¢ green, type II (15)	1,700.00	275.00
15	10¢ Washington, type III	1,750.00	285.00
16	10¢ green, type IV (15)	10,000.00	1,550.00
17	12¢ Washington	1,850.00	250.00

	Issues of 1857-61, Perf. 15	Un	U
	#18-24: Franklin (5)		
18	1¢ blue, type I	725.00	375.00
19	1¢ blue, type Ia	9,500.00	2,500.00
20	1¢ blue, type II	425.00	140.00
21	1¢ blue, type III	4,250.00	1,250.00
22	1¢ blue, type IIIa	650.00	250.00
23	1¢ blue, type IV	1,750.00	300.00
24	1¢ blue, type V	110.00	22.50
	#25-26a: Washington (11)		
25	3¢ rose, type I	650.00	27.50
26	3¢ dull red, type II	45.00	2.75
26a	3¢ dull red, type IIa	110.00	20.00
	#27-29: Jefferson (12)		
27	5¢ brick red, type I	7,500.00	1,000.00
28	5¢ red brown, type I	1,350.00	285.00
28A	5¢ Indian red, type I	9,000.00	1,500.00
29	5¢ brown, type I	750.00	225.00
30	5¢ Jefferson, type II	750.00	900.00
30A	5¢ orange brown		
	Jefferson, type II (30)	450.00	185.00
	#31-35: Washington (15)		
31	10¢ green, type I	5,000.00	525.00
32	10¢ green, type II	1,650.00	170.00
33	10¢ green, type III	1,750.00	185.00
34	10¢ green, type IV	15,000.00	1,600.00
35	10¢ green, type V	175.00	57.50
36	12¢ black Washington		
	(17)	325.00	85.00
37	24¢ Washington	600.00	220.00
38	30¢ Franklin	750.00	285.00
39	90¢ Washington	1,450.00	2,750.00
	90¢ Same, with pen cancel	—	1,000.00

Note: Beware of forged cancellations of
#39. Genuine cancellations are rare.

	Issues of 1875: Government Reprints, Printed by the Continental Bank Note Co., White Paper, Without Gum, Perf. 12		
40	1¢ bright blue Franklin (5)	550.00	—
41	3¢ scarlet Washington (11)	2,850.00	—
42	5¢ orange brown		
	Jefferson (30)	950.00	—
43	10¢ blue green		
	Washington (15)	2,250.00	—

	1875 continued, Reprints, Perf. 12	Un	U
44	12¢ greenish black		
	Washington (17)	2,600.00	—
45	24¢ blackish violet		
	Washington (37)	2,850.00	—
46	30¢ yellow orange Franklin		
	(38)	2,850.00	—
47	90¢ deep blue		
	Washington (39)	4,250.00	—

48-54 not assigned

Following the outbreak of the Civil War, the U.S. Government demonetized all previous issues.

**Issues of 1861,
Printed by the National Bank Note Co.,
Thin, Semi-Transparent Paper**

		Un	U
55	1¢ Franklin	17,000.00	—
56	3¢ Washington	700.00	—
57	5¢ brown Jefferson	12,500.00	—
58	10¢ Washington	5,500.00	—
59	12¢ Washington	35,000.00	—
60	24¢ dk. vio. Washington		
	(70)	6,000.00	—
61	30¢ red org. Franklin		
	(71)	16,000.00	—
62	90¢ dull blue		
	Washington (72)	20,000.00	—
62B	10¢ dark green		
	Washington (58)	5,500.00	450.00

#55-62 were not used for postage and do not exist in a canceled state. Paper of the following issues is more opaque.

Issues of 1861-62

		Un	U
63	1¢ Franklin	110.00	17.50
64	3¢ Washington	3,500.00	250.00
65	3¢ rose Washington (64)	50.00	1.10
66	3¢ lake Washington (64)	1,650.00	
67	5¢ Jefferson	4,000.00	375.00
68	10¢ Washington	250.00	30.00
69	12¢ Washington	450.00	50.00
70	24¢ Washington	550.00	77.50
71	30¢ Franklin	450.00	65.00
72	90¢ Washington	1,200.00	250.00

Issues of 1861-66

		Un	U
73	2¢ Andrew Jackson	110.00	22.50

		Un	U
74	3¢ scarlet Washington		
	(64)	4,500.00	—
75	5¢ red brown Jefferson		
	(67)	1,200.00	210.00
76	5¢ brn. Jefferson (67)	300.00	52.50
77	15¢ Abraham Lincoln	450.00	65.00
78	24¢ lilac Washington (70)	275.00	50.00

#74 was not regularly issued.

Grills on U.S. Stamps

Between 1867 and 1870, postage stamps were embossed with grills to prevent re-use of canceled stamps. The pyramid-shaped grills absorbed cancellation ink, making it virtually impossible to remove a postmark chemically.

Issues of 1867, With Grills

Grills A, B, C: Points Up

A. Grill Covers Entire Stamp

		Un	U
79	3¢ rose Washington		
	(64)	1,650.00	425.00
80	5¢ brn. Jefferson (67)	40,000.00	—
81	30¢ org. Franklin (71)	—	32,500.00

B. Grill about 18 x 15 mm.

82	3¢ rose Washington (64)	—	45,000.00

C. Grill about 13 x 16 mm.

83	3¢ rose Washington (64)	1,600.00	375.00

Grills, D, Z, E, F: Points Down

D. Grill about 12 x 14 mm.

84	2¢ blk. Jackson (73)	3,000.00	900.00
85	3¢ rose Washington (64)	1,350.00	425.00

Z. Grill about 11 x 14 mm.

85A	1¢ bl. Franklin (63)	—	110,000.00
85B	2¢ blk. Jackson (73)	1,200.00	350.00
85C	3¢ rose Washington (64)	3,500.00	950.00
85D	10¢ green Washington		
	(68)	—	25,000.00
85E	12¢ black Washington		
	(69)	1,550.00	550.00
85F	15¢ blk. Lincoln (77)	—	35,000.00

E. Grill about 11 x 13 mm.

86	1¢ blue Franklin (63)	750.00	250.00
87	2¢ black Jackson (73)	325.00	70.00
88	3¢ rose Washington (64)	275.00	12.50
89	10¢ grn. Washington (68)	1,200.00	175.00
90	12¢ blk. Washington (69)	1,400.00	190.00

55   56   57   58   59

62   63   64   67   68   69

70   71   72   73   77

Man of the World

Legislator, diplomat and author; scientist, musician and inventor; architect, philosopher and planter: Thomas Jefferson (#57, 67, 75-76), our nation's third President, was a Renaissance man born in the Age of Reason.

112   113   114   115   116

117   118   120   121   122

134   135   136   137   138

139   140   141   142   143

144

	1867 continued, With Grill, Perf. 12	Un	U
91	15¢ black Lincoln (77)	3,000.00	455.00
	F. Grill about 9 x 13 mm.		
92	1¢ blue Franklin (63)	325.00	100.00
93	2¢ black Jackson (73)	120.00	25.00
94	3¢ red Washington (64)	85.00	2.50
95	5¢ brown Jefferson (67)	850.00	275.00
96	10¢ yellow green		
	Washington (68)	650.00	110.00
97	12¢ blk. Washington (69)	675.00	115.00
98	15¢ black Lincoln (77)	675.00	125.00
99	24¢ gray lilac		
	Washington (70)	1,250.00	475.00
100	30¢ orange Franklin (71)	1,400.00	375.00
101	90¢ blue Washington		
	(72)	4,000.00	950.00

Reissues of 1861-66 in 1875, Without Grill

		Un	U
102	1¢ blue Franklin (63)	*500.00*	*800.00*
103	2¢ black Jackson (73)	*2,500.00*	*4,000.00*
104	3¢ brown red		
	Washington (64)	*3,250.00*	*4,250.00*
105	5¢ brown Jefferson (67)	*1,800.00*	*2,250.00*
106	10¢ grn. Washington (68)	*2,100.00*	*3,750.00*
107	12¢ blk. Washington (69)	*3,000.00*	*4,500.00*
108	15¢ black Lincoln (77)	*3,000.00*	*4,750.00*
109	24¢ deep violet		
	Washington (70)	*4,000.00*	*6,000.00*
110	30¢ brownish orange		
	Franklin (71)	*4,500.00*	*7,000.00*
111	90¢ blue		
	Washington (72)	*5,750.00*	*18,500.00*

Issues of 1869, With Grill Measuring 9½ x 9 mm.

112	1¢ Franklin	225.00	60.00
113	2¢ Post Rider	160.00	25.00
114	3¢ Locomotive	135.00	5.50
115	6¢ Washington	775.00	95.00
116	10¢ Shield and Eagle	850.00	95.00
117	12¢ S. S. Adriatic	750.00	90.00
118	15¢ Columbus		
	Landing, type I	1,750.00	250.00
119	15¢ brown and blue		
	Columbus Landing,		
	type II (118)	850.00	125.00
119b	Center inverted	*145,000.00*	*17,500.00*

		Un	U
120	24¢ Declaration of		
	Independence	2,500.00	450.00
120b	Center inverted	*125,000.00*	*16,500.00*
121	30¢ Shield, Eagle		
	and Flags	2,250.00	225.00
121b	Flags inverted	*120,000.00*	*45,000.00*
122	90¢ Lincoln	7,000.00	1,200.00

Reissues of 1869 in 1875, Without Grill, Hard, White Paper

123	1¢ Buff (112)	325.00	225.00
124	2¢ brown (113)	375.00	325.00
125	3¢ blue (114)	3,000.00	1,500.00
126	6¢ blue (115)	850.00	550.00
127	10¢ yellow (116)	1,400.00	1,200.00
128	12¢ green (117)	1,500.00	1,200.00
129	15¢ brown and blue		
	Columbus Landing,		
	type III (118)	1,300.00	550.00
130	24¢ grn. & vio. (120)	1,250.00	550.00
131	30¢ bl. & car. (121)	1,750.00	1,000.00
132	90¢ car. & blk. (122)	5,500.00	*6,000.00*

Reissue of 1869 in 1880, Soft, Porous Paper

133	1¢ buff (112)	200.00	135.00

Issues of 1870-71, With Grill, White Wove Paper, No Secret Marks

134	1¢ Franklin	475.00	55.00
135	2¢ Jackson	325.00	37.50
136	3¢ Washington	265.00	10.00
137	6¢ Lincoln	1,500.00	250.00
138	7¢ Edwin M. Stanton	1,000.00	225.00
139	10¢ Jefferson	1,350.00	400.00
140	12¢ Henry Clay	*12,000.00*	1,500.00
141	15¢ Daniel Webster	1,700.00	700.00
142	24¢ General Winfield		
	Scott	—	*10,500.00*
143	30¢ Alexander		
	Hamilton	4,000.00	825.00
144	90¢ Commodore Perry	5,500.00	750.00

It is generally accepted as fact that the Continental Bank Note Co. printed and delivered a quantity of 24¢ stamps. They are impossible to distinguish from those printed by the National Bank Note Co.

	1870-71 continued, Perf. 12, Without Grill, White Wove Paper	Un	U
145	1¢ ultra. Franklin (134)	150.00	6.50
146	2¢ red brn. Jackson		
	(135)	57.50	4.50
147	3¢ green Washington		
	(136)	110.00	.50
148	6¢ carmine Lincoln (137)	210.00	12.00
149	7¢ verm. Stanton (138)	300.00	50.00
150	10¢ brown Jefferson (139)	210.00	12.00
151	12¢ dull violet Clay (140)	500.00	60.00
152	15¢ bright orange Webster		
	(141)	475.00	60.00
153	24¢ purple W. Scott (142)	550.00	80.00
154	30¢ black Hamilton (143)	900.00	95.00
155	90¢ carmine Perry (144)	1,200.00	175.00

Issues of 1873, Without Grill, White Wove Paper, Thin to Thick, Secret Marks

		Un	U
156	1¢ Franklin	50.00	1.75
157	2¢ Jackson	140.00	7.00
158	3¢ Washington	45.00	.15
159	6¢ Lincoln	190.00	9.00
160	7¢ Stanton	375.00	55.00
161	10¢ Jefferson	200.00	10.00
162	12¢ Clay	550.00	65.00
163	15¢ Webster	525.00	60.00
164	not assigned		
165	30¢ Hamilton	600.00	60.00
166	90¢ Perry	1,250.00	185.00

Issues of 1875, Special Printing, Hard, White Wove Paper, Without Gum, Secret Marks

Although perforated, these stamps were usually cut apart with scissors. As a result, the perforations are often much mutilated and the design is frequently damaged.

		Un	U
167	1¢ ultra. Franklin (156)	7,500.00	—
168	2¢ dark brown		
	Jackson (157)	3,500.00	—
169	3¢ blue green		
	Washington (158)	9,500.00	—
170	6¢ dull rose Lincoln		
	(159)	8,500.00	—
171	7¢ reddish vermilion		
	Stanton (160)	2,100.00	—
172	10¢ pale brown		
	Jefferson (161)	7,750.00	—

		Un	U
173	12¢ dark violet Clay		
	(162)	2,750.00	—
174	15¢ bright orange		
	Webster (163)	7,750.00	—
175	24¢ dull purple		
	W. Scott (142)	1,850.00	—
176	30¢ greenish black		
	Hamilton (165)	7,000.00	—
177	90¢ violet car. Perry		
	(166)	7,000.00	—

Yellowish Wove Paper

		Un	U
178	2¢ vermilion Jackson		
	(157), June	150.00	5.50
179	5¢ Zachary Taylor,		
	June	165.00	9.00

Special Printing, Hard, White Wove Paper, Without Gum

		Un	U
180	2¢ carmine vermilion		
	Jackson (157)	17,000.00	—
181	5¢ bright blue Taylor		
	(179)	32,500.00	—

Issues of 1879, Printed by the American Bank Note Co. Soft, Porous Paper, Thin to Thick

		Un	U
182	1¢ dark ultramarine		
	Franklin (156)	110.00	1.20
183	2¢ vermilion Jackson		
	(157)	50.00	1.20
184	3¢ green Washington		
	(158)	42.50	.10
185	5¢ blue Taylor (179)	200.00	7.50
186	6¢ pink Lincoln (159)	400.00	12.00
187	10¢ brown Jefferson (139)		
	(no secret mark)	700.00	14.00
188	10¢ brown Jefferson (161)		
	(with secret mark)	425.00	15.00
189	15¢ red orange		
	Webster (163)	150.00	14.00
190	30¢ full black Hamilton		
	(165)	475.00	30.00
191	90¢ carmine Perry (166)	1,000.00	150.00

156

157

158

159

160

161

162

163

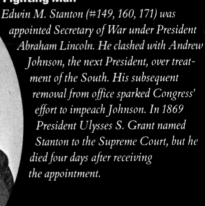
179

A Fighting Man

Edwin M. Stanton (#149, 160, 171) was appointed Secretary of War under President Abraham Lincoln. He clashed with Andrew Johnson, the next President, over treatment of the South. His subsequent removal from office sparked Congress' effort to impeach Johnson. In 1869 President Ulysses S. Grant named Stanton to the Supreme Court, but he died four days after receiving the appointment.

205

206

207

208

209

210

211

212

219

220

221

222

223

224

225

226

227

228

229

Perry Makes Japan Link

Commodore Matthew Perry (#229) sailed the first U.S. Navy ships into Tokyo Bay on July 8, 1853, then a year later arranged a treaty protecting American sailors and property in Japanese waters. The treaty opened Japan's ports to world trade (#1021) and, within 50 years, the island country had become a great world power.

		Un	U

Issues of 1880, Special Printing, Printed by the American Bank Note Co., Soft, Porous Paper, Without Gum, Perf. 12

		Un	U
192	1¢ dark ultramarine		
	Franklin (156)	9,000.00	—
193	2¢ black brown		
	Jackson (157)	5,750.00	—
194	3¢ blue green		
	Washington (158)	13,500.00	—
195	6¢ dull rose Lincoln		
	(159)	9,500.00	—
196	7¢ scarlet vermilion		
	Stanton (160)	2,100.00	—
197	10¢ deep brown		
	Jefferson (161)	8,750.00	—
198	12¢ blackish purple		
	Clay (162)	4,000.00	—
199	15¢ orange Webster		
	(163)	8,250.00	—
200	24¢ dark violet		
	W. Scott (142)	2,750.00	—
201	30¢ greenish black		
	Hamilton (165)	7,000.00	—
202	90¢ dull car. Perry (166)	7,000.00	—
203	2¢ scarlet vermilion		
	Jackson (157)	16,000.00	—
204	5¢ deep blue Taylor		
	(179)	28,500.00	—

Issue of 1882

205	5¢ yellow brown		
	Garfield, Apr. 10	100.00	4.00

Special Printing, Soft, Porous Paper, Without Gum

205C	5¢ gray brown (205)	16,500.00	—

Issues of 1881-82, Designs of 1873 Re-engraved

206	1¢ Franklin, Aug. 1881	32.50	.40
207	3¢ Washington,		
	July 16, 1881	37.50	.12
208	6¢ Lincoln, June 1882	225.00	45.00
209	10¢ Jefferson, Apr. 1882	70.00	2.50

Issues of 1883

210	2¢ Washington, Oct. 1	30.00	.08
211	4¢ Jackson, Oct. 1	130.00	7.50

		Un	U

Special Printing, Soft, Porous Paper

211B	2¢ pale red brown		
	Washington (210)	700.00	—
211D	4¢ deep blue green		
	Jackson (211) no gum	12,500.00	—

Issues of 1887

212	1¢ Franklin, June	55.00	.65
213	2¢ green Washington		
	(210), Sept. 10	22.50	.08
214	3¢ vermilion		
	Washington (207), Oct. 3	42.50	37.50

Issues of 1888

215	4¢ carmine Jackson		
	(211), Nov.	130.00	11.00
216	5¢ indigo Garfield		
	(205), Feb.	130.00	6.50
217	30¢ orange brown		
	Hamilton (165), Jan.	300.00	70.00
218	90¢ purple Perry		
	(166), Feb.	675.00	130.00

Issues of 1890-93

219	1¢ Franklin,		
	Feb. 22, 1890	18.50	.10
219D	2¢ lake Washington		
	(220), Feb. 22, 1890	135.00	.45
220	2¢ carmine, 1890	15.00	.05
221	3¢ Jackson,		
	Feb. 22, 1890	50.00	4.50
222	4¢ Lincoln, June 2, 1890	50.00	1.50
223	5¢ Ulysses S. Grant,		
	June 2, 1890	50.00	1.50
224	6¢ Garfield, Feb. 22, 1890	55.00	15.00
225	8¢ William T. Sherman,		
	Mar. 21, 1893	40.00	8.50
226	10¢ Webster, Feb. 22, 1890	95.00	1.75
227	15¢ Clay, Feb. 22, 1890	135.00	15.00
228	30¢ Jefferson,		
	Feb. 22, 1890	200.00	20.00
229	90¢ Perry, Feb. 22, 1890	325.00	90.00

	1893 continued	Un	U	PB/LP	#	FDC	Q
	Columbian Exposition Issue, Printed by the American Bank Note Co., Jan. 2 (8¢ March), Perf. 12						
230	1¢ Columbus Sights Land	22.50	.30	350.00	(6)	*3,000.00*	449,195,550
231	2¢ Landing of Columbus	21.00	.06	300.00	(6)	*2,400.00*	1,464,588,750
232	3¢ The Santa Maria	50.00	15.00	650.00	(6)	*6,000.00*	11,501,250
233	4¢ ultramarine Fleet of Columbus	70.00	6.00	950.00	(6)	*6,000.00*	19,181,550
233a	4¢ blue (error) (233)	*7,000.00*	*2,500.00*				
234	5¢ Columbus Seeking Aid	80.00	7.00	1,350.00	(6)	*6,250.00*	35,248,250
235	6¢ Columbus at Barcelona	70.00	20.00	1,050.00	(6)	*6,750.00*	4,707,550
236	8¢ Columbus Restored to Favor	55.00	8.00	650.00	(6)		10,656,550
237	10¢ Columbus Presenting						
	Indians	120.00	6.50	3,000.00	(6)	*7,500.00*	16,516,950
238	15¢ Columbus Announcing						
	His Discovery	200.00	65.00	*4,750.00*	(6)		1,576,950
239	30¢ Columbus at La Rabida	275.00	90.00	*7,000.00*	(6)		617,250
240	50¢ Recall of Columbus	325.00	140.00	*9,500.00*	(6)		243,750
241	$1 Isabella Pledging						
	Her Jewels	1,150.00	550.00	*20,000.00*	(6)		55,050
242	$2 Columbus in Chains	1,250.00	500.00	*22,000.00*	(6)	*15,000.00*	45,550
243	$3 Columbus Describing His						
	Third Voyage	2,600.00	1,100.00	*45,000.00*	(6)		27,650
244	$4 Isabella and Columbus	3,400.00	1,450.00	*90,000.00*	(6)		26,350
245	$5 Portrait of Columbus	3,600.00	1,700.00	*100,000.00*	(6)		27,350

The *Nina*, the *Pinta* and...

The **Santa Maria** (#232), the flagship on which Columbus sailed, was only about 75 to 90 feet long. It carried a crew of 40 men and took 36 days to cross the Atlantic Ocean. On Christmas Eve in 1492 the ship was wrecked on a reef near the present-day Cap-Haitien in the Republic of Haiti.

230

231

232

233

234

235

236

237

238

239

240

241

242

243

244

245

246   248   253   254   255   256

257   258   259   260   261   262

263

Watermark 191

Sherman's March

During the Civil War, General William Sherman (#257, 273) waged a campaign that not only beat Southern forces but devastated Georgia as well. He cut a destructive path to the sea and reached the coast in time to present President Lincoln the city of Atlanta as a Christmas gift in 1864.

Bureau Issues Starting in 1894, the Bureau of Engraving and Printing at Washington has produced all U.S. postage stamps except #909-921, 1335, 1355, 1410-1418, 1789, 1804, 1825, 1833, 2023, 2038, 2065-66, 2073, 2080, 2087, 2091, 2093, 2102, 2110, 2137-41, 2153, 2159-64, 2167, 2203-04, 2210-11, 2220-23, 2240-43, 2250 and 2337-38.

	Issues of 1894, **Perf. 12, Unwmkd.**	Un	U	PB/LP	#	FDC	Q
246	1¢ Franklin, Oct.	22.50	3.00	300.00	(6)		
247	1¢ blue Franklin (246)	55.00	1.25	600.00	(6)		
248	2¢ pink Washington, type I, Oct.	17.50	2.00	200.00	(6)		
	#249-252: Washington (248)						
249	2¢ carmine lake, type I	125.00	1.35	1,250.00	(6)		
250	2¢ carmine, type I	21.00	.25	300.00	(6)		
251	2¢ carmine, type II	175.00	2.50	2,100.00	(6)		
252	2¢ carmine, type III	100.00	3.25	1,200.00	(6)		
253	3¢ Jackson, Sept.	80.00	6.25	1,000.00	(6)		
254	4¢ Lincoln, Sept.	90.00	2.50	1,250.00	(6)		
255	5¢ Grant, Sept.	80.00	3.50	875.00	(6)		
256	6¢ Garfield, July	140.00	15.00	1,500.00	(6)		
257	8¢ Sherman, Mar.	110.00	11.50	1,100.00	(6)		
258	10¢ Webster, Sept.	175.00	7.50	2,400.00	(6)		
259	15¢ Clay, Oct.	250.00	45.00	3,750.00	(6)		
260	50¢ Jefferson, Nov.	325.00	75.00	6,000.00	(6)		
261	$1 Perry, type I, Nov.	850.00	250.00	*15,000.00*	(6)		
261A	$1 black Perry, type II (261), Nov.	1,850.00	475.00	*25,000.00*	(6)		
262	$2 James Madison, Dec.	2,100.00	650.00	*35,000.00*	(6)		
263	$5 John Marshall, Dec.	3,250.00	1,150.00	—	(6)		
	Issues of 1895, Wmkd. (191)						
264	1¢ blue Franklin (246), Apr.	5.00	.10	185.00	(6)		
	#265-267: Washington (248)						
265	2¢ carmine Washington, type I, May 1	25.00	.65	350.00	(6)		
266	2¢ carmine, type II	20.00	2.50	325.00	(6)		
267	2¢ carmine, type III	4.50	.05	135.00	(6)		
268	3¢ purple Jackson (253), Oct.	35.00	1.00	575.00	(6)		
269	4¢ dk. brn. Lincoln (254), June	37.50	1.10	600.00	(6)		
270	5¢ choc. Grant (255), June 11	35.00	1.75	600.00	(6)		
271	6¢ dull brn. Garfield (256), Aug.	65.00	3.50	1,100.00	(6)		
272	8¢ vio. brn. Sherman (257), July	45.00	1.00	700.00	(6)		
273	10¢ dk. grn. Webster (258), June	60.00	1.20	1,150.00	(6)		
274	15¢ dk. bl. Clay (259), Sept.	160.00	8.25	3,000.00	(6)		
275	50¢ or. Jefferson (260), Nov.	235.00	20.00	6,000.00	(6)		
276	$1 black Perry, type I (261), Aug.	550.00	70.00	*10,000.00*	(6)		
276A	$1 blk. Perry, type II (261)	1,200.00	135.00	*20,000.00*	(6)		
277	$2 brt. blue Madison (262), Aug.	900.00	290.00	*18,500.00*	(6)		
278	$5 dk. grn. Marshall (263), Aug.	2,000.00	425.00	*60,000.00*	(6)		

	Issues of 1898-1900, Perf. 12, Wmkd. (191) (279Be issued in 1900, rest in 1898)	Un	U	PB/LP	#	FDC	Q
279	1¢ deep green Franklin						
	(246), Jan.	10.00	.06	175.00	(6)		
279B	2¢ red Washington,						
	type III (248)	9.00	.05	160.00	(6)		
279Be	Booklet pane of 6,						
	Apr. 1900	350.00	200.00				
280	4¢ rose brown Lincoln						
	(254), Oct.	32.50	.70	600.00	(6)		
281	5¢ dark blue Grant (255), Mar.	35.00	.65	650.00	(6)		
282	6¢ lake Garfield (256), Dec.	50.00	2.00	900.00	(6)		
282C	10¢ Webster, type I, Nov.	160.00	2.00	2,500.00	(6)		
283	10¢ Webster, type II	95.00	1.75	1,500.00	(6)		
284	15¢ olive green Clay (259),						
	Nov.	125.00	7.50	2,250.00	(6)		
	Trans-Mississippi Exposition Issue, June 17						
285	1¢ Marquette on the						
	Mississippi	27.50	5.50	325.00	(6)	4,500.00	70,993,400
286	2¢ Farming in the West	25.00	1.50	300.00	(6)	4,000.00	159,720,800
287	4¢ Indian Hunting Buffalo	140.00	22.50	1,700.00	(6)		4,924,500
288	5¢ Fremont on the						
	Rocky Mountains	125.00	20.00	1,500.00	(6)	5,000.00	7,694,180
289	8¢ Troops Guarding						
	Wagon Train	165.00	40.00	2,650.00	(6)	7,500.00	2,927,200
290	10¢ Hardships of Emigration	185.00	20.00	3,500.00	(6)		4,629,760
291	50¢ Western Mining						
	Prospector	725.00	165.00	20,000.00	(6)	9,000.00	530,400
292	$1 Western Cattle in Storm	1,750.00	625.00	52,500.00	(6)		56,900
293	$2 Mississippi River Bridge,						
	St. Louis	2,650.00	875.00	115,000.00	(6)		56,200
	Issue of 1901, Pan-American Exposition Issue, May 1						
294	1¢ Great Lakes Steamer	20.00	4.00	275.00	(6)	3,500.00	91,401,500
294a	Center inverted	10,000.00	4,500.00	44,000.00	(3)		
295	2¢ An Early Locomotive	20.00	1.10	275.00	(6)	3,000.00	209,759,700
295a	Center inverted	45,000.00	13,500.00				
296	4¢ Closed Coach Automobile	110.00	20.00	2,500.00	(6)	4,250.00	5,737,100
296a	Center inverted	13,000.00	—	67,500.00	(4)		
297	5¢ Bridge at Niagara Falls	125.00	20.00	2,750.00	(6)	4,500.00	7,201,300
298	8¢ Sault Ste. Marie						
	Canal Locks	150.00	75.00	4,750.00	(6)		4,921,700
299	10¢ American Line Steamship	225.00	35.00	7,500.00	(6)		5,043,700

282C   283   285   286

287   288   289

290   291   292

293   294   294a   295

295a   296   296a   297

298   299

300   301   302   303   304

305   306   307   308   309   310

311   312   313   319

323   324   325

326   327

	Issues of 1902-07, Perf. 12, Wmkd. **(191)** (all issued 1903 except #300b, 301c, 306, 308)	Un	U	PB/LP	#	FDC	Q
300	1¢ Franklin, Feb.	10.00	.05	185.00	(6)		
300b	Bklt. pane of 6, Mar. 6, 1907	*500.00*	*250.00*				
301	2¢ Washington, Jan. 17	12.50	.05	200.00	(6)	*2,750.00*	
301c	Bklt. pane of 6, Jan. 24	*425.00*	*250.00*				
302	3¢ Jackson, Feb.	45.00	3.00	850.00	(6)		
303	4¢ Grant, Feb.	45.00	1.00	850.00	(6)		
304	5¢ Lincoln, Feb.	55.00	1.00	950.00	(6)		
305	6¢ Garfield, Feb.	60.00	2.25	1,000.00	(6)		
306	8¢ M. Washington, Dec. 1902	40.00	2.00	700.00	(6)		
307	10¢ Webster, Feb.	60.00	1.50	1,150.00	(6)		
308	13¢ B. Harrison, Nov. 18, 1902	40.00	8.50	650.00	(6)		
309	15¢ Clay, Mar. 27	135.00	6.00	3,000.00	(6)		
310	50¢ Jefferson, Mar. 23	400.00	27.50	7,500.00	(6)		
311	$1 David G. Farragut, June 5	700.00	60.00	*16,500.00*	(6)		
312	$2 Madison, June 5	950.00	200.00	*25,000.00*	(6)		
313	$5 Marshall, June 5	2,500.00	650.00	*62,500.00*	(6)		
	For listings of #312 and 313 with Perf. 10, see #479 and 480.						
	Issues of 1906-08, Imperf. (All issued 1908 except #314)						
314	1¢ bl. grn. Franklin (300), 1906	30.00	21.00	275.00	(6)		
314A	4¢ brown Grant (303), Apr.	*17,500.00*	*9,000.00*				
315	5¢ bl. Lincoln (304), May 12	550.00	250.00	4,750.00	(6)		
	#314A was issued imperforate, but all copies were privately perforated at the sides.						
	Coil Stamps, Perf. 12 Horizontally						
316	1¢ blue green pair						
	Franklin (300), Feb. 18	*22,500.00*		*55,000.00*			
317	5¢ blue pair Lincoln (304)	*5,500.00*		*7,500.00*			
	Perf. 12 Vertically						
318	1¢ blue green pair Franklin						
	(300), July 31	*4,250.00*	—	*6,250.00*			
	Issue of 1903, Perf. 12, Shield-shaped Background						
319	2¢ Washington, Nov. 12	6.00	.05	100.00	(6)		
319g	Bklt. pane of 6	110.00	*20.00*				
	Issue of 1906, Washington (319), Imperf.						
320	2¢ carmine, Oct. 2	30.00	21.00	300.00	(6)		
	Issues of 1908, Coil Stamps (319), Perf. 12 Horizontally						
321	2¢ carmine pair, Feb. 18	*35,000.00*	—				
	Perf. 12 Vertically						
322	2¢ carmine pair, July 31	*5,500.00*	—	*7,500.00*			
	Issues of 1904, Louisiana Purchase Exposition Issue, Apr. 30, Perf. 12						
323	1¢ Robert R. Livingston	27.50	5.00	275.00	(6)	*3,000.00*	79,779,200
324	2¢ Thomas Jefferson	25.00	1.50	275.00	(6)	*2,750.00*	192,732,400
325	3¢ James Monroe	95.00	35.00	950.00	(6)	*3,250.00*	4,542,600
326	5¢ William McKinley	110.00	25.00	1,100.00	(6)	*5,500.00*	6,926,700
327	10¢ Map of Louisiana Purchase	185.00	35.00	2,500.00	(6)	*7,500.00*	4,011,200

	Issues of 1907	Un	U	PB/LP	#	FDC	Q
	Jamestown Exposition Issue, Apr. 26, Perf. 12						
328	1¢ Captain John Smith	20.00	4.00	300.00	(6)	*3,250.00*	77,728,794
329	2¢ Founding of Jamestown	27.50	3.00	425.00	(6)	*4,000.00*	149,497,994
330	5¢ Pocahontas	110.00	30.00	2,900.00	(6)		7,980,594
	Issues of 1908-09, Wmkd. (191)						
331	1¢ Franklin, Dec. 1908	8.00	.05	80.00	(6)		
331a	Bklt. pane of 6	165.00	*35.00*				
332	2¢ Washington, Nov. 1908	7.50	.05	75.00	(6)		
332a	Bklt. pane of 6,						
	Nov. 16, 1908	125.00	*35.00*				
333	3¢ Washington, type I,						
	Dec. 1908	32.50	3.00	375.00	(6)		
334	4¢ Washington, Dec. 1908	37.50	1.00	375.00	(6)		
335	5¢ Washington, Dec. 1908	50.00	2.00	625.00	(6)		
336	6¢ Washington, Jan. 1909	60.00	4.50	900.00	(6)		
337	8¢ Washington, Dec. 1908	42.50	2.50	475.00	(6)		
338	10¢ Washington, Jan. 1909	70.00	1.50	1,000.00	(6)		
339	13¢ Washington, Jan. 1909	40.00	25.00	475.00	(6)		
340	15¢ Washington, Jan. 1909	65.00	5.75	650.00	(6)		
341	50¢ Washington, Jan. 13, 1909	300.00	17.50	*7,500.00*	(6)		
342	$1 Washington, Jan. 29, 1909	450.00	90.00	*12,500.00*	(6)		
	Imperf.						
343	1¢ grn. Franklin (331), Dec. 1908	8.00	3.50	90.00	(6)		
344	2¢ car. Washington (332),						
	Dec. 10, 1908	11.00	3.00	130.00	(6)		
	#345-347: Washington (333)						
345	3¢ dp. vio., type I, Mar. 3, 1909	25.00	13.50	300.00	(6)		
346	4¢ or. brown, Feb. 25, 1909	40.00	20.00	450.00	(6)		
347	5¢ blue, Feb. 25, 1909	60.00	35.00	650.00	(6)		
	Issues of 1908-10, Coil Stamps, Perf. 12 Horizontally						
	#350-351, 354-356: Washington (333)						
348	1¢ green Franklin (331),						
	Dec. 29, 1908	25.00	13.00	175.00			
349	2¢ car. Wash. (332), Jan. 1909	45.00	6.00	250.00			
350	4¢ or. brn., Aug. 15, 1910	110.00	75.00	800.00			
351	5¢ blue, Jan. 1909	130.00	85.00	850.00			
	Issues of 1909, Coil Stamps, Perf. 12 Vertically						
352	1¢ green Franklin (331), Jan.	55.00	18.50	300.00			
353	2¢ car. Washington (332), Jan. 12	45.00	6.00	300.00			
354	4¢ orange brown, Feb. 23	120.00	50.00	800.00			
355	5¢ blue, Feb. 23	130.00	70.00	850.00			
356	10¢ yellow, Jan. 7	1,300.00	400.00	7,500.00			
	Issues of 1909, Bluish Paper, Perf. 12						
357	1¢ green Franklin (331), Feb. 16	110.00	100.00	3,200.00	(6)		
358	2¢ car. Washington (332), Feb. 16	100.00	75.00	1,750.00	(6)		

328   329   330

331   332   333   334

335   336   337   338

339   340   341   342

Smith Saves Colony

Had it not been for the resourcefulness and leadership of Captain John Smith (#328), the first permanent English settlement in the New World—established at Jamestown, Virginia (#329) in 1607—might have been wiped out by disease, starvation and massacres.

367

368

370

371

372

373

Watermark 190

Hudson-Fulton Celebration

*In 1609, Henry Hudson sailed on the **Half Moon**, discovering the New York river named for him. In 1807, on the same river, Robert Fulton's **Clermont** made the first successful commercial steamboat run (#372-373).*

	1909 continued, Bluish Paper, Perf. 12, Wmkd. (191)	Un	U	PB/LP	#	FDC	Q
359	3¢ deep violet, type I	1,650.00	1,250.00	*16,500.00*	(6)		
360	4¢ orange brown	*15,000.00*	—	*60,000.00*	(3)		
361	5¢ blue	3,500.00	4,000.00	*35,000.00*	(6)		
362	6¢ red orange	1,000.00	650.00	*11,000.00*	(6)		
363	8¢ olive green	*15,000.00*	—	*55,000.00*	(3)		
364	10¢ yellow	1,050.00	700.00	*12,000.00*	(6)		
365	13¢ blue green	2,100.00	1,100.00	*17,500.00*	(6)		
366	15¢ pale ultramarine	1,000.00	700.00	*9,500.00*	(6)		
	Lincoln Memorial Issue, Feb. 12						
367	2¢ Lincoln, Perf. 12	7.00	2.75	160.00	(6)	*350.00*	148,387,191
368	2¢ Lincoln, Imperf.	30.00	25.00	300.00	(6)	*3,500.00*	1,273,900
369	2¢ Lincoln, bluish paper, Perf. 12	225.00	200.00	*4,250.00*	(6)		637,000
	Alaska-Yukon Exposition Issue, June 1						
370	2¢ William Seward, Perf. 12	12.00	2.25	300.00	(6)	*1,800.00*	152,887,311
371	2¢ William Seward, Imperf.	45.00	30.00	400.00	(6)		525,400
	Hudson-Fulton Celebration Issue, Sept. 25						
372	2¢ Half Moon & Clermont, Perf. 12	16.00	4.75	350.00	(6)	*850.00*	72,634,631
373	2¢ Half Moon & Clermont, Imperf.	50.00	30.00	450.00	(6)	*2,000.00*	216,480
	Issues of 1910-11, Wmkd. (190) #376-382: Washington (333)						
374	1¢ grn. Franklin (331),						
	Nov. 23, 1910	7.50	.06	85.00	(6)		
374a	Bklt. pane of 6, Oct. 7, 1910	135.00	*30.00*				
375	2¢ car. Washington (332),						
	Nov. 23, 1910	7.00	.05	85.00	(6)		
375a	Bklt. pane of 6, Nov. 30, 1910	110.00	*25.00*				
376	3¢ dp. vio., type I, Jan. 16, 1911	18.50	1.50	175.00	(6)		
377	4¢ brown, Jan. 20, 1911	27.50	.50	225.00	(6)		
378	5¢ blue, Jan. 25, 1911	27.50	.50	265.00	(6)		
379	6¢ red orange, Jan. 25, 1911	37.50	.75	450.00	(6)		
380	8¢ olive green, Feb. 8, 1911	115.00	13.50	1,750.00	(6)		
381	10¢ yellow, Jan. 24, 1911	110.00	4.00	1,250.00	(6)		
382	15¢ pale ultra., Mar. 1, 1911	275.00	15.00	2,750.00	(6)		
	Issues of Jan. 3, 1911, Imperf.						
383	1¢ green Franklin (331)	4.00	3.00	65.00	(6)		
384	2¢ car. Washington (332)	6.00	2.00	200.00	(6)		
	Issues of Nov. 1, 1910, Coil Stamps, Perf. 12 Horizontally						
385	1¢ green Franklin (331)	25.00	12.00	225.00			
386	2¢ car. Washington (332)	45.00	11.00	375.00			
	Issues of 1910-11, Coil Stamps, Perf. 12 Vertically						
387	1¢ grn. Franklin (331), Nov. 1, 1910	75.00	22.50	350.00			
388	2¢ car. Washington						
	(332), Nov. 1, 1910	550.00	75.00	3,750.00			
389	3¢ dp. vio. Washington,						
	type I (333), Jan. 24, 1911	*13,000.00*	*5,500.00*	—			

	Issues of 1910-13 continued, Perf. 8½ Horizontally, Wmkd. (190)	Un	U	PB/LP	#	FDC	Q
390	1¢ grn. Franklin (331), 1910	5.00	3.25	27.50			
391	2¢ car. Washington (332), 1910	32.50	8.50	175.00			
	Perf. 8½ Vertically #394-396: Washington (333)						
392	1¢ green Franklin (331), 1910	20.00	15.00	125.00			
393	2¢ car. Washington (332), 1910	40.00	6.00	200.00			
394	3¢ dp. vio., type I, Sept. 18, 1911	50.00	27.50	300.00			
395	4¢ brown, Apr. 15, 1912	50.00	27.50	300.00			
396	5¢ blue, Mar. 1913	50.00	27.50	300.00			
	Issues of 1913, Panama Pacific Exposition Issue, Perf. 12						
397	1¢ Balboa, Jan. 1	17.50	1.75	175.00	(6)	*3,250.00*	167,398,463
398	2¢ Locks, Panama Canal, Jan.	20.00	.50	300.00	(6)		251,856,543
399	5¢ Golden Gate, Jan. 1	80.00	11.00	2,250.00	(6)	*4,000.00*	14,544,363
400	10¢ Discovery of, San Francisco						
	Bay, Jan. 1	160.00	25.00	3,000.00	(6)		8,484,182
400A	10¢ orange (400), Aug.	250.00	20.00	*9,500.00*	(6)		
	1914-15, Perf. 10						
401	1¢ green (397), Dec. 1914	27.50	6.50	375.00	(6)		167,398,463
402	2¢ carm. (398), Feb. 1915	90.00	1.50	1,850.00	(6)		251,856,543
403	5¢ blue (399), Feb. 1915	190.00	17.50	4,500.00	(6)		14,544,363
404	10¢ or. (400), July 1915	1,250.00	75.00	*15,000.00*	(6)		8,484,182
	Issues of 1912-14, Perf. 12, #405-413: Washington (333)						
405	1¢ green, Feb. 1912	7.50	.06	115.00	(6)		
405b	Bklt. pane of 6, Feb. 8, 1912	65.00	*7.50*				
406	2¢ carmine, type I, 1912	6.50	.05	165.00	(6)		
406a	Bklt. pane of 6, Feb. 8, 1912	70.00	*17.50*				
407	7¢ black, Apr. 1914	100.00	8.00	1,250.00	(6)		
	Imperf.						
408	1¢ green, Mar. 1912	1.50	.60	70.00	(6)		
409	2¢ carmine, type I, Mar. 1912	1.65	.60	70.00	(6)		
	Coil Stamps. Perf. 8½ Horizontally						
410	1¢ green, Mar. 1912	6.25	3.50	35.00			
411	2¢ carm., type I, Mar. 1912	8.50	3.75	45.00			
	Coil Stamps, Perf. 8½ Vertically						
412	1¢ green, Mar. 18, 1912	21.00	5.00	90.00			
413	2¢ carm., type I, Mar. 1912	35.00	.60	175.00			
	Perf. 12 #414-423: Franklin (414)						
414	8¢ Franklin, Feb. 1912	40.00	1.50	475.00	(6)		
415	9¢ Franklin, Apr. 1914	55.00	15.00	750.00	(6)		
416	10¢ Franklin, Jan. 1912	40.00	.30	525.00	(6)		
417	12¢ Franklin, Apr. 1914	47.50	4.50	550.00	(6)		
418	15¢ Franklin, Feb. 1912	80.00	3.50	750.00	(6)		
419	20¢ Franklin, Apr. 1914	175.00	16.00	2,000.00	(6)		
420	30¢ Franklin, Apr. 1914	125.00	16.00	1,750.00	(6)		
421	50¢ Franklin, Apr. 29, 1914	500.00	17.50	9,000.00	(6)		

397 398 399 400

400a 405 406 407 414

415 416 417 418 419

420 421 423 513 523

524

	1912-14 continued, Perf. 12, Wmkd. (191)	Un	U	PB/LP	#	FDC	Q
422	50¢ violet (421), Feb. 12, 1912	250.00	17.50	5,500.00	(6)		
423	$1 Franklin, Feb. 12, 1912	575.00	70.00	*12,500.00*	(6)		
	Issues of 1914-15, Perf. 10, Wmkd. (190) #424-430: Washington (333)						
424	1¢ green, Sept. 5, 1914	2.75	.06	45.00	(6)		
424d	Bklt. pane of 6, Jan. 6, 1914	4.00	.75				
425	2¢ rose red, type I, Sept. 5, 1914	2.50	.05	30.00	(6)		
425e	Bklt. pane of 6, Jan. 6, 1914	15.00	*3.00*				
426	3¢ deep violet, type I,						
	Sept. 18, 1914	13.50	1.25	135.00	(6)		
427	4¢ brown, Sept. 7, 1914	35.00	.40	400.00	(6)		
428	5¢ blue, Sept. 14, 1914	30.00	.40	285.00	(6)		
429	6¢ red orange, Sept. 28, 1914	37.50	1.20	300.00	(6)		
430	7¢ black, Sept. 10, 1914	90.00	4.25	850.00	(6)		
	#431-440: Franklin (414)						
431	8¢ pale olive green,						
	Sept. 26, 1914	37.50	1.50	400.00	(6)		
432	9¢ salmon red, Oct. 6, 1914	50.00	8.50	550.00	(6)		
433	10¢ orange yellow, Sept. 9, 1914	47.50	.25	550.00	(6)		
434	11¢ dark green, Aug. 11, 1915	22.50	7.00	200.00	(6)		
435	12¢ claret brown, Sept. 10, 1914	25.00	4.50	250.00	(6)		
437	15¢ gray, Sept. 16, 1914	115.00	7.25	850.00	(6)		
438	20¢ ultramarine, Sept. 19, 1914	225.00	4.00	2,500.00	(6)		
439	30¢ orange red, Sept. 19, 1914	275.00	20.00	3,500.00	(6)		
440	50¢ violet, Dec. 10, 1914	800.00	20.00	11,000.00	(6)		
	Issues of 1914, Coil Stamps, Perf. 10 Horizontally #441-459: Washington (333)						
441	1¢ green, Nov. 14	1.00	.90	7.50			
442	2¢ carmine, type I, July 22	10.00	7.50	57.50			
	Coil Stamps, Perf. 10 Vertically						
443	1¢ green, May 29	22.50	6.00	115.00			
444	2¢ carmine, type I, Apr. 25	30.00	1.50	175.00			
445	3¢ violet, type I, Dec. 18	225.00	110.00	1,100.00			
446	4¢ brown, Oct. 2	130.00	35.00	650.00			
447	5¢ blue, July 30	45.00	22.50	225.00			
	Issues of 1915-16, Coil Stamps, Perf. 10 Horizontally (Rotary Press, Designs 18½-19 x 22½ mm.)						
448	1¢ green, Dec. 12, 1915	8.50	3.00	47.50			
449	2¢ red, type I, Dec. 5, 1915	1,600.00	160.00	7,500.00			
450	2¢ carmine, type III, Feb. 1916	12.00	3.00	60.00			

	Issues of 1914-16, Coil Stamps, **Perf. 10 Vertically** (Rotary Press, Designs 19½-20 x 22 mm.)	Un	U	PB/LP	#	FDC	Q
452	1¢ green, Nov. 11, 1914	12.00	1.75	80.00			
453	2¢ red, type I, July 3, 1914	120.00	4.50	600.00			
454	2¢ carmine, type II, June 1915	115.00	13.50	575.00			
455	2¢ carmine, type III, Dec. 1915	10.00	1.00	60.00			
456	3¢ violet, type I, Feb. 18, 1916	300.00	95.00	1,300.00			
457	4¢ brown, Feb. 18, 1916	30.00	18.00	165.00			
458	5¢ blue, Mar. 9, 1916	30.00	18.00	165.00			
	Issue of 1914, Imperf., Coil						
459	2¢ carmine, type I, June 30	450.00	*600.00*	2,100.00			
	Issues of 1915, Perf. 10, Wmkd. (191)						
460	$1 violet black Franklin						
	(423), Feb. 8	975.00	95.00	*12,500.00*	(6)		
	Perf. 11						
461	2¢ pale carmine red, type I,						
	Washington (333), June 17	100.00	85.00	950.00	(6)		
	Privately perforated copies of #409 have been made to resemble #461.						
	From 1916 to date, all postage stamps except #519 and #832b are on unwatermarked paper.						
	Issues of 1916-17, Perf. 10, Unwmkd. #462-469: Washington (333)						
462	1¢ green, Sept. 27, 1916	8.50	.20	150.00	(6)		
462a	Bklt. pane of 6, Oct. 15, 1916	12.00	*1.00*				
463	2¢ carmine, type I, Sept. 25, 1916	5.00	.10	120.00	(6)		
463a	Bklt. pane of 6, Oct. 8, 1916	85.00	*20.00*				
464	3¢ violet, type I, Nov. 11, 1916	80.00	11.00	1,350.00	(6)		
465	4¢ orange brown, Oct. 7, 1916	45.00	1.75	650.00	(6)		
466	5¢ blue, Oct. 17, 1916	80.00	1.75	900.00	(6)		
467	5¢ carmine (error in plate of 2¢)						
	Mar. 7, 1917	750.00	525.00	135.00	(6)		
468	6¢ red orange, Oct. 10, 1916	95.00	7.50	1,150.00	(6)		
469	7¢ black, Oct. 10, 1916	125.00	13.00	1,350.00	(6)		
	#470-478: Franklin (414)						
470	8¢ olive green, Nov. 13, 1916	55.00	6.50	525.00	(6)		
471	9¢ salmon red, Nov. 16, 1916	60.00	16.00	675.00	(6)		
472	10¢ orange yellow, Oct. 17, 1916	120.00	1.00	1,350.00	(6)		
473	11¢ dark green, Nov. 16, 1916	32.50	17.50	325.00	(6)		
474	12¢ claret brown, Oct. 10, 1916	50.00	5.00	550.00	(6)		
475	15¢ gray, Nov. 16, 1916	175.00	12.00	2,500.00	(6)		
476	20¢ lt. ultra., Dec. 5, 1916	250.00	12.50	3,500.00	(6)		
477	50¢ light violet, Mar. 2, 1917	1,400.00	75.00	*25,000.00*	(6)		
478	$1 violet black, Dec. 22, 1916	950.00	22.50	*13,000.00*	(6)		
479	$2 dark blue Madison (312),						
	Mar. 22, 1917	500.00	45.00	6,000.00	(6)		
480	$5 light green Marshall (313),						
	Mar. 22, 1917	400.00	47.50	4,500.00	(6)		

	Issues of 1916-17, Imperf., Unwmkd.	Un	U	PB/LP	#	FDC	Q
	#481-496: Washington (333)						
481	1¢ green, Nov. 1916	1.00	.75	15.00	(6)		
482	2¢ carmine, type I, Dec. 8, 1916	1.25	1.25	25.00	(6)		
482a	2¢ deep rose, type 1a	—	6,000.00				
483	3¢ violet, type I, Oct. 13, 1917	15.00	8.50	175.00	(6)		
484	3¢ violet, type II, Oct. 13, 1917	11.00	4.00	135.00	(6)		
485	5¢ carmine (error in plate of 2¢),						
	Mar. 1917	13,000		300.00	(6)		
	Issues of 1916-22, Coil Stamps, Perf. 10 Horizontally						
486	1¢ green, Jan. 1918	1.00	.15	4.50			
487	2¢ carmine, type II, Nov. 15, 1916	18.00	2.50	135.00			
488	2¢ carmine, type III, 1919	3.00	1.50	20.00			
489	3¢ violet, type I, Oct. 10, 1917	6.50	1.00	37.50			
	Coil Stamps, Perf. 10 Vertically						
490	1¢ green, Nov. 17, 1916	.75	.15	4.75			
491	2¢ carmine, type II,						
	Nov. 17, 1916	1,450.00	225.00	7,000.00			
492	2¢ carmine, type III, 1916	11.00	.15	65.00			
493	3¢ violet, type I, July 23, 1917	21.00	3.00	140.00			
494	3¢ violet, type II, Feb. 4, 1918	11.50	.60	75.00			
495	4¢ orange brown, Apr. 15, 1917	12.50	3.50	85.00			
496	5¢ blue, Jan. 15, 1919	4.50	.60	30.00			
497	10¢ or. yel. Franklin (416),						
	Jan. 31, 1922	26.50	8.50	150.00		1,750.00	
	Issues of 1917-19, Perf. 11						
	#498-507: Washington (333)						
498	1¢ green, Mar. 1917	.30	.05	17.50	(6)		
498e	Bklt. pane of 6, Apr. 6, 1917	1.75	.35				
498f	Bklt. pane of 30	550.00					
499	2¢ rose, type I, Mar. 1917	.25	.05	14.00	(6)		
499e	Bklt. pane of 6, Mar. 31, 1917	2.00	.50				
499f	Bklt. pane of 30	9,000.00					
500	2¢ deep rose, type Ia, 1917	275.00	130.00	2,250.00	(6)		
501	3¢ light violet, type I, Mar. 1917	17.50	.10	175.00	(6)		
501b	Bklt. pane of 6, Oct. 1917	75.00	15.00				
502	3¢ dark violet, type II, 1917	20.00	.25	210.00	(6)		
502b	Bklt. pane of 6,						
	Feb. 25, 1918	50.00	10.00				
503	4¢ brown, Mar. 1917	13.00	.20	185.00	(6)		
504	5¢ blue, Mar. 1917	10.10	.08	150.00	(6)		
505	5¢ rose (error in plate of 2¢),						
	Mar. 23, 1917	550.00	400.00	35.00	(6)		
506	6¢ red orange, Mar. 1917	15.00	.30	210.00	(6)		
507	7¢ black, Mar. 1917	32.50	1.50	325.00	(6)		

	1917-19 continued, Unwmkd., Perf. 11	Un	U	PB/LP	#	FDC	Q
	#508-518: Franklin (414)						
508	8¢ olive bistre, Mar. 1917	13.50	.70	200.00	(6)		
509	9¢ salmon red, Mar. 1917	17.50	2.75	190.00	(6)		
510	10¢ orange yellow, Mar. 1917	20.00	.10	250.00	(6)		
511	11¢ light green, May 1917	10.00	3.75	135.00	(6)		
512	12¢ claret brown, May 1917	10.50	.45	150.00	(6)		
513	13¢ apple green, Jan. 10, 1919	12.00	7.00	140.00	(6)		
514	15¢ gray, May 1917	50.00	1.00	675.00	(6)		
515	20¢ light ultramarine, May 1917	60.00	.30	750.00	(6)		
516	30¢ orange red, May 1917	50.00	.95	600.00	(6)		
517	50¢ red violet, May 1917	95.00	.65	1,500.00	(6)		
518	$1 violet brown, May 1917	75.00	1.75	1,200.00	(6)		
	Issue of 1917, Wmkd. (191)						
519	2¢ carmine Washington						
	(332), Oct. 10	250.00	275.00	2,500.00	(6)		
	Privately perforated copies of #344 have been made to resemble #519.						
520-22 not assigned.							
	Issues of 1918, Aug., Unwmkd.						
523	$2 orange red and black						
	Franklin (547)	800.00	200.00	*18,500.00*	(8)		
524	$5 deep green and black						
	Franklin (547)	350.00	30.00	*6,000.00*	(8)		
	Issues of 1918-20						
	#525-535: Washington (333)						
525	1¢ gray green, Dec. 1918	2.25	.60	30.00	(6)		
526	2¢ carmine, type IV,						
	Mar. 15, 1920	32.50	4.00	275.00	(6)	*800.00*	
527	2¢ carmine, type V, 1920	17.50	1.00	150.00	(6)		
528	2¢ carmine, type Va, 1920	8.00	.15	65.00	(6)		
528A	2¢ carmine, type VI, 1920	55.00	1.00	400.00	(6)		
528B	2¢ carmine, type VII, 1920	20.00	.12	165.00	(6)		
529	3¢ violet, type III, 1918	3.00	.10	70.00	(6)		
530	3¢ purple, type IV, 1918	.70	.06	12.00	(6)		
	Imperf.						
531	1¢ green, Jan. 1920	10.00	8.00	100.00	(6)		
532	2¢ car. rose, type IV, 1920	47.50	27.50	350.00	(6)		
533	2¢ carmine, type V, 1920	235.00	70.00	2,000.00	(6)		
534	2¢ carmine, type Va, 1920	12.50	9.00	110.00	(6)		
534A	2¢ carmine, type VI, 1920	42.50	25.00	375.00	(6)		
534B	2¢ carmine, type VII, 1920	1,550.00	425.00	*12,500.00*	(6)		
535	3¢ violet, type IV, 1918	8.50	6.50	70.00	(6)		
	Issues of 1919, Perf. 12½						
536	1¢ gray green Washington						
	(333), Aug.	15.00	15.00	200.00	(6)		

	1919 continued, Perf. 12½	Un	U	PB/LP	#	FDC	Q
537	3¢ Allied Victory, Mar. 3	11.00	4.25	150.00	(6)	*700.00*	99,585,200
	#538-546: Washington (333)						
	Perf. 11x10						
538	1¢ green, June	10.00	9.00	110.00	(4)		
539	2¢ carmine rose, type II	2,350.00	750.00	*15,000.00*	(4)		
540	2¢ carm. rose, type III, June 14	11.00	9.00	115.00	(4)		
541	3¢ violet, type II, June	37.50	35.00	400.00	(4)		
	Issue of 1920, Perf. 10x11						
542	1¢ green, May 26	11.00	1.00	175.00	(6)	700.00	
	Issue of 1921, Perf. 10 (Design 19 x 22½ mm)						
543	1¢ green	.60	.06	20.00	(4)		
	Issues of 1923, Perf. 11 (Design 19 x 22½ mm)						
544	1¢ green, 19x22½ mm	*6,500.00*	1,750.00				
	Issues of 1921, Perf. 11 (Designs 19½-20 x 22 mm)						
545	1¢ green, 19½-20x22mm	150.00	110.00	1,100.00	(4)		
546	2¢ carmine rose, type III	100.00	90.00	850.00	(4)		
	Issues of 1920						
547	$2 Franklin	300.00	40.00	7,000.00	(8)		
	Pilgrim Tercentenary Issue, Dec. 21						
548	1¢ The Mayflower	5.50	3.00	55.00	(6)	*700.00*	137,978,207
549	2¢ Landing of the Pilgrims	8.50	2.25	80.00	(6)	*625.00*	196,037,327
550	5¢ Signing of the Compact	52.50	18.50	650.00	(6)		11,321,607
	Issues of 1922-25						
551	½¢ Nathan Hale, Apr. 14, 1925	.15	.06	7.00	(6)	22.50	
552	1¢ Franklin, Jan. 15, 1923	2.25	.05	25.00	(6)	32.50	
552a	Bklt. pane of 6, Aug. 11, 1923	5.50	*.50*				
553	1½¢ Harding, May 19, 1925	3.50	.20	40.00	(6)	35.00	
554	2¢ Washington, Jan. 15, 1923	1.75	.05	25.00	(6)	45.00	
554c	Bklt. pane of 6, Feb. 10, 1923	7.00	*1.00*				
555	3¢ Lincoln, Feb. 12, 1923	21.00	1.25	210.00	(6)	37.50	
556	4¢ M. Washington, Jan. 15, 1923	22.50	.20	225.00	(6)	50.00	
557	5¢ T. Roosevelt, Oct. 22, 1922	22.50	.08	250.00	(6)	*125.00*	
558	6¢ Garfield, Nov. 20, 1922	40.00	.85	425.00	(6)	200.00	
559	7¢ McKinley, May 1, 1923	10.00	.75	90.00	(6)	100.00	
560	8¢ Grant, May 1, 1923	55.00	.85	725.00	(6)	100.00	
561	9¢ Jefferson, Jan. 15, 1923	18.00	1.25	210.00	(6)	100.00	
562	10¢ Monroe, Jan. 15, 1923	24.00	.10	300.00	(6)	100.00	
563	11¢ Hayes, Oct. 4, 1922	2.00	.25	35.00	(6)	550.00	
564	12¢ Cleveland, Mar. 20, 1923	8.50	.08	90.00	(6)	*135.00*	
565	14¢ American Indian, 1923	5.00	.85	60.00	(6)	300.00	
566	15¢ Statue of Liberty, 1922	27.50	.06	300.00	(6)	350.00	
567	20¢ Golden Gate, 1923	27.50	.06	300.00	(6)	*400.00*	
568	25¢ Niagara Falls, 1922	24.00	.50	250.00	(6)	*600.00*	
569	30¢ Buffalo, Mar. 20, 1923	45.00	.35	450.00	(6)	*725.00*	

537   547   548   549

550   551   552   553   554

555   556   557   558   559

560   561   562   563   564

565   566   567   568   569

570   571   572   573

	1922-25 continued, Perf. 11	Un	U	PB/LP	#	FDC	Q
570	50¢ Arlington Amphitheater,						
	Nov. 11, 1922	75.00	.12	900.00	(6)	1,000.00	
571	$1 Lincoln Memorial,						
	Feb. 12, 1923	50.00	.45	500.00	(6)	4,000.00	
572	$2 U.S. Capitol, Mar. 20, 1923	145.00	11.00	1,650.00	(6)	10,000.00	
573	$5 Head of Freedom,						
	Capitol Dome, Mar. 20, 1923	375.00	15.00	5,500.00	(8)	11,000.00	
574 not assigned							
	Issues of 1923-25, Imperf.						
575	1¢ green Franklin (552),						
	Mar. 20, 1923	10.00	3.50	100.00	(6)		
576	1½¢ yellow brown Harding						
	(553), Apr. 4, 1925	2.25	1.75	30.00	(6)	45.00	
577	2¢ carmine Washington (554)	2.50	2.00	30.00	(6)		
	For listings of other perforated stamps of issues 551-571 see:						
	#578 and 579		Perf. 11x10				
	#581 to 591		Perf. 10				
	#594 and 595		Perf. 11				
	#622 and 623		Perf. 11				
	#632 to 642, 653, 692 to 696		Perf. 11x10½				
	#697 to 701		Perf. 10½x11				
	Issues of 1923-26, Perf. 11x10						
578	1¢ green Franklin (552)	80.00	65.00	750.00	(4)		
579	2¢ carmine Washington (554)	.57.50	50.00	450.00	(4)		
580 not assigned							

	Issues of 1923-29, Perf. 10	Un	U	PB/LP	#	FDC	Q
581	1¢ green Franklin (552), 1923	10.00	.65	125.00	(4)	2,000.00	
582	1½¢ brown Harding (553), 1925	5.00	.60	45.00	(4)	47.50	
583	2¢ car. Washington (554), 1924	2.50	.05	30.00	(4)		
583a	Bklt. pane of 6, Aug. 27, 1926	75.00	25.00				
584	3¢ violet Lincoln (555), 1925	27.50	1.75	250.00	(4)	55.00	
585	4¢ yellow brown						
	M. Washington (556), 1925	17.00	.40	175.00	(4)	55.00	
586	5¢ blue T. Roosevelt (557), 1925	16.00	.18	165.00	(4)	55.00	
587	6¢ red or. Garfield (558), 1925	7.50	.40	70.00	(4)	70.00	
588	7¢ black McKinley (559), 1926	11.50	5.00	110.00	(4)	70.00	
589	8¢ olive green Grant (560), 1926	27.50	3.00	250.00	(4)	72.50	
590	9¢ rose Jefferson, (561), 1926	5.00	2.25	45.00	(4)	75.00	
591	10¢ or. Monroe (562), 1925	75.00	.10	675.00	(4)	100.00	

592-93 not assigned.

	Perf. 11						
594	1¢ green Franklin (552), design						
	19¾x22¼mm	7,000.00	2,500.00				
595	2¢ carmine Washington (554),						
	design 19¾x22¼mm	225.00	175.00	1,500.00	(4)		
596	1¢ green Franklin,						
	design 19¼x22¾mm (552)	—	13,500.00				

	Coil Stamps, Perf. 10 Vertically						
597	1¢ grn. Franklin (552), 1923	.35	.06	2.25		450.00	
598	1½¢ br. Harding (553), 1925	.75	.10	5.25		55.00	
599	2¢ carmine Washington (554),						
	type I, 1929	.30	.05	2.00		850.00	
599A	2¢ carmine Washington (554),						
	type II, 1929	140.00	12.00	800.00			
600	3¢ violet Lincoln (555), 1924	8.00	.08	35.00		72.50	
601	4¢ yellow brown						
	M. Washington (556), 1923	4.50	.40	27.50			
602	5¢ dark blue						
	T. Roosevelt (557), 1924	2.00	.18	10.00		75.00	
603	10¢ or. Monroe (562), 1924	4.00	.08	27.50		95.00	

	Perf. 10 Horizontally						
604	1¢ yel. grn. Franklin (552), 1924	.25	.08	3.00		85.00	
605	1½¢ yel. brn. Harding (553), 1925	.30	.15	2.75		55.00	
606	2¢ car. Washington (554), 1923	.30	.12	2.00		80.00	

607-09 not assigned.

	Issue of 1923	Un	U	PB/LP	#	FDC	Q
	Harding Memorial Issue, Perf. 11						
610	2¢ Harding, Sept. 1	.75	.10	30.00	(6)	40.00	1,459,487,085
	Imperf.						
611	2¢ Harding (610), Nov. 15	11.00	6.00	140.00	(6)	100.00	770,000
	Rotary Press Printing (19¼ x 22¾mm)						
612	2¢ blk. Perf. 10 (610), Sept. 12	25.00	2.50	375.00	(4)	110.00	99,950,300
613	2¢ black Perf. 11 (610)	—	13,500.00				
	Issues of 1924, Huguenot-Walloon Tercentary Issue, May 1, Perf. 11						
614	1¢ Ship *Nieu Nederland*	4.50	4.50	50.00	(6)	27.50	51,378,023
615	2¢ Walloons' Landing at						
	Fort Orange (Albany)	7.50	3.50	85.00	(6)	35.00	77,753,423
616	5¢ Huguenot Monument						
	to Jan Ribault at Mayport, FL	45.00	22.50	450.00	(6)	70.00	5,659,023
	Issues of 1925, Lexington-Concord Issue, Apr. 4						
617	1¢ Washington at Cambridge	4.50	4.50	50.00	(6)	27.50	15,615,000
618	2¢ "The Birth of Liberty," by						
	Henry Sandham	8.00	7.50	95.00	(6)	35.00	26,596,600
619	5¢ "The Minute Man," by						
	Daniel Chester French	40.00	20.00	400.00	(6)	50.00	5,348,800
	Norse-American Issue, May 18						
620	2¢ Sloop *Restaurationen*	7.00	5.00	225.00	(8)	25.00	9,104,983
621	5¢ Viking Ship	22.50	21.00	750.00	(8)	45.00	1,900,983
	Issues of 1925-26						
622	13¢ Benjamin Harrison,						
	Jan. 11, 1926	17.50	.65	200.00	(6)	35.00	
623	17¢ Woodrow Wilson,						
	Dec. 28, 1925	25.00	.35	250.00	(6)	30.00	
624-626 not assigned.							
	Issues of 1926						
627	2¢ Independence						
	Sesquicentennial Exposition, May 10	4.00	.60	50.00	(6)	14.00	307,731,900
628	5¢ John Ericsson Memorial,						
	May 29	10.00	5.00	110.00	(6)	22.50	20,280,500
629	2¢ Battle of White Plains,						
	Oct. 18	2.75	2.25	50.00	(6)	6.25	40,639,485
	International Philatelic Exhibition Issue, Oct. 18, Souvenir Sheet, Perf. 11						
630	2¢ Battle of White Plains, sheet of 25 with						
	selvage inscription (629)	500.00	425.00			1,500.00	107,398
	Imperf. (Rotary Press, Design 18½-19 x 22½ mm)						
631	1½¢ Harding (553), Aug. 27	2.25	2.10	70.00	(4)	35.00	

610

614

615

616

617

618

619

620

621

622

623

627

629

628

630

643

644

645

646

647

648

649

650

651

654

657

Let There Be Light

On October 21, 1879, Thomas Edison developed the first incandescent electric lamp (#654-656).

	Issues of 1926-34	Un	U	PB/LP	#	FDC	Q
	Perf. 11x10½						
632	1¢ green Franklin (552), 1927	.15	.05	2.00	(4)	55.00	
632a	Bklt. pane of 6, Nov. 10, 1927	3.50	.25				
633	1½¢ Harding (553), May 17, 1927	2.50	.08	90.00	(4)	55.00	
634	2¢ carmine Washington (554), type I						
	Dec. 10, 1926	.15	.05	1.20	(4)	57.50	
634d	Bklt. pane of 6, Feb. 25, 1927	1.00	.15				
634A	2¢ carmine Washington (554), type II						
	Dec. 1928	350.00	25.00	2,100.00	(4)		
635	3¢ violet Lincoln (555), 1927	.50	.05	7.00	(4)	47.50	
635a	3¢ brt. vio. Lincoln, 1934	.30	.05			22.50	
636	4¢ yellow brown						
	M. Washington (556), 1927	3.50	.08	100.00	(4)	55.00	
637	5¢ dk. bl. T. Roosevelt (557), 1927	3.00	.05	21.00	(4)	55.00	
638	6¢ red Garfield (558), 1927	3.00	.05	21.00	(4)	65.00	
639	7¢ black McKinley (559), 1927	3.00	.08	21.00	(4)	67.50	
640	8¢ olive green Grant (560), 1927	3.00	.05	21.00	(4)	70.00	
641	9¢ or. red Jefferson (561), 1927	3.00	.05	21.00	(4)	85.00	
642	10¢ orange Monroe (562), 1927	5.50	.05	35.00	(4)	90.00	
	Issues of 1927, Perf. 11						
643	2¢ Vermont Sesquicentennial, Aug. 3	1.50	1.65	40.00	(6)	6.00	39,974,900
644	2¢ Burgoyne Campaign, Aug. 3	5.00	3.75	65.00	(6)	16.50	25,628,450
	Issues of 1928						
645	2¢ Valley Forge, May 26	1.10	.65	40.00	(6)	5.00	101,330,328
	Perf. 11x10½						
646	2¢ Battle of Monmouth, Oct. 20	1.50	1.50	40.00	(4)	17.50	9.779,896
647	2¢ Hawaii 150th Anniv., Aug. 13	7.00	6.00	150.00	(4)	17.50	5,519,897
648	5¢ Hawaii 150th Anniv., Aug. 13	20.00	17.50	300.00	(4)	32.50	1,459,897
	Aeronautics Conference Issue, Dec. 12, Perf. 11						
649	2¢ Wright Airplane	1.50	1.40	17.50	(6)	10.00	51,342,273
650	5¢ Globe and Airplane	8.50	5.00	90.00	(6)	15.00	10,319,700
	Issues of 1929						
651	2¢ George Rogers Clark, Feb. 25	.85	.80	16.00	(6)	7.50	16,684,674
652 not assigned.							
	Perf. 11x10½						
653	½¢ olive brown Nathan Hale						
	(551), May 25	.05	.05	1.00	(4)	30.00	
	Electric Light's Golden Jubilee Issue, June 5, Perf. 11						
654	2¢ Thomas Edison's First Lamp	.90	1.00	35.00	(6)	13.00	31,679,200
	Perf. 11x10½						
655	2¢ carmine rose (654), June 11	.85	.25	55.00	(4)	90.00	210,119,474
	Coil Stamp, Perf. 10 Vertically						
656	2¢ carmine rose (654), June 11	20.00	2.00	90.00		100.00	133,530,000
	Perf. 11						
657	2¢ Sullivan Expedition, June 17	1.00	.90	35.00	(6)	4.50	51,451,880

	1929 continued	Un	U	PB/LP	#	FDC	Q
	658-668 Overprinted "Kans.", May 1, Perf. 11x10½						
658	1¢ green Franklin	2.00	1.65	25.00	(4)	27.50	13,390,000
659	1½¢ brown Harding (553)	3.00	3.00	40.00	(4)	27.50	8,240,000
660	2¢ carmine Washington (554)	3.00	.65	40.00	(4)	27.50	87,410,000
661	3¢ violet Lincoln (555)	17.50	12.00	175.00	(4)	30.00	2,540,000
662	4¢ yellow brown						
	M. Washington (556)	17.50	7.50	175.00	(4)	32.50	2,290,000
663	5¢ deep blue T. Roosevelt						
	(557)	13.00	9.00	150.00	(4)	35.00	2,700,000
664	6¢ red orange Garfield (558)	30.00	17.50	400.00	(4)	42.50	1,450,000
665	7¢ black McKinley (559)	27.50	22.50	400.00	(4)	42.50	1,320,000
666	8¢ olive green Grant (560)	85.00	72.50	800.00	(4)	80.00	1,530,000
667	9¢ light rose Jefferson (561)	13.00	11.00	175.00	(4)	72.50	1,130,000
668	10¢ orange yel. Monroe (562)	22.50	11.00	325.00	(4)	85.00	2,860,000
	669-679 Overprinted "Nebr.", May 1						
669	1¢ green Franklin	2.00	2.00	25.00	(4)	27.50	8,220,000
670	1½¢ brown Harding (553)	3.00	2.25	40.00	(4)	25.00	8,990,000
671	2¢ carmine Washington (554)	2.00	.85	25.00	(4)	25.00	73,220,000
672	3¢ violet Lincoln (555)	12.00	8.75	150.00	(4)	32.50	2,110,000
673	4¢ yellow brown						
	M. Washington (556)	17.50	11.00	200.00	(4)	37.50	1,600,000
674	5¢ deep blue T. Roosevelt						
	(557)	16.00	13.50	210.00	(4)	37.50	1,860,000
675	6¢ red orange Garfield (558)	42.50	19.00	500.00	(4)	55.00	980,000
676	7¢ black McKinley (559)	22.50	15.00	275.00	(4)	57.50	850,000
677	8¢ olive green Grant (560)	32.50	22.50	375.00	(4)	60.00	1,480,000
678	9¢ light rose Jefferson (561)	37.50	25.00	400.00	(4)	62.50	530,000
679	10¢ orange yel. Monroe (562)	110.00	17.50	900.00	(4)	70.00	1,890,000
	Warning: Excellent forgeries of the Kansas and Nebraska overprints exist.						
	Perf. 11						
680	2¢ Battle of Fallen Timbers,						
	Sept. 14	1.00	1.00	40.00	(6)	5.00	29,338,274
681	2¢ Ohio River Canalization, Oct. 19	.80	.80	32.50	(6)	4.50	32,680,900
	Issues of 1930						
682	2¢ Massachusetts Bay Colony, Apr. 8	.80	.60	40.00	(6)	5.25	74,000,774
683	2¢ Carolina-Charleston,						
	Apr. 10	1.65	1.60	65.00	(6)	5.50	25,215,574
	Perf. 11x10½						
684	1½¢ Warren G. Harding, Dec. 1	.25	.05	1.50	(4)	6.25	
685	4¢ William H. Taft, June 4	.75	.06	10.00	(4)	10.00	
	Coil Stamps, Perf. 10 Vertically						
686	1½¢ brown Harding (684), Dec. 1	2.10	.07	7.50		7.50	
687	4¢ brown Taft (685), June 4	4.00	.50	15.00		30.00	

658

669

680

681

682

683

684

685

Battle of Fallen Timbers

On August 20, 1794, U.S. General "Mad Anthony" Wayne defeated 2,000 Indians gathered along the Maumee River near what is now Toledo, Ohio. Encouraged by the British—who hoped to regain the Northwest Territory—Potawatomi, Chippewa, Ottawa and Shawnee warriors met and fought Wayne's forces in a field strewn with fallen trees (#680). Wayne's decisive victory assured peaceful colonial settlement in Ohio.

688

689

690

702

703

704

705

706

707

708

709

710

711

712

		Un	U	PB/LP	#	FDC	Q
	1930 continued, Perf. 11						
688	2¢ Battle of Braddock's Field,						
	July 9	1.40	1.40	55.00	(6)	6.00	25,609,470
689	2¢ Gen. von Steuben, Sept. 17	.80	.75	35.00	(6)	6.00	66,487,000
	Issues of 1931						
690	2¢ Gen. Pulaski, Jan. 16	.25	.18	17.50	(6)	5.00	96,559,400
691 not assigned							
	Perf. 11x10½						
692	11¢ lt. blue Hayes (563), Sept. 4	3.00	.10	19.00	(4)	80.00	
693	12¢ br. vio. Cleveland (564),						
	Aug. 25	6.50	.06	35.00	(4)	80.00	
694	13¢ yellow gr. Harrison (622),						
	Sept. 4	2.50	.10	18.00	(4)	85.00	
695	14¢ dk. bl. Indian (565), Sept. 8	4.00	.30	25.00	(4)	85.00	
696	15¢ gray Statue of Liberty						
	(566), Aug. 27	10.00	.06	60.00	(4)	100.00	
	Perf. 10½x11						
697	17¢ blk. Wilson (623), July 25	5.00	.25	30.00	(4)	325.00	
698	20¢ carmine rose Golden						
	Gate (567), Sept. 8	12.00	.05	65.00	(4)	185.00	
699	25¢ blue green Niagara						
	Falls (568), July 25	11.00	.08	62.50	(4)	350.00	
700	30¢ brown Buffalo (569), Sept. 8	18.50	.07	100.00	(4)	275.00	
701	50¢ lilac Amphitheater (570),						
	Sept.4	55.00	.07	300.00	(4)	425.00	
	Perf. 11						
702	2¢ Red Cross, May 21	.15	.12	2.25	(4)	4.00	99,074,600
703	2¢ Yorktown, Oct. 12	.40	.35	3.50	(4)	5.00	25,006,400
	Issues of 1932, Washington Bicentennial Issue, Jan., 1, Perf. 11x10½						
704	½¢ Portrait by Charles W. Peale	.08	.05	4.00	(4)	5.00	87,969,700
705	1¢ Bust by Jean Antoine Houdon	.13	.05	5.00	(4)	5.50	1,265,555,100
706	1½¢ Portrait by Charles W. Peale	.55	.08	22.50	(4)	5.50	304,926,800
707	2¢ Portrait by Gilbert Stuart	.10	.05	1.50	(4)	5.50	4,222,198,300
708	3¢ Portrait by Charles W. Peale	.60	.06	16.00	(4)	5.75	456,198,500
709	4¢ Portrait by Charles P. Polk	.25	.06	5.00	(4)	5.75	151,201,300
710	5¢ Portrait by Charles W. Peale	2.25	.10	24.00	(4)	6.00	170,565,100
711	6¢ Portrait by John Trumbull	6.00	.06	75.00	(4)	6.75	111,739,400
712	7¢ Portrait by John Trumbull	.30	.20	6.00	(4)	6.75	83,257,400
713	8¢ Portrait by Charles B.J.F.						
	Saint Memin	4.50	.90	70.00	(4)	6.75	96,506,100
714	9¢ Portrait by W. Williams	4.00	.25	45.00	(4)	7.75	75,709,200
715	10¢ Portrait by Gilbert Stuart	15.00	.10	150.00	(4)	10.00	147,216,000
	Olympic Winter Games Issue, Jan. 25, Perf. 11						
716	2¢ Ski Jumper	.50	.25	17.50	(6)	7.50	51,102,800
	Perf. 11x10½						
717	2¢ Arbor Day, Apr. 22	.18	.08	12.50	(4)	5.00	100,869,300

	1932 continued	Un	U	PB/LP	#	FDC	Q
	Olympic Summer Games Issue, June 15, Perf. 11x10½						
718	3¢ Runner at Starting Mark	2.25	.06	25.00	(4)	7.50	168,885,300
719	5¢ Myron's Discobolus	3.50	.30	40.00	(4)	9.50	52,376,100
720	3¢ Washington, June 16	.15	.05	1.50	(4)	10.00	
720b	Bklt. pane of 6, July 25	22.50	5.00				
	Coil Stamps, Perf. 10 Vertically						
721	3¢ deep violet (720), June 24	3.00	.08	14.00		.20.00	
	Perf. 10 Horizontally						
722	3¢ deep violet (720), Oct. 12	1.85	.45	10.00		20.00	
	Perf. 10 Vertically						
723	6¢ Garfield (558), Aug. 18	12.50	.25	75.00		20.00	
	Perf. 11						
724	3¢ William Penn, Oct. 24	.35	.25	18.50	(6)	3.00	49,949,000
725	3¢ Daniel Webster, Oct. 24	.50	.40	30.00	(6)	3.00	49,538,500
	Issues of 1933						
726	3¢ Georgia Settlement, Feb. 12	.35	.25	20.00	(6)	3.00	61,719,200
	Perf. 10½x11						
727	3¢ Peace of 1783, Apr. 19	.15	.10	6.50	(4)	3.50	73,382,400
	Century of Progress Issue, May 25						
728	1¢ Restoration of Fort Dearborn	.12	.06	2.50	(4)	3.00	348,266,800
729	3¢ Federal Building at Chicago	.18	.05	3.50	(4)	3.00	480,239,300
	American Philatelic Society Issue, Souvenir Sheets, Aug. 25, Without Gum, Imperf.						
730	1¢ deep yellow green						
	sheet of 25 (728)	35.00	35.00			120.00	456,704
730a	Single stamp from sheet	1.00	.50			3.25	11,417,600

Disk-Thrower Is a Glorious Copy

Discobolus (#719), or Disk-Thrower, is considered one of the finest examples of ancient Greek sculpture. Yet it is only a copy of the original by Myron, a Greek who lived in the 5th century B.C. Noted for his ability to portray athletes and animals, Myron's work survives only through Roman copies and written description.

718

719

720

723

724

725

726

727

728

729

731

732

733

734

736

737

739

741

	1933 continued	Un	U	PB/LP	#	FDC	Q
	American Philatelic Society Issue, Souvenir Sheet, Aug. 25, Without Gum, Imperf. (See also #730-30a)						
731	3¢ deep violet, sheet of 25 (729)	30.00	30.00			120.00	441,172
731a	Single stamp from sheet	.85	.50			3.25	11,029,300
	Perf. 10½x11						
732	3¢ NRA, Aug. 15	.14	.05	1.75	(4)	3.25	1,978,707,300
	Perf. 11						
733	3¢ Byrd Antarctic Expedition II, Oct. 9	.85	.85	25.00	(6)	6.00	5,735,944
734	5¢ Kosciuszko, Oct. 13	.85	.40	45.00	(6)	5.50	45,137,700
	Issues of 1934						
	National Stamp Exhibition Issue, Souvenir Sheet, Feb. 10, Without Gum, Imperf.						
735	3¢ dk. blue sheet of 6 (733)	22.50	20.00			55.00	811,404
735a	Single stamp from sheet	2.50	2.50			6.00	4,868,424
	Perf. 11						
736	3¢ Maryland Tercentary, Mar. 23	.20	.20	13.50	(6)	1.60	46,258,300
	Mothers of America Issue, May 2, Perf. 11x10½						
737	3¢ Portrait of his Mother, by James A. McNeill Whistler	.15	.06	1.75	(4)	1.60	193,239,100
	Perf. 11						
738	3¢ deep violet (737)	.20	.20	7.25	(6)	1.60	15,432,200
739	3¢ Wisconsin Tercentary, July 7	.20	.12	7.00	(6)	1.60	64,525,400
	National Parks Issue (See also #742-749)						
740	1¢ El Capitan, Yosemite (California), July 16	.10	.06	1.50	(6)	2.25	84,896,350
741	2¢ Grand Canyon (Arizona), July 24	.15	.06	2.00	(6)	2.25	74,400,200

Awesome Wonder

Established as a National Park in 1919, the Grand Canyon (#741), with its breathtaking panorama, is one of the world's outstanding spectacles. The Colorado River and the forces of nature joined to chisel the barren rock into beautiful layers, cliffs, terraces, buttes, peaks and canyons within a canyon.

	1934 continued, Perf. 11	Un	U	PB/LP	#	FDC	Q
742	3¢ Mirror Lake, Mt. Rainier						
	(Washington), Aug. 3	.20	.06	3.00	(6)	2.50	95,089,000
743	4¢ Cliff Palace, Mesa Verde						
	(Colorado), Sept. 25	.55	.50	11.00	(6)	3.25	19,178,650
744	5¢ Old Faithful, Yellowstone						
	(Wyoming), July 30	1.10	.90	16.00	(6)	3.25	30,980,100
745	6¢ Crater Lake (Oregon), Sept. 5	2.00	1.25	30.00	(6)	4.00	16,923,350
746	7¢ Great Head, Acadia Park						
	(Maine), Oct. 2	1.00	1.00	20.00	(6)	4.00	15,988,250
747	8¢ Great White Throne,						
	Zion Park (Utah), Sept. 18	2.85	2.50	30.00	(6)	*4.25*	15,288,700
748	9¢ Mt. Rockwell and Two Medicine						
	Lake, Glacier National Park						
	(Montana), Aug. 27	3.00	.90	30.00	(6)	4.50	17,472,600
749	10¢ Great Smoky Mountains						
	(North Carolina), Oct. 8	5.00	1.35	50.00	(6)	10.00	18,874,300
	American Philatelic Society Issue, Souvenir Sheet, Imperf.						
750	3¢ deep violet sheet of 6						
	(742), Aug. 28	40.00	35.00			55.00	511,391
750a	Single stamp from sheet	4.50	4.50			6.25	3,068,346
	Trans-Mississippi Philatelic Exposition Issue, Souvenir Sheet, Imperf.						
751	1¢ green sheet of 6						
	(740), Oct. 10	15.00	15.00			40.00	793,551
751a	Single stamp from sheet	1.75	1.75			4.50	4,761,306
	Issues of 1935, Special Printing (#752 to 771 inclusive), March 15,						
	Without Gum, Perf. 10½x11						
752	3¢ vio. Peace of 1783 (727) Mar. 15	.20	.15	16.00	(4)	10.00	3,274,556
	Perf. 11						
753	3¢ blue Byrd Antarctic						
	Expedition II (733)	.60	.60	25.00	(6)	12.00	2,040,760
	Imperf.						
754	3¢ deep violet Portrait of						
	Whistler's Mother (737)	1.00	.60	35.00	(6)	12.00	2,389,288
755	3¢ deep violet Wisconsin						
	Tercentary (739)	1.00	.60	35.00	(6)	12.00	2,294,948
756	1¢ green Yosemite (740)	.30	.20	5.50	(6)	12.00	3,217,636
757	2¢ red Grand Canyon (741)	.40	.35	6.50	(6)	12.00	2,746,640
758	3¢ dp. vio. Mt. Rainier (742)	.75	.70	20.00	(6)	13.00	2,168,088
759	4¢ brown Mesa Verde (743)	2.00	2.00	27.50	(6)	13.00	1,822,684
760	5¢ blue Yellowstone (744)	2.75	2.25	35.00	(6)	13.00	1,724,576
761	6¢ dk. blue Crater Lake (745)	4.00	2.75	47.50	(6)	13.00	1,647,696
762	7¢ black Acadia (746)	3.00	2.50	42.50	(6)	13.00	1,682,948
763	8¢ sage green Zion (747)	3.50	2.75	55.00	(6)	15.00	1,638,644
764	9¢ red orange Glacier (748)	3.75	2.75	60.00	(6)	15.00	1,625,224
765	10¢ gray blk. Smoky Mts. (749)	6.25	5.50	72.50	(6)	15.00	1,644,900

742

743

744

745

746

747

748

749

750

751

772

773

774

775

776

777

778

782

783

784

	1935 continued, Imperf.	Un	U	PB/LP	#	FDC	Q
766	1¢ yellow green (728)						
	Pane of 25	35.00	35.00				98,712
766a	Single stamp from pane	1.00	.50			11.00	2,467,800
767	3¢ violet (729)						
	Pane of 25	30.00	30.00				85,914
767a	Single stamp from pane	.85	.50			11.00	2,147,850
768	3¢ dark blue (733)						
	Pane of 6	22.50	20.00				
768a	Single stamp from pane	2.50	2.50			13.00	1,603,200
769	1¢ green (740)						
	Pane of 6	15.00	12.00				279,960
769a	Single stamp from pane	1.75	1.75			8.00	1,679,760
770	3¢ deep violet (742)						
	Pane of 6	35.00	25.00				215,920
770a	Single stamp from pane	3.75	3.75			10.00	1,295,520
771	16¢ dk. bl. Great Seal of U.S.	3.00	3.00	65.00	(6)	25.00	1,370,560
	For perforate variety, see #CE2.						
	Perf. 11x10½						
772	3¢ Connecticut Settlement,						
	Apr. 26	.15	.06	2.00	(4)	8.00	70,726,800
773	3¢ California Pacific International						
	Exposition, May 29	.12	.06	2.00	(4)	8.00	100,839,600
	Perf. 11						
774	3¢ Boulder Dam, Sept. 30	.12	.06	2.75	(6)	10.00	73,610,650
	Perf. 11x10½						
775	3¢ Michigan Statehood, Nov. 1	.12	.06	2.00	(4)	8.00	75,823,900
	Issues of 1936						
776	3¢ Republic of Texas Independence,						
	Mar. 2	.12	.06	2.00	(4)	12.50	124,324,500
	Perf. 10½x11						
777	3¢ Rhode Island Settlement, May 4	.15	.06	2.00	(4)	8.00	67,127,650
	Third International Philatelic Exhibition Issue, Souvenir Sheet, May 9, Imperf.						
778	Violet, sheet of 4 different stamps						
	(772, 773, 775 and 776)	3.50	3.50			13.00	2,809,039
779-81 not assigned							
	Perf. 11x10½						
782	3¢ Arkansas Statehood, June 15	.12	.06	2.00	(4)	8.00	72,992,650
783	3¢ Oregon Territory, July 14	.12	.06	2.00	(4)	8.50	74,407,450
784	3¢ Susan B. Anthony, Aug. 26	.10	.05	.75	(4)	15.00	269,522,200

	Issues of 1936-37	Un	U	PB/LP	#	FDC	Q
	Army Issue, Perf. 11x10½						
785	1¢ George Washington,						
	Nathanael Green and Mount Vernon,						
	Dec. 15, 1936	.10	.06	1.00	(4)	5.00	105,196,150
786	2¢ Andrew Jackson, Winfield Scott						
	and the Hermitage, Jan. 15, 1937	.15	.06	1.10	(4)	5.00	93,848,500
787	3¢ Generals Sherman, Grant						
	and Sheridan, Feb. 18, 1937	.20	.08	1.50	(4)	5.00	87,741,150
788	4¢ Generals Robert E. Lee,						
	"Stonewall" Jackson and						
	Stratford Hall, Mar. 23, 1937	.65	.15	13.00	(4)	5.50	35,794,150
789	5¢ U.S. Military Academy at						
	West Point, May 26, 1937	1.00	.15	15.00	(4)	5.50	36,839,250
	Navy Issue						
790	1¢ John Paul Jones, John Barry,						
	Bon Homme Richard and *Lexington*,						
	Dec. 15, 1936	.10	.06	1.00	(4)	5.00	104,773,450
791	2¢ Stephen Decatur,						
	Thomas Macdonough and						
	Saratoga, Jan. 15, 1937	.15	.06	1.10	(4)	5.00	92,054,550
792	3¢ David G. Farragut and						
	David D. Porter, *Hartford* and						
	Powhatan, Feb. 18, 1937	.20	.08	1.50	(4)	5.00	93,291,650
793	4¢ Admirals William T. Sampson,						
	George Dewey and Winfield						
	S. Schley, Mar. 23, 1937	.65	.15	13.00	(4)	5.50	34,552,950
794	5¢ Seal of U.S. Naval Academy						
	and Naval Cadets, May 26, 1937	1.00	.15	15.00	(4)	5.50	36,819,050
	Issues of 1937						
795	3¢ Northwest Territory Ordinance,						
	July 13	.12	.06	2.00	(4)	6.00	84,825,250
	Perf. 11						
796	5¢ Virginia Dare, Aug. 18	.35	.25	10.00	(6)	7.00	25,040,400
	Society of Philatelic Americans Issue, Souvenir Sheet, Aug. 26, Imperf.						
797	10¢ blue green (749)	1.25	.85			6.00	5,277,445
	Perf. 11x10½						
798	3¢ Constitution Sesquicentennial,						
	Sept. 17	.15	.07	1.65	(4)	6.50	99,882,300
	Territorial Issue, Perf. 10½x11						
799	3¢ Hawaii, Oct. 18	.15	.07	2.00	(4)	7.00	78,454,450
	Perf. 11x10½						
800	3¢ Alaska, Nov. 12	.15	.07	2.00	(4)	7.00	77,004,200
801	3¢ Puerto Rico, Nov. 25	.15	.07	2.00	(4)	7.00	81,292,450
802	3¢ Virgin Islands, Dec. 15	.15	.07	2.00	(4)	7.00	76,474,550

785

786

787

788

789

790

791

792

793

794

795

796

798

799

800

801

802

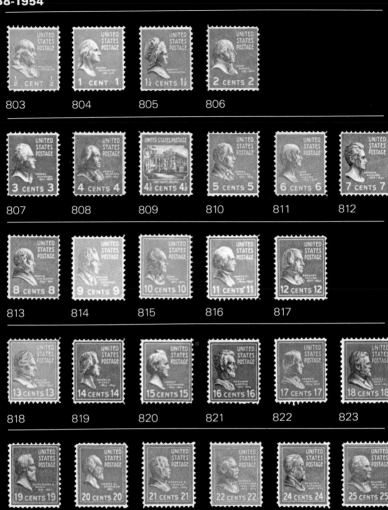

803   804   805   806

807   808   809   810   811   812

813   814   815   816   817

818   819   820   821   822   823

824   825   826   827   828   829

830   831   832   833   834

Issues of 1938-54		Un	U	PB/LP	#	FDC		Q
Presidential Issue, Perf. 11x10½ (#804b, 806b, 807a issued in 1939, 832b in 1951, 832c in 1954; rest in 1938)								
803	½¢ Benjamin Franklin, May 19	.05	.05	.40	(4)	1.25		
804	1¢ George Washington, Apr. 25	.06	.05	.25	(4)	2.00		
804b	Bklt. pane of 6, Jan. 1939	1.75	.20					
805	1½¢ Martha Washington, May 5	.06	.05	.30	(4)	2.00		
806	2¢ John Adams, June 3	.06	.05	.35	(4)	2.00		
806b	Bklt. pane of 6, Jan. 1939	4.25	.50					
807	3¢ Thomas Jefferson, June 16	.10	.05	.50	(4)	2.00		
807a	Bklt. pane of 6, Jan. 1939	8.50	.50					
808	4¢ James Madison, July 1	.45	.05	2.75	(4)	2.00		
809	4½¢ White House, July 11	.20	.06	1.60	(4)	2.50		
810	5¢ James Monroe, July 21	.40	.05	2.00	(4)	2.25		
811	6¢ John Q. Adams, July 28	.45	.05	2.00	(4)	2.25		
812	7¢ Andrew Jackson, Aug. 4	.50	.05	2.50	(4)	2.50		
813	8¢ Martin Van Buren, Aug. 11	.65	.05	3.25	(4)	2.50		
814	9¢ William H. Harrison, Aug 18	.70	.05	3.50	(4)	2.65		
815	10¢ John Tyler, Sept. 2	.50	.05	2.50	(4)	2.75		
816	11¢ James K. Polk, Sept. 8	1.00	.08	5.00	(4)	2.75		
817	12¢ Zachary Taylor, Sept. 14	1.90	.06	9.50	(4)	3.00		
818	13¢ Millard Fillmore, Sept. 22	2.00	.08	10.00	(4)	3.00		
819	14¢ Franklin Pierce, Oct. 6	1.75	.10	8.75	(4)	3.25		
820	15¢ James Buchanan, Oct. 13	.75	.05	3.75	(4)	3.25		
821	16¢ Abraham Lincoln, Oct. 20	1.75	.35	8.75	(4)	3.50		
822	17¢ Andrew Johnson, Oct. 27	1.50	.12	7.50	(4)	3.75		
823	18¢ Ulysses S. Grant, Nov. 3	3.25	.08	16.00	(4)	4.25		
824	19¢ Rutherford B. Hayes, Nov. 10	2.00	.50	10.00	(4)	4.25		
825	20¢ James A. Garfield, Nov. 10	1.20	.05	6.00	(4)	4.50		
826	21¢ Chester A. Arthur, Nov. 22	2.25	.10	12.50	(4)	5.00		
827	22¢ Grover Cleveland, Nov. 22	2.25	.50	11.50	(4)	5.25		
828	24¢ Benjamin Harrison, Dec. 2	7.00	.25	35.00	(4)	5.25		
829	25¢ William McKinley, Dec. 2	1.40	.05	7.00	(4)	6.50		
830	30¢ Theodore Roosevelt, Dec. 8	9.00	.05	45.00	(4)	10.00		
831	50¢ William Howard Taft, Dec. 8	13.50	.06	67.50	(4)	20.00		
	Perf. 11							
832	$1 Woodrow Wilson, Aug. 29	12.50	.10	62.50	(4)	55.00		
	Wmkd. USIR							
832b	purple and black, 1951	350.00	90.00					
	Unwmkd.							
832c	red violet and black,							
	Aug. 31, 1954	8.00	.15	40.00		30.00		
833	$2 Warren G. Harding, Sept. 29	32.50	6.00	165.00	(4)	110.00		
834	$5 Calvin Coolidge, Nov. 17	125.00	5.50	625.00	(4)	190.00		

This series was in use for approximately 16 years when the Liberty Series began replacing it. Various shades of these stamps are in existence because of numerous reprintings.

	1938 continued, Perf. 11x10½	Un	U	PB/LP	#	FDC	Q
835	3¢ Constitution Ratification,						
	June 21	.25	.08	5.50	(4)	6.50	73,043,650
	Perf. 11						
836	3¢ Swedish-Finnish Settlement,						
	June 27	.25	.10	6.00	(6)	6.00	58,564,368
	Perf. 11x10½						
837	3¢ Northwest Territory Settlement,						
	July 15	.25	.08	15.00	(4)	6.00	65,939,500
838	3¢ Iowa Territorial Centennial,						
	Aug. 24	.25	.08	9.00	(4)	6.00	47,064,300
	Issues of 1939, Coil Stamps, Jan. 20, Perf. 10 Vertically						
839	1¢ green Washington (804)	.25	.06	1.50		7.00	
840	1½¢ bistre brown						
	M. Washington (805)	.30	.06	1.50		7.00	
841	2¢ rose carmine Adams (806)	.30	.05	1.75		7.00	
842	3¢ deep violet Jefferson (807)	.75	.05	3.00		8.00	
843	4¢ red violet Madison (808)	9.00	.35	35.00		10.00	
844	4½¢ dk. gray White House (809)	.60	.45	4.00		10.00	
845	5¢ bright blue Monroe (810)	6.50	.35	30.00		11.00	
846	6¢ red or. J.Q. Adams (811)	1.40	.20	8.75		16.00	
847	10¢ brown red Tyler (815)	15.00	.40	60.00		22.00	
	Jan. 27, Perf. 10 Horizontally						
848	1¢ green Washington (804)	1.00	.12	3.75		7.00	
849	1½¢ bistre brown						
	M. Washington (805)	1.50	.40	4.75		9.00	
850	2¢ rose carmine Adams (806)	3.50	.50	9.00		11.00	
851	3¢ deep violet Jefferson (807)	2.75	.45	7.50		13.50	
	Perf. 10½x11						
852	3¢ Golden Gate Exposition. Feb. 18	.12	.06	1.75	(4)	5.00	114,439,600
853	3¢ New York World's Fair, Apr. 1	.15	.06	2.00	(4)	8.00	101,699,550
	Perf. 11						
854	3¢ Washington's Inauguration,						
	Apr. 30	.35	.10	4.25	(6)	5.00	72,764,550
	Perf. 11x10½						
855	3¢ Baseball, June 12	.35	.08	4.00	(4)	18.00	81,269,600
	Perf. 11						
856	3¢ Panama Canal, Aug. 15	.30	.08	6.00	(6)	5.00	67,813,350
	Perf. 10½x11						
857	3¢ Printing, Sept. 25	.15	.08	1.65	(4)	5.00	71,394,750
	Perf. 11x10½						
858	3¢ 50th Anniv. of Statehood						
	(Montana, North Dakota, South						
	Dakota, Washington), Nov. 2	.15	.08	1.65	(4)	5.00	66,835,000

835

836

837

838

852

853

854

855

856

857

858

U.S. Constitution Ratified

Before the U.S. Constitution could be put into effect, its ratification (#835), or acceptance, was required by at least 9 of the 13 original states. Ratification was hotly debated because some people feared the loss of individual liberties under a federal government. New Hampshire was the ninth state to ratify the Constitution, thereby putting the document in force on June 21, 1788, more than nine months after the Constitution was created.

859   860   861   862   863

864   865   866   867   868

869   870   871   872   873

874   875   876   877   878

879   880   881   882   883

	Issues of 1940	Un	U	PB/LP	#	FDC	Q
	Famous Americans Issue, Perf. 10½x11						
	Authors						
859	1¢ Washington Irving, Jan. 29	.08	.06	1.10	(4)	1.75	56,348,320
860	2¢ James Fenimore Cooper, Jan. 29	.10	.08	1.25	(4)	1.75	53,177,110
861	3¢ Ralph Waldo Emerson, Feb. 5	.12	.06	2.00	(4)	1.75	53,260,270
862	5¢ Louisa May Alcott, Feb. 5	.35	.30	11.00	(4)	4.50	22,104,950
863	10¢ Samuel L. Clemens (Mark Twain), Feb. 13	2.50	2.35	50.00	(4)	7.50	13,201,270
	Poets						
864	1¢ Henry W. Longfellow, Feb. 16	.12	.08	1.75	(4)	1.75	51,603,580
865	2¢ John Greenleaf Whittier, Feb. 16	.10	.08	1.75	(4)	1.75	52,100,510
866	3¢ James Russell Lowell, Feb. 20	.18	.06	3.50	(4)	1.75	51,666,580
867	5¢ Walt Whitman, Feb. 20	.35	.25	11.00	(4)	4.00	22,207,780
868	10¢ James Whitcomb Riley, Feb. 24	3.25	3.00	45.00	(4)	7.50	11,835,530
	Educators						
869	1¢ Horace Mann, Mar. 14	.09	.08	1.75	(4)	1.75	52,471,160
870	2¢ Mark Hopkins, Mar. 14	.10	.06	1.40	(4)	1.75	52,366,440
871	3¢ Charles W. Eliot, Mar. 28	.30	.06	3.25	(4)	1.75	51,636,270
872	5¢ Frances E. Willard, Mar. 28	.50	.35	12.00	(4)	4.00	20,729,030
873	10¢ Booker T. Washington, Apr. 7	2.25	2.25	32.50	(4)	7.50	14,125,580
	Scientists						
874	1¢ John James Audubon, Apr. 8	.08	.06	1.00	(4)	1.75	59,409,000
875	2¢ Dr. Crawford W. Long, Apr. 8	.10	.06	1.20	(4)	1.75	57,888,600
876	3¢ Luther Burbank, Apr. 17	.10	.06	1.75	(4)	2.75	58,273,180
877	5¢ Dr. Walter Reed, Apr. 17	.30	.25	9.00	(4)	4.00	23,779,000
878	10¢ Jane Addams, Apr. 26	2.00	2.00	32.50	(4)	7.50	15,112,580
	Composers						
879	1¢ Stephen Collins Foster, May 3	.08	.06	1.25	(4)	1.75	57,322,790
880	2¢ John Philip Sousa, May 3	.10	.06	1.25	(4)	1.75	58,281,580
881	3¢ Victor Herbert, May 13	.15	.06	1.75	(4)	1.75	56,398,790
882	5¢ Edward A. MacDowell, May 13	.60	.30	12.50	(4)	4.00	21,147,000
883	10¢ Ethelbert Nevin, June 10	5.00	2.25	50.00	(4)	7.00	13,328,000

	1940 continued, Perf. 10½x11	Un	U	PB/LP	#	FDC	Q
	Artists						
884	1¢ Gilbert Charles Stuart, Sept. 5	.08	.06	1.10	(4)	1.75	54,389,510
885	2¢ James A. McNeill Whistler,						
	Sept. 5	.10	.06	1.10	(4)	1.75	53,636,580
886	3¢ Augustus Saint-Gaudens,						
	Sept. 16	.10	.06	1.25	(4)	1.75	55,313,230
887	5¢ Daniel Chester French,						
	Sept. 16	.40	.22	11.50	(4)	3.50	21,720,580
888	10¢ Frederic Remington,						
	Sept. 30	2.50	2.25	35.00	(4)	7.00	13,600,580
	Inventors						
889	1¢ Eli Whitney, Oct. 7	.12	.08	2.50	(4)	1.75	47,599,580
890	2¢ Samuel F.B. Morse, Oct. 7	.10	.06	1.30	(4)	1.75	53,766,510
891	3¢ Cyrus Hall McCormick, Oct. 14	.20	.06	2.50	(4)	1.75	54,193,580
892	5¢ Elias Howe, Oct. 14	1.25	.40	20.00	(4)	4.50	20,264,580
893	10¢ Alexander Graham Bell,						
	Oct. 28	14.50	3.25	100.00	(4)	12.50	13,726,580
	Perf. 11x10½						
894	3¢ Pony Express, Apr. 3	.50	.15	6.50	(4)	6.00	46,497,400
	Perf. 10½x11						
895	3¢ Pan American Union, Apr. 14	.40	.12	5.50	(4)	4.50	47,700,000
	Perf. 11x10½						
896	3¢ Idaho Statehood, July 3	.20	.08	3.50	(4)	4.50	50,618,150
	Perf. 10½x11						
897	3¢ Wyoming Statehood, July 10	.20	.08	2.75	(4)	4.50	50,034,400
	Perf. 11x10½						
898	3¢ Coronado Expedition, Sept. 7	.20	.08	2.75	(4)	4.50	60,943,700
	National Defense Issue, Oct. 16						
899	1¢ Statue of Liberty	.05	.05	.70	(4)	4.25	
900	2¢ 90mm Anti-aircraft Gun	.06	.05	.70	(4)	4.25	
901	3¢ Torch of Enlightenment	.12	.05	1.40	(4)	4.25	
	Perf. 10½x11						
902	3¢ Thirteenth Amendment,						
	Oct. 20	.25	.15	6.00	(4)	5.00	44,389,550
	Issue of 1941, Perf. 11x10½						
903	3¢ Vermont Statehood, Mar. 4	.22	.10	2.50	(4)	4.50	54,574,550
	Issues of 1942						
904	3¢ Kentucky Statehood, June 1	.15	.12	2.25	(4)	4.00	63,558,400
905	3¢ Win the War, July 4	.10	.05	.60	(4)	3.75	

884

885

886

887

888

889

890

891

892

893

894

895

896

897

898

899

900

901

902

903

904

905

906   907   908

909   910   911

912   913   914

915   916   917

918   919   920

921   922   923

	1942 continued, Perf. 11x10½	Un	U	PB/LP	#	FDC	Q
906	5¢ Chinese Resistance, July 7	.35	.30	18.50	(4)	5.75	21,272,800
	Issues of 1943						
907	2¢ Allied Nations, Jan. 14	.08	.05	.50	(4)	3.50	1,671,564,200
908	1¢ Four Freedoms, Feb. 12	.06	.05	1.00	(4)	3.50	1,227,334,200
	Issue of 1943-44, Overrun Countries Issue, Perf. 12						
909	5¢ Poland, June 22	.35	.20			6.00	19,999,646
910	5¢ Czechoslovakia, July 12	.30	.15			5.00	19,999,646
911	5¢ Norway, July 27	.25	.12			4.00	19,999,646
912	5¢ Luxembourg, Aug. 10	.25	.12			4.00	19,999,646
913	5¢ Netherlands, Aug. 24	.25	.12			4.00	19,999,646
914	5¢ Belgium, Sept. 14	.25	.12			4.00	19,999,646
915	5¢ France, Sept. 28	.25	.10			4.00	19,999,646
916	5¢ Greece, Oct. 12	.85	.60			4.00	14,999,646
917	5¢ Yugoslavia, Oct. 26	.50	.40			4.00	14,999,646
918	5¢ Albania, Nov. 9	.50	.40			4.00	14,999,646
919	5¢ Austria, Nov. 23	.30	.25			4.00	14,999,646
920	5¢ Denmark, Dec. 7	.50	.50			4.00	14,999,646
921	5¢ Korea, Nov. 2, 1944	.28	.25			5.00	14,999,646
	Issues of 1944, Perf. 11x10½						
922	3¢ Transcontinental Railroad,						
	May 10	.20	.15	2.50	(4)	6.00	61,303,000
923	3¢ Steamship, May 22	.15	.15	2.50	(4)	4.00	61,001,450

Country Divided

An Asian country and peninsula, Korea (#921) is one land but two nations. In the south is the Republic of Korea, and in the north is a communist nation, the Democratic People's Republic. This division resulted indirectly from Japan's takeover of Korea in 1910. After Japan was defeated in World War II, U.S. forces occupied the southern half of Korea and Russian forces the northern half, with a separate government formed in each section. After the failure of plans to reunite Korea, the two existing nations were established in 1948.

	1944 continued, Perf. 11x10½	Un	U	PB/LP	#	FDC	Q
924	3¢ Telegraph, May 24	.12	.10	1.60	(4)	3.50	60,605,000
925	3¢ Philippines, Sept. 27	.12	.12	3.00	(4)	3.50	50,129,350
926	3¢ Motion Pictures, Oct. 31	.12	.10	2.00	(4)	3.50	53,479,400
	Issues of 1945						
927	3¢ Florida Statehood, Mar. 3	.10	.08	1.00	(4)	3.50	61,617,350
928	5¢ United Nations Conference,						
	Apr. 25	.12	.08	.70	(4)	3.50	75,500,000
	Perf. 10½x11						
929	3¢ Iwo Jima (Marines), July 11	.10	.05	.50	(4)	5.25	137,321,000
	Issues of 1945-46, Franklin D. Roosevelt Issue, Perf. 11x10½						
930	1¢ Roosevelt and Hyde Park						
	Residence, July 26, 1945	.05	.05	.30	(4)	2.50	128,140,000
931	2¢ Roosevelt and "The Little						
	White House" at Warm Springs, Ga.,						
	Aug. 24, 1945	.08	.08	.40	(4)	2.50	67,255,000
932	3¢ Roosevelt and White House,						
	June 27, 1945	.10	.08	.65	(4)	2.50	133,870,000
933	5¢ Roosevelt, Map of Western						
	Hemisphere and Four Freedoms,						
	Jan. 30, 1946	.12	.08	.75	(4)	3.00	76,455,400
934	3¢ Army, Sept. 28	.10	.05	.60	(4)	3.50	128,357,750
935	3¢ Navy, Oct. 27	.10	.05	.60	(4)	3.50	135,863,000
936	3¢ Coast Guard, Nov. 10	.10	.05	.60	(4)	3.50	111,616,700
937	3¢ Alfred E. Smith, Nov. 26	.10	.05	.50	(4)	2.50	308,587,700
938	3¢ Texas Statehood, Dec. 29	.10	.05	.50	(4)	3.50	170,640,000
	Issues of 1946						
939	3¢ Merchant Marine, Feb. 26	.10	.05	.50	(4)	2.50	135,927,000

$2-Billion Business

Motion pictures (#926) have become big business since their inception in 1894, with Americans spending nearly $2 billion on movies every year. Early films were shown in nickelodeons, where viewers watched silent films and listened to piano accompaniment—all for five cents!

924

925

926

927

928

929

930

931

932

933

934

935

940

941

942

943

944

945

946

947

948

949

	1946 continued, Perf. 11x10½	Un	U	PB/LP	#	FDC	Q
940	3¢ Veterans of World War II, May 9	.10	.05	.55	(4)	2.50	260,339,100
941	3¢ Tennesse Statehood, June 1	.10	.05	.50	(4)	2.50	132,274,500
942	3¢ Iowa Statehood, Aug. 3	.10	.05	.50	(4)	2.50	132,430,000
943	3¢ Smithsonian Institution, Aug. 10	.10	.05	.50	(4)	2.50	139,209,500
944	3¢ Kearny Expedition, Oct. 16	.10	.05	.50	(4)	2.50	114,684,450
	Issues of 1947, Perf. 10½x11						
945	3¢ Thomas A. Edison, Feb. 11	.10	.05	.50	(4)	2.50	156,540,510
	Perf. 11x10½						
946	3¢ Joseph Pulitzer, Apr. 10	.10	.05	.50	(4)	2.50	120,452,600
947	3¢ First U.S. Postage Stamps						
	Centenary, May 17	.10	.05	.50	(4)	2.50	127,104,300
	Centenary International Philatelic Exhibition Issue, Souvenir Sheet, May 19, Imperf.						
948	Souvenir sheet of 2	1.10	1.00			3.00	10,299,600
948a	5¢ blue, single stamp from sheet	.30	.30				
948b	10¢ brown orange, single stamp						
	from sheet	.40	.30				
	Perf. 11x10½						
949	3¢ Doctors, June 9	.10	.05	.50	(4)	1.50	132,902,000
950	3¢ Utah Settlement, July 24	.10	.05	.50	(4)	1.50	131,968,000
951	3¢ U.S. Frigate Constitution, Oct. 21	.10	.05	.50	(4)	1.50	131,488,000
	Perf. 10½x11						
952	3¢ Everglades National Park, Dec. 5	.10	.05	.50	(4)	1.50	122,362,000

An Apple a Day...

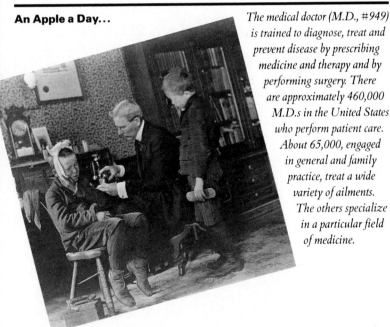

The medical doctor (M.D., #949) is trained to diagnose, treat and prevent disease by prescribing medicine and therapy and by performing surgery. There are approximately 460,000 M.D.s in the United States who perform patient care. About 65,000, engaged in general and family practice, treat a wide variety of ailments. The others specialize in a particular field of medicine.

	Issues of 1948, Perf. 10½x11	Un	U	PB/LP	#	FDC	Q
953	3¢ Dr. George Washington Carver,						
	Jan. 5	.10	.05	.50	(4)	1.50	121,548,000
	Perf. 11x10½						
954	3¢ California Gold, Jan. 24	.10	.05	.50	(4)	1.50	131,109,500
955	3¢ Mississippi Territory, Apr. 7	.10	.05	.50	(4)	1.50	122,650,500
956	3¢ Four Chaplains, May 28	.10	.05	.50	(4)	1.50	121,953,500
957	3¢ Wisconsin Statehood, May 29	.10	.05	.50	(4)	1.50	115,250,000
958	5¢ Swedish Pioneer, June 4	.15	.10	1.00	(4)	1.50	64,198,500
959	3¢ Progress of Women, July 19	.10	.05	.50	(4)	1.50	117,642,500
	Perf. 10½x11						
960	3¢ William Allen White, July 31	.10	.06	.60	(4)	1.50	77,649,600
	Perf. 11x10½						
961	3¢ U.S.-Canada Friendship, Aug. 2	.10	.05	.50	(4)	1.50	113,474,500
962	3¢ Francis Scott Key, Aug. 9	.10	.05	.50	(4)	1.50	120,868,500
963	3¢ Salute to Youth, Aug. 11	.10	.06	.50	(4)	1.50	77,800,500
964	3¢ Oregon Territory, Aug. 14	.10	.10	.90	(4)	1.50	52,214,000
	Perf. 10½x11						
965	3¢ Harlan F. Stone, Aug. 25	.10	.08	1.70	(4)	1.50	53,958,100
966	3¢ Palomar Mountain Observatory,						
	Aug. 30	.12	.10	2.50	(4)	1.50	61,120,010
	Perf. 11x10½						
967	3¢ Clara Barton, Sept. 7	.10	.08	.60	(4)	1.25	57,823,000
968	3¢ Poultry Industry, Sept. 9	.12	.08	.80	(4)	1.25	52,975,000
	Perf. 10½x11						
969	3¢ Gold Star Mothers, Sept. 21	.12	.08	.65	(4)	1.50	77,149,000
	Perf. 11x10½						
970	3¢ Fort Kearny, Sept. 22	.12	.08	.65	(4)	1.50	58,332,000
971	3¢ Volunteer Firemen, Oct. 4	.12	.08	.75	(4)	1.50	56,228,000

953

954

955

956

957

958

959

960

961

962

963

964

965

966

967

968

969

970

971

972

973

974

975

976

977

978

979

980

981

982

983

984

985

986

987

988

989

990

	1948 continued, Perf. 11x10½	Un	U	PB/LP	#	FDC	Q
972	3¢ Indian Centennial, Oct. 15	.12	.08	.75	(4)	1.25	57,832,000
973	3¢ Rough Riders, Oct. 27	.12	.10	1.20	(4)	1.25	53,875,000
974	3¢ Juliette Gordon Low, Oct. 29	.12	.08	.65	(4)	1.25	63,834,000
	Perf. 10½x11						
975	3¢ Will Rogers, Nov. 4	.12	.08	1.00	(4)	1.25	67,162,200
976	3¢ Fort Bliss, Nov. 5	.15	.08	1.50	(4)	1.25	64,561,000
	Perf. 11x10½						
977	3¢ Moina Michael, Nov. 9	.12	.08	.65	(4)	1.25	64,079,500
978	3¢ Gettysburg Address, Nov. 19	.12	.08	.70	(4)	1.25	63,388,00
	Perf. 10½x11						
979	3¢ American Turners, Nov. 20	.12	.08	.55	(4)	1.25	62,285,000
980	3¢ Joel Chandler Harris, Dec. 9	.12	.08	.85	(4)	1.25	57,492,610
	Issues of 1949, Perf. 11x10½						
981	3¢ Minnesota Territory, Mar. 3	.10	.05	.50	(4)	1.25	99,190,000
982	3¢ Washington and Lee University,						
	Apr. 12	.10	.05	.50	(4)	1.25	104,790,000
983	3¢ Puerto Rico Election, Apr. 27	.10	.05	.50	(4)	1.25	108,805,000
984	3¢ Annapolis Settlement, May 23	.10	.05	.50	(4)	1.25	107,340,000
985	3¢ Grand Army of the Republic,						
	Aug. 29	.10	.05	.50	(4)	1.25	117,020,000
	Perf. 10½x11						
986	3¢ Edgar Allen Poe, Oct. 7	.10	.05	.60	(4)	1.25	122,633,000
	Issues of 1950, Perf. 11x10½						
987	3¢ American Bankers Association,						
	Jan. 3	.10	.05	.50	(4)	1.25	130,960,000
	Perf. 10½x11						
988	3¢ Samuel Gompers, Jan. 27	.10	.05	.65	(4)	1.25	128,478,000
	National Capital Sesquicentennial Issue, Perf. 10½x11, 11x10½ (See also #991-992)						
989	3¢ Statue of Freedom on Capitol						
	Dome, Apr. 27	.10	.05	.50	(4)	1.25	132,090,000
990	3¢ Executive Mansion, June 12	.10	.05	.50	(4)	1.25	130,050,000

	1950 continued	Un	U	PB/LP	#	FDC	Q
	National Capital Sesquicentennial Issue continued, Perf. 10½x11, 11x10½ (See also #989-990)						
991	3¢ Supreme Court, Aug. 2	.10	.05	.50	(4)	1.25	131,350,000
992	3¢ U.S. Capitol, Nov. 22	.10	.05	.50	(4)	1.25	129,980,000
	Perf. 11x10½						
993	3¢ Railroad Engineers, Apr. 29	.10	.05	.50	(4)	1.25	122,315,000
994	3¢ Kansas City, Mo., June 3	.10	.05	.50	(4)	1.25	122,170,000
995	3¢ Boy Scouts, June 30	.10	.06	.55	(4)	2.00	131,635,000
996	3¢ Indiana Territory, July 4	.10	.05	.50	(4)	1.25	121,860,000
997	3¢ California Statehood, Sept. 9	.10	.05	.50	(4)	1.25	121,120,000
	Issues of 1951						
998	3¢ United Confederate Veterans, May 30	.10	.05	.50	(4)	1.25	119,120,000
999	3¢ Nevada Settlement, July 14	.10	.05	.50	(4)	1.25	112,125,000
1000	3¢ Landing of Cadillac, July 24	.10	.05	.50	(4)	1.25	114,140,000
1001	3¢ Colorado Statehood, Aug. 1	.10	.05	.50	(4)	1.25	114,490,000
1002	3¢ American Chemical Society, Sept. 4	.10	.05	.50	(4)	1.25	117,200,000
1003	3¢ Battle of Brooklyn, Dec. 10	.10	.05	.50	(4)	1.25	116,130,000
	Issues of 1952						
1004	3¢ Betsy Ross, Jan. 2	.10	.05	.50	(4)	1.25	116,175,000
1005	3¢ 4-H Club, Jan. 15	.10	.05	.60	(4)	1.25	115,945,000
1006	3¢ B&O Railroad, Feb. 28	.10	.05	.50	(4)	1.50	112,540,000
1007	3¢ American Auto Association, Mar. 4	.10	.05	.60	(4)	.85	117,415,000
1008	3¢ NATO, Apr. 4	.10	.05	.55	(4)	.85	2,899,580,000
1009	3¢ Grand Coulee Dam, May 15	.10	.05	.50	(4)	.85	114,540,000

NATO

On April 4, 1949 the United States, Canada, France, Great Britain, the Netherlands, Belgium, Denmark, the United Kingdom and Portugal signed the North Atlantic Treaty (#1008), which formally states: "An armed attack against one or more of them in Europe and North America shall be considered an attack against all."

WASHINGTON 1800-1950
NATIONAL CAPITAL SESQUICENTENNIAL
UNITED STATES POSTAGE

991

WASHINGTON
NATIONAL CAPITAL
SESQUICENTENNIAL
UNITED STATES OF AMERICA

992

HONORING RAILROAD ENGINEERS OF AMERICA
UNITED STATES POSTAGE

993

U.S. POSTAGE
KANSAS CITY, MISSOURI
CENTENNIAL

994

ON MY HONOR
I WILL DO MY BEST
BOY SCOUTS
OF AMERICA
UNITED STATES POSTAGE

995

INDIANA TERRITORY
SESQUICENTENNIAL
UNITED STATES POSTAGE

996

CALIFORNIA
CENTENNIAL OF STATEHOOD
UNITED STATES POSTAGE

997

FINAL REUNION UNITED CONFEDERATE VETERANS
UCV
3 CENTS
UNITED STATES POSTAGE

998

NEVADA
SETTLEMENT CENTENNIAL
UNITED STATES POSTAGE

999

U S POSTAGE
THE LANDING OF CADILLAC AT DETROIT 1701 1951

1000

3¢ U·S·POSTAGE
COLORADO
1876 1951
75TH ANNIVERSARY OF STATEHOOD

1001

AMERICAN CHEMICAL SOCIETY
DIAMOND JUBILEE 1876 1951
ACS
3¢ U.S.POSTAGE 3¢

1002

UNITED STATES POSTAGE
WASHINGTON SAVES HIS ARMY AT BROOKLYN

1003

200TH ANNIVERSARY · THE BIRTH OF BETSY ROSS

1004

TO MAKE THE BEST BETTER
THE 4-H CLUBS
UNITED STATES POSTAGE

1005

UNITED STATES POSTAGE
THE BALTIMORE & OHIO RAILROAD CHARTERED FEB 28 1827
125 YEARS OF RAIL TRANSPORTATION

1006

AMERICAN AUTOMOBILE ASSOCIATION
50TH ANNIVERSARY
1902 1952
U.S.POSTAGE 3¢

1007

NATO
PEACE·STRENGTH·FREEDOM

1008

3¢ U.S.POSTAGE
1902 1952 RECLAMATION

1009

1010

1011

1012

1013

1014

1015

1016

1017

1018

1019

1020

1021

1022

1023

1024

1025

1026

1027

120

	1952 continued, Perf. 11x10½	Un	U	PB/LP	#	FDC	Q
1010	3¢ Arrival of Lafayette, June 13	.10	.05	.50	(4)	.85	113,135,000
	Perf. 10½x11						
1011	3¢ Mt. Rushmore Mem., Aug. 11	.10	.05	.60	(4)	.85	116,255,000
	Perf. 11x10½						
1012	3¢ Engineering, Sept. 6	.10	.05	.50	(4)	.85	113,860,000
1013	3¢ Service Women, Sept. 11	.10	.05	.50	(4)	.85	124,260,000
1014	3¢ Gutenberg Bible, Sept. 30	.10	.05	.50	(4)	.85	115,735,000
1015	3¢ Newspaper Boys, Oct. 4	.10	.05	.50	(4)	.85	115,430,000
1016	3¢ International Red Cross, Nov. 21	.10	.05	.50	(4)	.85	136,220,000
	Issues of 1953						
1017	3¢ National Guard, Feb. 23	.10	.05	.50	(4)	.85	114,894,000
1018	3¢ Ohio Statehood, Mar. 2	.10	.05	.80	(4)	.85	118,706,000
1019	3¢ Washington Territory, Mar. 2	.10	.05	.50	(4)	.85	114,190,000
1020	3¢ Louisiana Purchase, Apr. 30	.10	.05	.50	(4)	.85	113,990,000
1021	5¢ Opening of Japan, July 14	.15	.10	1.40	(4)	.85	89,289,600
1022	3¢ American Bar Association, Aug. 24	.10	.05	.50	(4)	.85	114,865,000
1023	3¢ Sagamore Hill, Sept. 14	.10	.05	.50	(4)	1.00	115,780,000
1024	3¢ Future Farmers, Oct. 13	.10	.05	.50	(4)	.85	115,244,600
1025	3¢ Trucking Industry, Oct. 27	.10	.05	.50	(4)	.85	123,709,600
1026	3¢ General Patton, Nov. 11	.10	.05	.60	(4)	.85	114,798,600
1027	3¢ New York City Settlement, Nov. 20	.10	.05	.60	(4)	.85	115,759,600

Food for Thought

The first medium of mass communication, printing (#1014) has provided the foundation both for education and business in our society. The history of modern printing can be traced to Johannes Gutenberg, who invented movable type around 1440. Prior to his invention, books were either copied by hand or printed with hand-carved blocks. By adapting a grape and cheese press, Gutenberg was able to print about 300 copies a day.

	1953 continued, Perf. 11x10½	Un	U	PB/LP	#	FDC	Q
1028	3¢ Gadsden Purchase, Dec. 30	.10	.05	.50	(4)	.85	116,134,600
	Issues of 1954						
1029	3¢ Columbia University, Jan. 4	.10	.05	.50	(4)	.85	118,540,000
	Liberty Issue, 1954-61, Perf. 11x10½, 10½x11						
1030	½¢ Franklin, Oct. 24, 1954	.05	.05	.30	(4)	.85	Unlimited
1031	1¢ Washington, Aug. 26, 1954	.05	.05	.25	(4)	.85	Unlimited
1031A	1¼¢ Palace of the Governors,						
	Santa Fe, June 17, 1960	.05	.05	1.75	(4)	.85	Unlimited
1032	1½¢ Mt. Vernon, Feb. 22, 1956	.08	.05	7.50	(4)	.60	Unlimited
1033	2¢ Jefferson, Sept. 15, 1954	.05	.05	.25	(4)	.60	Unlimited
1034	2½¢ Bunker Hill Monument and						
	Massachusetts Flag, June 17, 1959	.08	.05	2.00	(4)	.60	Unlimited
1035	3¢ Statue of Liberty, 1954	.08	.05	.40	(4)	.60	Unlimited
1035a	Bklt. pane of 6, June 30, 1954	3.00	.50				
1036	4¢ Lincoln, Nov. 19, 1954	.10	.05	.50	(4)	.60	Unlimited
1036a	Bklt. pane of 6, July 31, 1958	2.00	.50				
1037	4½¢ The Hermitage, Mar. 16, 1959	.15	.08	1.75	(4)	.60	Unlimited
1038	5¢ James Monroe, Dec. 2, 1954	.17	.05	.85	(4)	.60	Unlimited
1039	6¢ T. Roosevelt, Nov. 18, 1955	.40	.05	2.00	(4)	.65	Unlimited
1040	7¢ Wilson, Jan. 10, 1956	.25	.05	1.50	(4)	.70	Unlimited
	Perf. 11						
1041	8¢ Statue of Liberty, Apr. 9, 1954	.30	.06	5.00	(4)	.80	Unlimited
1042	8¢ Statue of Liberty,						
	redrawn, Mar. 22, 1958	.30	.05	1.75	(4)	.60	Unlimited
	Perf. 11x10½, 10½x11						
1042A	8¢ Gen. John J. Pershing,						
	Nov. 17, 1961	.25	.05	1.50	(4)	.60	Unlimited
1043	9¢ The Alamo, June 14, 1956	.30	.05	1.50	(4)	1.50	Unlimited
1044	10¢ Independence Hall, 1956	.35	.05	1.65	(4)	.90	Unlimited
	Perf. 11						
1044A	11¢ Statue of Liberty, 1961	.30	.06	1.50	(4)	.90	Unlimited
	Perf. 11x10½, 10½x11						
1045	12¢ Benjamin Harrison, June 6, 1959	.55	.05	2.75	(4)	.90	Unlimited
1046	15¢ John Jay, Dec. 12, 1958	.85	.05	4.25	(4)	1.00	Unlimited
1047	20¢ Monticello, Apr. 13, 1956	.90	.05	4.50	(4)	1.20	Unlimited
1048	25¢ Paul Revere, April 18, 1958	2.75	.05	13.75	(4)	1.30	Unlimited
1049	30¢ Robert E. Lee, Sept. 21, 1955	2.00	.08	10.00	(4)	1.50	Unlimited
1050	40¢ John Marshall, Sept. 24, 1955	3.50	.10	17.50	(4)	1.75	Unlimited
1051	50¢ Susan B. Anthony, 1955	3.25	.05	16.00	(4)	6.00	Unlimited
1052	$1 Patrick Henry, Oct. 7, 1955	10.00	.06	50.00	(4)	13.00	Unlimited
	Perf. 11						
1053	$5 Alexander Hamilton, 1956	100.00	8.00	500.00	(4)	75.00	Unlimited

1028

1029

1030

1031

1031A

1032

1033

1034

1035

1036

1037

1038

1039

1040

1041

1042

1042A

1043

1044

1044A

1045

1046

1047

1048

1049

1050

1051

1052

1053

1060

1061

1062

1063

1064

1065

1066

1067

1068

1069

1070

1071

1072

1073

1074

	Issues of 1954-65, Coil Stamps, Perf. 10 Horizontally	Un	U	PB/LP	#	FDC	Q
1054	1¢ dark green Washington						
	(1031), Oct. 8, 1954	.35	.12	2.00		.75	Unlimited
1054A	1¼¢ turquoise, Palace of the						
	Governors (1031A), June 17, 1960	.25	.20	3.00		1.00	Unlimited
	Perf. 10 Vertically						
1055	2¢ rose carmine						
	Jefferson (1033), Oct. 22, 1954	.10	.05	.75		.75	Unlimited
1056	2½¢ gray blue, Bunker Hill Monument,						
	Mass. Flag (1034), Sept. 9, 1959	.55	.35	7.50		1.20	Unlimited
1057	3¢ deep violet Statue of Liberty						
	(1035), July 20, 1954	.15	.05	1.00		.75	Unlimited
1058	4¢ red violet Lincoln (1036),						
	July 31, 1958	.15	.05	1.20		.75	Unlimited
	Perf. 10 Horizontally						
1059	4½¢ bl. grn. Hermitage (1037),						
	May 1, 1959	3.25	1.20	20.00		1.75	Unlimited
	Perf. 10 Vertically						
1059A	25¢ grn. Revere (1048), 1965	.70	.30	3.25		1.20	Unlimited
	Issues of 1954, Perf. 11x10½						
1060	3¢ Nebraska Territory, May 7	.10	.05	.50	(4)	.75	115,810,000
1061	3¢ Kansas Territory, May 31	.10	.05	.50	(4)	.75	113,603,700
	Perf. 10½x11						
1062	3¢ George Eastman, July 12	.10	.05	.60	(4)	.75	128,002,000
	Perf. 11x10½						
1063	3¢ Lewis and Clark, July 28	.10	.05	.50	(4)	.75	116,078,150
	Issues of 1955, Perf. 10½x11						
1064	3¢ Pennsylvania Academy						
	of the Fine Arts, Jan. 15	.10	.05	.50	(4)	.75	116,139,800
	Perf. 11x10½						
1065	3¢ Land-Grant Colleges, Feb. 12	.10	.05	.50	(4)	.75	120,484,800
1066	8¢ Rotary International, Feb. 23	.20	.12	1.50	(4)	.90	53,854,750
1067	3¢ Armed Forces Reserve, May 21	.10	.05	.50	(4)	.75	175,075,000
	Perf. 10½x11						
1068	3¢ New Hampshire, June 21	.10	.05	.50	(4)	.75	125,944,400
	Perf. 11x10½						
1069	3¢ Soo Locks, June 28	.10	.05	.50	(4)	.75	122,284,600
1070	3¢ Atoms for Peace, July 28	.12	.05	.70	(4)	.75	133,638,850
1071	3¢ Fort Ticonderoga, Sept. 18	.10	.05	.50	(4)	.75	118,664,600
	Perf. 10½x11						
1072	3¢ Andrew W. Mellon, Dec. 20	.10	.05	.60	(4)	.75	112,434,000
	Issues of 1956						
1073	3¢ Benjamin Franklin, Jan. 17	.10	.05	.50	(4)	.75	129,384,550
	Perf. 11x10½						
1074	3¢ Booker T. Washington, Apr. 5	.10	.05	.50	(4)	.75	121,184,600

	1956 continued	Un	U	PB/LP	#	FDC	Q
	Fifth International Philatelic Exhibition Issue, Souvenir Sheet, Apr. 28, Imperf.						
1075	Sheet of 2 stamps (1035, 1041),						
	Apr. 28	4.00	.350			7.50	2,900,731
1075a	3¢ deep violet (1035), single						
	stamp from sheet	1.35	1.10				
1075b	8¢ dark violet, blue and carmine						
	rose (1041), single						
	stamp from sheet	1.75	1.50				
	Apr. 30, Perf. 11x10½						
1076	3¢ New York Coliseum and						
	Columbus Monument	.10	.05	.50	(4)	.75	119,784,200
	Wildlife Conservation Issue						
1077	3¢ Wild Turkey, May 5	.12	.05	.65	(4)	1.10	123,159,400
1078	3¢ Pronghorn Antelope, June 22	.12	.05	.65	(4)	1.10	123,138,800
1079	3¢ King Salmon, Nov. 9	.12	.05	.65	(4)	1.10	109,275,000
	Perf. 10½x11						
1080	3¢ Pure Food and Drug Laws,						
	June 27	.10	.05	.50	(4)	.80	112,932,200
	Perf. 11x10½						
1081	3¢ Wheatland, Aug. 5	.10	.05	.50	(4) ·	.80	125,475,000
	Perf. 10½x11						
1082	3¢ Labor Day, Sept. 3	.10	.05	.50	(4)	.80	117,855,000
	Perf. 11x10½						
1083	3¢ Nassau Hall, Sept. 22	.10	.05	.50	(4)	.80	122,100,000
	Perf. 10½x11						
1084	3¢ Devils Tower, Sept. 24	.10	.05	.50	(4)	.80	118,180,000
	Perf. 11x10½						
1085	3¢ Children's Stamp, Dec. 15	.10	.05	.50	(4)	.80	100,975,000
	Issues of 1957						
1086	3¢ Alexander Hamilton, Jan. 11	.10	.05	.50	(4)	.80	115,299,450
	Perf. 10½x11						
1087	3¢ Polio, Jan. 15	.10	.05	.50	(4)	.80	186,949,627
	Perf. 11x10½						
1088	3¢ Coast and Geodetic Survey,						
	Feb. 11	.10	.05	.50	(4)	.80	115,235,000
1089	3¢ American Institute						
	of Architects, Feb. 23	.10	.05	.50	(4)	.80	106,647,500
	Perf. 10½x11						
1090	3¢ Steel Industry, May 22	.10	.05	.50	(4)	.80	112,010,000
	Perf. 11x10½						
1091	3¢ International Naval Review-						
	Jamestown Festival, June 10	.10	.05	.50	(4)	.80	118,470,000
1092	3¢ Oklahoma Statehood, June 14	.10	.05	.60	(4)	.80	102,230,000
1093	3¢ School Teachers, July 1	.10	.05	.50	(4)	.80	102,410,000

3¢ U.S.POSTAGE
FIFTH INTERNATIONAL PHILATELIC EXHIBITION
NEW YORK COLISEUM 1956

076

WILDLIFE CONSERVATION
WILD TURKEY
UNITED STATES POSTAGE 3

1077

WILDLIFE CONSERVATION
PRONGHORN ANTELOPE
3¢ UNITED STATES POSTAGE 3

1078

WILDLIFE CONSERVATION
KING SALMON
3¢ UNITED STATES POSTAGE 3

079

UNITED STATES POSTAGE
50TH ANNIVERSARY PURE FOOD AND DRUG LAWS

1080

UNITED STATES POSTAGE 3
WHEATLAND THE HOME OF JAMES BUCHANAN

1081

LABOR DAY
LABOR PEACE
U.S.POSTAGE 3

1082

200th ANNIVERSARY of NASSAU HALL 1756-1956
3¢ UNITED STATES POSTAGE 3

083

U.S.POSTAGE
50th ANNIVERSARY DEVILS TOWER NATIONAL MONUMENT
3¢

1084

FRIENDSHIP - THE KEY TO WORLD PEACE
CHILDREN'S STAMP 1956
3¢ UNITED STATES POSTAGE 3

1085

UNITED STATES POS
ALEXANDER HAMILTON

1086

MARCHING FEET AND HELPED FIGHT POLIO
3¢ UNITED STATES POSTAGE

087

COAST AND GEODETIC SURVEY
1807 1957
U.S.POSTAGE 3 CENTS

1088

CENTENNIAL
AMERICAN INSTITUTE OF ARCHITECTS 1957
3¢
UNITED STATES POSTAGE

1089

AMERICA AND STEEL GROWING TOGETHER
STEEL CENTENNIAL 1857-1957
U.S.POSTAGE 3¢

1090

INTERNATIONAL NAVAL REVIEW
1957
U.S.POSTAGE 3

1907 ARROWS TO ATOMS 1957
50 TH ANNIVERSARY OF OKLAHOMA STATEHOOD
3¢ UNITED STATES POSTAGE

HONORING THE TEACHERS OF AMERICA
NATIONAL EDUCATION ASSOCIATION 1857-1957
UNITED STATES POSTAGE 3

1094

1095

1096

1097

1098

1099

1100

1104

1105

1106

1107

1108

1109

1110

1111

	1957 continued, Perf. 11	Un	U	PB/LP	#	FDC	Q
1094	4¢ Flag, July 4	.10	.05	.60	(4)	.80	84,054,400
	Perf. 10½x11						
1095	3¢ Shipbuilding, Aug. 15	.10	.05	.70	(4)	.80	126,266,000
	Champion of Liberty Issue, Ramon Magsaysay, Aug. 31, Perf. 11						
1096	8¢ Bust of Magsaysay on Medal	.22	.15	1.75	(4)	.80	39,489,600
	Perf. 10½x11						
1097	3¢ Lafayette, Sept. 6	.10	.05	.50	(4)	.80	122,990,000
	Perf. 11						
1098	3¢ Wildlife Conservation, Nov. 22	.10	.05	.65	(4)	1.00	174,372,800
	Perf. 10½x11						
1099	3¢ Religious Freedom, Dec. 27	.10	.05	.50	(4)	.80	114,365,000
	Issues of 1958						
1100	3¢ Gardening-Horticulture, Mar. 15	.10	.05	.50	(4)	.80	122,765,200
1101-03 not assigned							
	Perf. 11x10½						
1104	3¢ Brussels Universal and						
	International Exhibition, Apr. 17	.10	.05	.50	(4)	.80	113,660,200
1105	3¢ James Monroe, Apr. 28	.10	.05	.60	(4)	.80	120,196,580
1106	3¢ Minnesota Statehood, May 11	.10	.05	.50	(4)	.80	120,805,200
	Perf. 11						
1107	3¢ International Geophysical						
	Year, May 31	.10	.05	.75	(4)	.80	125,815,200
	Perf. 11x10½						
1108	3¢ Gunston Hall, June 12	.10	.05	.50	(4)	.80	108,415,200
	Perf. 10½x11						
1109	3¢ Mackinac Bridge, June 25	.10	.05	.50	(4)	.80	107,195,200
	Champion of Liberty Issue, Simon Bolivar, July 24						
1110	4¢ Bust of Bolivar on Medal	.10	.05	.60	(4)	.80	115,745,280
	Perf. 11						
1111	8¢ Bust of Bolivar on Medal	.25	.15	5.00	(4)	.80	39,743,640
	Perf. 11x10½						
1112	4¢ Atlantic Cable, Aug. 15	.10	.05	.50	(4)	.80	114,570,200

	1958 continued	Un	U	PB/LP	#	FDC	Q
	Lincoln Sesquicentennial Issue, 1958-59, Perf. 10½x11, 11x10½						
1113	1¢ Portrait by George Healy,						
	Feb. 12, 1959	.05	.05	.40	(4)	.80	120,400,200
1114	3¢ Sculptured Head,						
	by Gutzon Borglum, Feb. 27, 1959	.10	.06	.60	(4)	.80	91,160,200
1115	4¢ Lincoln and Stephen Douglas						
	Debating, by Joseph Boggs Beale,						
	Aug. 27, 1958	.10	.05	.55	(4)	.80	114,860,200
1116	4¢ Statue in Lincoln Memorial						
	by Daniel Chester French,						
	May 30, 1959	.10	.05	.65	(4)	.80	126,500,000
	Issues of 1958, Champion of Liberty Issue, Lajos Kossuth, Sept. 19, Perf. 10½x11						
1117	4¢ Bust of Kossuth on Medal	.10	.05	.60	(4)	.80	120,561,280
	Perf. 11						
1118	8¢ Bust of Kossuth on Medal	.22	.12	3.50	(4)	.80	44,064,576
	Perf. 10½x11						
1119	4¢ Freedom of the Press, Sept. 22	.10	.05	.50	(4)	.80	118,390,200
	Perf. 11x10½						
1120	4¢ Overland Mail, Oct. 10	.10	.05	.50	(4)	.80	125,770,200
	Perf. 10½x11						
1121	4¢ Noah Webster, Oct. 16	.10	.05	.50	(4)	.80	114,114,280
	Perf. 11						
1122	4¢ Forest Conservation, Oct. 27	.10	.05	.60	(4)	.80	156,600,200
	Perf. 11x10½						
1123	4¢ Fort Duquesne, Nov. 25	.10	.05	.50	(4)	.80	124,200,200
	Issues of 1959						
1124	4¢ Oregon Statehood, Feb. 14	.10	.05	.50	(4)	.80	120,740,200
	Champion of Liberty Issue, José de San Martin, Feb. 25, Perf. 10½x11						
1125	4¢ Bust of San Martin on Medal	.10	.05	.55	(4)	.80	133,623,280
	Perf. 11						
1126	8¢ Bust of San Martin on Medal	.20	.12	1.75	(4)	.80	45,569,088
	Perf. 10½x11						
1127	4¢ NATO, Apr. 1	.10	.05	.50	(4)	.80	122,493,280
	Perf. 11x10½						
1128	4¢ Arctic Explorations, Apr. 6	.13	.05	.85	(4)	.80	131,260,200
1129	8¢ World Peace through World						
	Trade, Apr. 20	.20	.12	1.50	(4)	.80	47,125,200
1130	4¢ Silver Centennial, June 8	.10	.05	.50	(4)	.80	123,105,000
	Perf. 11						
1131	4¢ St. Lawrence Seaway, June 26	.10	.05	.50	(4)	.80	126,105,050

1113

1114

1115

1116

1117

1118

1119

1120

1121

1122

1123

1124

1125

1126

1127

1128

1129

1130

1131

1132

1133

1134

1135

1136

1137

1138

1139

1140

1141

1142

1143

1144

1145

1146

1147   1148

	1959 continued, Perf. 11	Un	U	PB/LP	#	FDC	Q
1132	4¢ 49-Star Flag, July 4	.10	.05	.50	(4)	.80	209,170,000
1133	4¢ Soil Conservation, Aug. 26	.10	.05	.65	(4)	.80	120,835,000
1134	4¢ Petroleum Industry, Aug. 27	.10	.05	.50	(4)	.80	115,715,000
	Perf. 11x10½						
1135	4¢ Dental Health, Sept. 14	.10	.05	.50	(4)	.80	118,445,000
	Champion of Liberty Issue, Ernst Reuter, Sept. 29, Perf. 10½x11						
1136	4¢ Bust of Reuter on Medal	.10	.05	.60	(4)	.80	111,685,000
	Perf. 11						
1137	8¢ Bust of Reuter on Medal	.20	.12	1.75	(4)	.80	43,099,200
	Perf. 10½x11						
1138	4¢ Dr. Ephraim McDowell, Dec. 3	.10	.05	.50	(4)	.80	115,444,000
	Issues of 1960-61, American Credo Issue, Perf. 11						
1139	4¢ Quotation from Washington's						
	Farewell Address, Jan. 20, 1960	.18	.05	1.00	(4)	1.25	126,470,000
1140	4¢ Benjamin Franklin Quotation,						
	Mar. 31, 1960	.18	.05	1.00	(4)	1.00	124,560,000
1141	4¢ Thomas Jefferson Quotation,						
	May 18, 1960	.18	.05	1.00	(4)	1.00	115,455,000
1142	4¢ Francis Scott Key Quotation,						
	Sept. 14, 1960	.18	.05	1.00	(4)	1.25	122,060,000
1143	4¢ Abraham Lincoln Quotation,						
	Nov. 19, 1960	.18	.05	1.00	(4)	1.25	120,540,000
1144	4¢ Patrick Henry Quotation,						
	Jan. 11, 1961	.18	.05	1.00	(4)	1.25	113,075,000
	Issues of 1960						
1145	4¢ Boy Scouts, Feb. 8	.10	.05	.50	(4)	1.25	139,325,000
	Olympic Winter Games Issue, Feb. 18, Perf. 10½x11						
1146	4¢ Olympic Rings and Snowflake	.10	.05	.50	(4)	.80	124,445,000
	Champion of Liberty Issue, Thomas G. Masaryk, Mar. 7						
1147	4¢ Bust of Masaryk on Medal	.10	.05	.60	(4)	.80	113,792,000
	Perf. 11						
1148	8¢ Bust of Masaryk on Medal	.20	.12	1.75	(4)	.80	44,215,200

1960 continued, Perf. 11x10½	Un	U	PB/LP	#	FDC	Q
1149 4¢ World Refugee Year, Apr. 7	.10	.05	.50	(4)	.80	113,195,000
Perf. 11						
1150 4¢ Water Conservation, Apr. 18	.10	.05	.65	(4)	.80	121,805,000
Perf. 10½x11						
1151 4¢ SEATO, May 31	.10	.05	.50	(4)	.80	115,353,000
Perf. 11x10½						
1152 4¢ American Woman, June 2	.10	.05	.50	(4)	.80	111,080,000
Perf. 11						
1153 4¢ 50-Star Flag, July 4	.10	.05	.50	(4)	.80	153,025,000
Perf. 11x10½						
1154 4¢ Pony Express, July 19	.10	.05	.50	(4)	.80	119,665,000
Perf. 10½x11						
1155 4¢ Employ the Handicapped, Aug. 28	.10	.05	.50	(4)	.80	117,855,000
1156 4¢ World Forestry Congress, Aug. 29	.10	.05	.50	(4)	.80	118,185,000
Perf. 11						
1157 4¢ Mexican Independence, Sept. 16	.10	.05	.50	(4)	.80	112,260,000
1158 4¢ U.S.-Japan Treaty, Sept. 28	.10	.05	.50	(4)	.80	125,010,000
Champion of Liberty Issue, Ignacy Jan Paderewski, Oct. 8, Perf. 10½x11						
1159 4¢ Bust of Paderewski on Medal	.10	.05	.55	(4)	.80	119,798,000
Perf. 11						
1160 8¢ Bust of Paderewski on Medal	.20	.12	1.75	(4)	.80	42,696,000
Perf. 10½x11						
1161 4¢ Sen. Robert A. Taft Memorial, Oct. 10	.10	.05	.50	(4)	.80	106,610,000
Perf. 11x10½						
1162 4¢ Wheels of Freedom, Oct. 15	.10	.05	.50	(4)	.80	109,695,000
Perf. 11						
1163 4¢ Boys' Club of America, Oct. 18	.10	.05	.50	(4)	.80	123,690,000
1164 4¢ First Automated Post Office, Oct. 20	.10	.05	.50	(4)	.80	123,970,000
Champion of Liberty Issue, Gustaf Mannerheim, Oct. 26, Perf. 10½x11						
1165 4¢ Bust of Mannerheim on Medal	.10	.05	.55	(4)	.80	124,796,000
Perf. 11						
1166 8¢ Bust of Mannerheim on Medal	.20	.12	1.75	(4)	.80	42,076,800

1149

1150

1151

1152

1153

1154

1155

1156

1157

1158

1159

1160

1161

1162

1163

1164

1165

1166

1167

1168

1169

1170

1171

1172

1173

1174

1175

1176

1177

1178

1179

1180

1181

1182

1183

1184

	1960 continued, Perf. 11	Un	U	PB/LP	#	FDC	Q
1167	4¢ Camp Fire Girls, Nov. 1	.10	.05	.50	(4)	.80	116,210,000
	Champion of Liberty Issue, Giusseppe Garibaldi, Nov. 2, Perf. 10½x11						
1168	4¢ Bust of Garibaldi on Medal	.10	.05	.55	(4)	.80	126,252,000
	Perf. 11						
1169	8¢ Bust of Garibaldi on Medal	.20	.12	1.75	(4)	.80	42,746,400
	Perf. 10½x11						
1170	4¢ Sen. Walter F. George						
	Memorial, Nov. 5	.10	.05	.50	(4)	.80	124,117,000
1171	4¢ Andrew Carnegie, Nov. 25	.10	.05	.50	(4)	.80	119,840,000
1172	4¢ John Foster Dulles Memorial,						
	Dec. 6	.10	.05	.55	(4)	.80	117,187,000
	Perf. 11x10½						
1173	4¢ Echo 1-Communications for						
	Peace, Dec. 15	.35	.12	2.25	(4)	1.75	124,390,000
	Issues of 1961, Champion of Liberty Issue, Mahatma Gandhi, Jan. 26, Perf. 10½x11						
1174	4¢ Bust of Gandhi on Medal	.10	.05	.55	(4)	.80	112,966,000
	Perf. 11						
1175	8¢ Bust of Gandhi on Medal	.20	.12	2.00	(4)	.80	41,644,200
1176	4¢ Range Conservation, Feb. 2	.10	.05	.65	(4)	.75	110,850,000
	Perf. 10½x11						
1177	4¢ Horace Greeley, Feb. 3	.10	.05	.55	(4)	.75	98,616,000
	Issues of 1961-65, Civil War Centennial Issue, Perf. 11x10½						
1178	4¢ Fort Sumter, Apr. 12, 1961	.18	.05	1.10	(4)	1.75	101,125,000
1179	4¢ Shiloh, Apr. 7, 1962	.15	.05	1.00	(4)	1.75	124,865,000
	Perf. 11						
1180	5¢ Gettysburg, July 1, 1963	.15	.05	1.00	(4)	1.75	79,905,000
1181	5¢ Wilderness, May 5, 1964	.15	.05	1.00	(4)	1.75	125,410,000
1182	5¢ Appomattox, Apr. 9, 1965	.15	.05	1.10	(4)	1.75	112,845,000
	Issues of 1961 continued						
1183	4¢ Kansas Statehood, May 10	.10	.05	.55	(4)	.75	106,210,000
	Perf. 11x10½						
1184	4¢ Sen. George W. Norris, July 11	.10	.05	.55	(4)	.75	110,810,000

	1961 continued, Perf. 11x10½	Un	U	PB/LP	#	FDC	Q
1185	4¢ Naval Aviation, Aug. 20	.10	.05	.55	(4)	.90	116,995,000
	Perf. 10½x11						
1186	4¢ Workmen's Compensation, Sept. 4	.10	.05	.55	(4)	.75	121,015,000
	Perf. 11						
1187	4¢ Frederic Remington, Oct. 4	.12	.05	1.00	(4)	.75	111,600,000
	Perf. 10½x11						
1188	4¢ Republic of China, Oct. 10	.10	.05	.55	(4)	.75	110,620,000
1189	4¢ Naismith-Basketball, Nov. 6	.10	.05	.55	(4)	1.50	109,110,000
	Perf. 11						
1190	4¢ Nursing, Dec. 28	.10	.05	.70	(4)	.75	145,350,000
	Issues of 1962						
1191	4¢ New Mexico Statehood, Jan. 6	.10	.05	.55	(4)	.75	112,870,000
1192	4¢ Arizona Statehood, Feb. 14	.10	.05	.65	(4)	.75	121,820,000
1193	4¢ Project Mercury, Feb. 20	.10	.10	.65	(4)	1.50	289,240,000
1194	4¢ Malaria Eradication, Mar. 30	.10	.05	.55	(4)	.75	120,155,000
	Perf. 10½x11						
1195	4¢ Charles Evans Hughes, Apr. 11	.10	.05	.55	(4)	.75	124,595,000
	Perf. 11						
1196	4¢ Seattle World's Fair, Apr. 25	.10	.05	.65	(4)	.75	147,310,000
1197	4¢ Louisiana Statehood, Apr. 30	.10	.05	.55	(4)	.75	118,690,000
	Perf. 11x10½						
1198	4¢ Homestead Act, May 20	.10	.05	.55	(4)	.75	122,730,000
1199	4¢ Girl Scouts, July 24	.10	.05	.55	(4)	1.00	126,515,000
1200	4¢ Sen. Brien McMahon, July 28	.10	.05	.65	(4)	.75	130,960,000
1201	4¢ Apprenticeship, Aug. 31	.10	.05	.55	(4)	.75	120,055,000

Colonists Learned Through Apprenticeships

Apprenticeship (#1201) played an important part in colonial American life. Apprentices, or learners, primarily were young boys from poor families who were placed with masters of crafts or trades. Under this system, the apprentice served the master while learning his craft, trade or profession. Today, apprenticeships are available in some 300 occupations.

1185

1186

1187

1188

1189

1190

1191

1192

1193

1194

1195

1196

1197

1198

1199

1200

1201

1202

1203

1204

1205

1206

1207

1208

1209

1213

1230

1231

1232

1233

1234

1235

1236

1237

	1962 continued, Perf. 11	Un	U	PB/LP	#	FDC	Q
1202	4¢ Sam Rayburn, Sept. 16	.10	.05	.55	(4)	.75	120,715,000
1203	4¢ Dag Hammarskjold, Oct. 23	.10	.05	.70	(4)	.75	121,440,000
1204	4¢ Dag Hammarskjold, Special						
	Printing black, brown and yellow						
	(yellow inverted), Nov. 16	.12	.08	4.00	(4)	6.00	40,270,000
	Christmas Issue, Nov. 1						
1205	4¢ Wreath and Candles	.10	.05	.50	(4)	.75	861,970,000
1206	4¢ Higher Education, Nov. 14	.10	.05	.55	(4)	.75	120,035,000
1207	4¢ Winslow Homer, Dec. 15	.15	.05	1.00	(4)	.75	117,870,000
	Issue of 1963						
1208	5¢ Flag over White House, Jan. 9	.12	.05	.55	(4)	.75	
	Regular Issues of 1962-63, Perf. 11x10½						
1209	1¢ Andrew Jackson, Mar. 22, 1963	.05	.05	.25	(4)	.75	
1210-12 not assigned							
1213	5¢ George Washington, Nov. 23, 1962	.12	.05	.75	(4)	.75	
1213a	Bklt. pane of 5 + label,						
	Nov. 23, 1962	2.00	.75				
1214-24 not assigned							
	Coil Stamps, Perf. 10 Vertically						
1225	1¢ green Jackson (1209),						
	May 31, 1963	.20	.05	.85		.75	
1226-28 not assigned							
1229	5¢ dk. blue gray Washington						
	(1213), Nov. 23, 1962	1.75	.05	4.75		.75	
	Issues of 1963, Perf. 11						
1230	5¢ Carolina Charter, Apr. 6	.12	.05	.60	(4)	.75	129,945,000
1231	5¢ Food for Peace-Freedom from						
	Hunger, June 4	.12	.05	.60	(4)	.75	135,620,000
1232	5¢ West Virginia Statehood, June 20	.12	.05	.60	(4)	.75	137,540,000
1233	5¢ Emancipation Proclamation,						
	Aug. 16	.12	.05	.60	(4)	.75	132,435,000
1234	5¢ Alliance for Progress, Aug. 17	.12	.05	.60	(4)	.75	135,520,000
	Perf. 10½x11						
1235	5¢ Cordell Hull, Oct. 5	.12	.05	.60	(4)	.75	131,420,000
	Perf. 11x10½						
1236	5¢ Eleanor Roosevelt, Oct. 11	.12	.05	.60	(4)	.75	133,170,000
	Perf. 11						
1237	5¢ The Sciences, Oct. 14	.12	.05	.60	(4)	.75	130,195,000

	1963 continued, Perf. 11	Un	U	PB/LP	#	FDC	Q
1238	5¢ City Mail Delivery, Oct. 26	.12	.05	.60	(4)	.75	128,450,000
1239	5¢ International Red Cross, Oct. 29	.12	.05	.60	(4)	.75	118,665,000
	Christmas Issue, Nov. 1						
1240	5¢ National Christmas Tree and White House	.12	.05	.60	(4)	.75	1,291,250,000
1241	5¢ John James Audubon, Dec. 7, (see also #C71)	.12	.05	.60	(4)	.75	175,175,000
	Issues of 1964, Perf. 10½x11						
1242	5¢ Sam Houston, Jan. 10	.12	.05	.60	(4)	.75	125,995,000
	Perf. 11						
1243	5¢ Charles M. Russell, Mar. 19	.15	.05	.75	(4)	.75	128,925,000
	Perf. 11x10½						
1244	5¢ New York World's Fair, Apr. 22	.12	.05	.60	(4)	.75	145,700,000
	Perf. 11						
1245	5¢ John Muir, Apr. 29	.12	.05	.60	(4)	.75	120,310,000
	Perf. 11x10½						
1246	5¢ President John Fitzgerald Kennedy Memorial, May 29	.12	.05	.60	(4)	.75	511,750,000
	Perf. 10½x11						
1247	5¢ New Jersey Settlement, June 15	.12	.05	.60	(4)	.75	123,845,000
	Perf. 11						
1248	5¢ Nevada Statehood, July 22	.12	.05	.60	(4)	.75	122,825,000
1249	5¢ Register and Vote, Aug. 1	.12	.05	.60	(4)	.75	453,090,000
	Perf. 10½x11						
1250	5¢ Shakespeare, Aug. 14	.12	.05	.60	(4)	.75	123,245,000
1251	5¢ Doctors Mayo, Sept. 11	.12	.05	.60	(4)	.75	123,355,000
	Perf. 11						
1252	5¢ American Music, Oct. 15	.12	.05	.60	(4)	.75	126,970,000
1253	5¢ Homemakers, Oct. 26	.12	.05	.60	(4)	.75	121,250,000

No Longer "Women Only"

Traditionally, women have managed households and cared for children. However, with more and more women entering the work force, the responsibilities of homemaking (#1253) increasingly are being shared by all household members.

CITY MAIL DELIVERY 1863-1963

5c UNITED STATES

1238

1963 INTERNATIONAL RED CROSS 1963

5c UNITED STATES POSTAGE

1239

CHRISTMAS 1963

UNITED STATES 5c

1240

Audubon, American Artist

U.S. Postage

1241

5c POSTAGE

Sam Houston

1242

5c U.S. POSTAGE

C. M. Russell American Artist

1243

NEW YORK WORLD'S FAIR 1964 1965

5c POSTAGE

1244

JOHN MUIR CONSERVATIONIST

5c UNITED STATES POSTAGE

1245

...THE GLOW FROM THAT FIRE CAN TRULY LIGHT...

5c 1917 JOHN FITZGERALD KENNEDY

1246

NEW JERSEY TERCENTENARY 1664 1964

5c UNITED STATES POSTAGE

1247

U.S. POSTAGE NEVADA STATEHOOD 1864 1964

1248

REGISTER VOTE

5c POSTAGE

1249

UNITED STATES

SHAKESPEARE

5

U.S. POSTAGE 5c

DOCTORS MAYO

AMERICAN MUSIC

U.S. POSTAGE 5 CENTS

1252

U.S. 5c HOMEMAKERS

1253

1254 1255
1256 1257

1258

1259

1260

1261

1262

1263

1264

1265

1266

1267

1268

1270

1272

	1964 continued	Un	U	PB/LP	#	FDC	Q
	Christmas Issue, Nov. 9, Perf. 11						
1254	5¢ Holly	.50	.05	3.25	(4)	.75	351,940,000
1255	5¢ Mistletoe	.50	.05	3.25	(4)	.75	351,940,000
1256	5¢ Poinsettia	.50	.05	3.25	(4)	.75	351,940,000
1257	5¢ Sprig of Conifer	.50	.05	3.25	(4)	.75	351,940,000
1257a	Block of four, #1254-1257	2.75	1.25			3.00	
	Perf. 10½x11						
1258	5¢ Verrazano-Narrows Bridge,						
	Nov. 21	.12	.05	.60	(4)	.75	120,005,000
	Perf. 11						
1259	5¢ Fine Arts, Dec. 2	.12	.05	.75	(4)	.75	125,800,000
	Perf. 10½x11						
1260	5¢ Amateur Radio, Dec. 15	.12	.05	.75	(4)	.75	122,230,000
	Issues of 1965, Perf. 11						
1261	5¢ Battle of New Orleans, Jan. 8	.12	.05	.75	(4)	.75	115,695,000
1262	5¢ Physical Fitness-Sokols, Feb. 15	.12	.05	.75	(4)	.75	115,095,000
1263	5¢ Crusade Against Cancer, Apr. 1	.12	.05	.75	(4)	.75	119,560,000
	Perf. 10½x11						
1264	5¢ Winston Churchill Memorial,						
	May 13	.12	.05	.75	(4)	.75	125,180,000
	Perf. 11						
1265	5¢ Magna Carta, June 15	.12	.05	.75	(4)	.75	120,135,000
1266	5¢ Inernational Cooperation Year-						
	United Nations, June 26	.12	.05	.75	(4)	.75	115,405,000
1267	5¢ Salvation Army, July 2	.12	.05	.75	(4)	.75	115,855,000
	Perf. 10½x11						
1268	5¢ Dante, July 17	.12	.05	.75	(4)	.75	115,340,000
1269	5¢ President Herbert Hoover						
	Memorial, Aug. 10	.12	.05	.75	(4)	.75	114,840,000
	Perf. 11						
1270	5¢ Robert Fulton, Aug. 19	.12	.05	.75	(4)	.75	116,140,000
1271	5¢ Florida Settlement, Aug. 28	.12	.05	1.00	(4)	.75	116,900,000
1272	5¢ Traffic Safety, Sept. 3	.12	.05	1.00	(4)	.75	114,085,000

		Un	U	PB/LP	#	FDC	Q
	1965 continued, Perf. 11						
1273	5¢ John Singleton Copley, Sept. 17	.15	.05	1.25	(4)	.75	114,880,000
1274	11¢ International Telecommunication						
	Union, Oct. 6	.50	.25	9.00	(4)	.75	26,995,000
1275	5¢ Adlai E. Stevenson, Oct. 23	.12	.05	.75	(4)	.75	128,495,000
	Christmas Issue, Nov. 2						
1276	5¢ Angel with Trumpet						
	(1840 Weathervane)	.12	.05	.60	(4)	.75	1,139,930,000
1277, 1296, 1300-02 not assigned							
	Issues of 1965-78, Prominent Americans Issue, Perf. 11x10½, 10½x11						
1278	1¢ Jefferson, Jan. 12, 1968	.05	.05	.25	(4)	.60	
1278a	Bklt. pane of 8, Jan. 12, 1968	1.00	.25				
1278b	Bklt. pane of 4 + 2 labels, 1971	.75	.20				
1279	1¼¢ Albert Gallatin, Jan. 30, 1967	.10	.05	25.00	(4)	.60	
1280	2¢ Frank Lloyd Wright, 1966	.05	.05	.30	(4)	.60	
1280a	Bklt. pane of 5+ label, 1968	1.20	.40				
1280c	Bklt. pane of 6, May 7, 1971	1.00	.35				
1281	3¢ Francis Parkman, Sept. 16, 1967	.06	.05	.40	(4)	.60	
1282	4¢ Lincoln, Nov. 19, 1965	.08	.05	.40	(4)	.60	
1283	5¢ Washington, Feb. 2, 1966	.10	.05	.50	(4)	.60	
1283B	5¢ redrawn, Nov. 17, 1967	.12	.05	1.00	(4)	.45	
1284	6¢ Franklin D. Roosevelt, 1966	.18	.05	.90	(4)	.45	
1284b	Bklt. pane of 8, Dec. 28, 1967	1.50	.50				
1284c	Bklt. pane of 5+ label, 1968	1.25	.50				
1285	8¢ Albert Einstein, Mar. 15, 1966	.30	.05	1.25	(4)	.50	
1286	10¢ Jackson, Mar. 15, 1967	.25	.05	2.00	(4)	.60	
1286A	12¢ Henry Ford, July 30, 1968	.35	.05	1.50	(4)	.50	
1287	13¢ Kennedy, May 29, 1967	.30	.05	1.65	(4)	.65	
1288	15¢ Oliver Wendell Holmes, 1968	.30	.06	1.50	(4)	.60	
	Perf. 10						
1288B	15¢ dk. rose claret Holmes (1288),						
	Single from booklet	.30	.05			.65	
1288Bc	Bklt. pane of 8, June 14, 1978	2.40	1.25				
	Perf. 11x10½, 10½x11						
1289	20¢ George C. Marshall, 1967	.60	.06	2.50	(4)	.80	
1290	25¢ Frederick Douglass, 1967	.70	.05	2.75	(4)	1.00	
1291	30¢ John Dewey, Oct. 21, 1968	.75	.08	3.50	(4)	1.20	
1292	40¢ Thomas Paine, Jan. 29, 1969	1.10	.10	4.25	(4)	1.60	
1293	50¢ Lucy Stone, Aug. 13, 1968	1.00	.05	5.00	(4)	3.25	
1294	$1 Eugene O'Neill, Oct. 16, 1967	2.40	.08	10.50	(4)	7.50	
1295	$5 John Bassett Moore, 1966	12.50	2.00	50.00	(4)	60.00	

1273

1274

1276

1275

1278

1279

1280

1281

1282

1283

1283B

1284

1285

1286

1286A

1287

1288

1289

1290

1291

1292

1293

1294

1295

1305

1306

1307

1308

1309

1310

1312

1313

1311

1314

1315

1316

1317

1318

1319

	Issues of 1966-81, Coil Stamps, Perf. 10 Horizontally	Un	U	PB/LP	#	FDC	Q
1297	3¢ violet Parkman (1281),						
	Nov. 4, 1975	.12	.05	.60		.75	
1298	6¢ gray brown F.D.R. (1284),						
	Dec. 28, 1967	.30	.05	3.00		.75	
	Perf. 10 Vertically						
1299	1¢ green Jefferson (1278),						
	Jan. 12, 1968	.06	.05	.35		.75	
1303	4¢ black Lincoln (1282),						
	May 28, 1966	.15	.05	2.25		.75	
1304	5¢ blue Washington (1283),						
	Sept. 8, 1966	.15	.05	.90		.75	
1304C	5¢ redrawn (1283B), 1981	.15	.05	.75			
1305	6¢ F.D.R. (1284), Feb. 28, 1968	.20	.05	1.25		.75	
1305E	15¢ rose claret Holmes						
	(1288), June 14, 1978	.30	.05	1.65		.75	
1305C	$1 dull purple Eugene O'Neill						
	(1294), Jan. 12, 1973	2.00	.20	6.00		3.00	
	Issues of 1966, Perf. 11						
1306	5¢ Migratory Bird Treaty, Mar. 16	.12	.05	.75	(4)	.75	116,835,000
1307	Humane Treatment of Animals,						
	Apr. 9	.12	.05	.90	(4)	.75	117,470,000
1308	5¢ Indiana Statehood, Apr. 16	.12	.05	.75	(4)	.75	123,770,000
1309	5¢ American Circus, May 2	.12	.05	.90	(4)	.75	131,270,000
	Sixth International Philatelic Exhibition Issue, May 21						
1310	5¢ Stamped Cover	.12	.05	.90	(4)	.75	122,285,000
	Souvenir Sheet, May 23, Imperf.						
1311	5¢ Stamped Cover (1310) and						
	Washington, D.C., Scene	.30	.15			.75	14,680,000
	Perf. 11						
1312	5¢ Bill of Rights, July 1	.12	.05	.75	(4)	.75	114,160,000
	Perf. 10½x11						
1313	5¢ Poland's Millennium, July 30	.12	.05	.90	(4)	.75	128,475,000
	Perf. 11						
1314	5¢ National Park Service, Aug. 25	.12	.05	.75	(4)	.75	119,535,000
1315	5¢ Marine Corps Reserve, Aug. 29	.12	.05	1.00	(4)	.75	125,110,000
1316	5¢ General Federation						
	of Women's Clubs, Sept. 12	.12	.05	1.00	(4)	.75	114,853,200
	American Folklore Issue, Johnny Appleseed, Sept. 24						
1317	5¢ Appleseed Carrying Shovel and						
	Seed Sack, Apple in Background	.12	.05	1.00	(4)	.75	124,290,000
1318	5¢ Beautification of America, Oct. 5	.12	.05	1.00	(4)	.75	128,460,000
1319	5¢ Great River Road, Oct. 21	.12	.05	1.00	(4)	.75	127,585,000

	1966 continued, Perf. 11	Un	U	PB/LP	#	FDC	Q
1320	5¢ Savings Bond-Servicemen,						
	Oct. 26	.12	.05	1.00	(4)	.75	115,875,000
	Christmas Issue, Nov. 1						
1321	5¢ Madonna and Child, by						
	Hans Memling	.12	.05	.75	(4)	.75	1,173,547,000
1322	5¢ Mary Cassatt, Nov. 17	.20	.05	2.75	(4)	.75	114,015,000
	Issues of 1967						
1323	5¢ National Grange, Apr. 17	.12	.05	.90	(4)	.75	121,105,000
1324	5¢ Canada, May 25	.12	.05	.90	(4)	.75	132,045,000
1325	5¢ Erie Canal, July 4	.12	.05	.90	(4)	.75	118,780,000
1326	5¢ Search for Peace-						
	Lions International, July 5	.12	.05	.90	(4)	.75	121,985,000
1327	5¢ Henry David Thoreau, July 12	.12	.05	.90	(4)	.75	111,850,000
1328	5¢ Nebraska Statehood, July, 29	.12	.05	.90	(4)	.75	117,225,000
1329	5¢ Voice of America, Aug. 1	.12	.05	1.00	(4)	.75	111,515,000
	American Folklore Issue, Davy Crockett, Aug. 17						
1330	5¢ Davy Crockett with Rifle, and						
	Scrub Pine	.12	.05	1.00	(4)	.75	114,270,000
	Accomplishments in Space Issue, Sept. 29						
1331	5¢ Space-Walking Astronaut	.90	.25			2.50	60,432,500
1331a	Attached pair, #1331-1332	2.00	1.50	8.00	(4)	8.00	
1332	5¢ Gemini 4 Capsule and Earth	.90	.25	8.00	(4)	2.50	60,432,500
1333	5¢ Urban Planning, Oct. 2	.15	.05	1.25	(4)	.75	110,675,000
1334	5¢ Finland Independence, Oct. 6	.15	.05	1.25	(4)	.75	110,670,000
	Perf. 12						
1335	5¢ Thomas Eakins, Nov. 2	.18	.05	1.50	(4)	.75	113,825,000
	Christmas Issue, Nov. 6, Perf. 11						
1336	5¢ Madonna and Child,						
	by Hans Memling	.12	.05	.60	(4)	.75	1,208,700,000
1337	5¢ Mississippi Statehood, Dec. 11	.15	.05	1.00	(4)	.75	113,330,000
	Issue of 1968						
1338	6¢ Flag over White House						
	(design 19 x 22 mm), Jan. 24, 1968	.12	.05	.60	(4)	.75	

1320

1321

1322

1323

1324

1325

1326

1327

1328

1329

1330

1331   1332

1333

1334

1335

1337   1338

1336

1339

1340

1341

1342

1343

1344

1345

1346

1347

1348

1349

1350

1351

1352

1353

1354

1355

	Issues of 1969-1971, Perf. 11x10½	Un	U	PB/LP	#	FDC	Q
1338D	6¢ dark blue, red and green (1338, design 18⅛ x 21 mm), Aug. 7, 1970	.20	.05	4.25	(20)	.75	
1338F	8¢ multicolored (1338), May 10, 1971	.20	.05	4.25	(20)	.75	
	Coil Stamps, Perf. 10 Vertically						
1338A	6¢ dark blue, red and green (1338), May 30, 1969	.20	.05	—		.75	
1338G	8¢ multicolored (1338), May 10, 1971	.20	.05	—		.75	
	Issues of 1968, Perf. 11						
1339	6¢ Illinois Statehood, Feb. 12	.18	.05	1.00	(4)	.75	141,350,000
1340	6¢ HemisFair '68, Mar. 30	.18	.05	1.00	(4)	.75	144,345,000
1341	$1 Airlift, Apr. 4	5.00	3.00	25.00	(4)	6.50	
1342	6¢ Support Our Youth-Elks, May 1	.18	.05	1.00	(4)	.75	147,120,000
1343	6¢ Law and Order, May 17	.18	.05	1.00	(4)	.75	130,125,000
1344	6¢ Register and Vote, June 27	.18	.05	1.00	(4)	.75	158,700,000
	Historic Flag Series, July 4						
1345	6¢ Fort Moultrie Flag, 1776	1.00	.50			4.00	23,153,000
1346	6¢ U.S. Flag, 1795-1818 (Fort McHenry Flag)	1.00	.50			4.00	25,153,000
1347	6¢ Washington's Cruisers Flag, 1775	.60	.50			4.00	23,153,000
1348	6¢ Bennington Flag, 1777	.60	.40			4.00	23,153,000
1349	6¢ Rhode Island Flag, 1775	.60	.45			4.00	23,153,000
1350	6¢ First Stars and Stripes Flag, 1777	.60	.35			4.00	23,153,000
1351	6¢ Bunker Hill Flag, 1775	.60	.35			4.00	23,153,000
1352	6¢ Grand Union Flag, 1776	.60	.35			4.00	23,153,000
1353	6¢ Philadelphia Light Horse Flag, 1775	.80	.35			4.00	23,153,000
1354	6¢ First Navy Jack, 1775	.80	.40			4.00	23,153,000
	Plate Block, #1345-1354			18.00	(20)		
1354a	#1345-1354 printed se-tenant in vertical rows of 10	8.25	7.50				
	Perf. 12						
1355	6¢ Walt Disney, Sept. 11	.20	.05	1.25	(4)	1.00	153,015,000

	1968 continued, Perf. 11	Un	U	PB/LP	#	FDC	Q
1356	6¢ Father Marquette, Sept. 20	.20	.05	1.00	(4)	.75	132,560,000
	American Folklore Issue, Daniel Boone, Sept. 26						
1357	6¢ Pennsylvania Rifle, Powder Horn,						
	Tomahawk, Pipe and Knife	.20	.05	1.00	(4)	.75	130,385,000
1358	6¢ Arkansas River Navigation,						
	Oct. 1	.20	.05	1.00	(4)	.75	132,265,000
1359	6¢ Leif Erikson, Oct. 9	.20	.05	1.00	(4)	.75	128,710,000
	Perf. 11x10½						
1360	6¢ Cherokee Strip, Oct. 15	.20	.05	1.00	(4)	.75	124,775,000
	Perf. 11						
1361	6¢ John Trumbull, Oct. 18	.25	.05	1.25	(4)	.75	128,295,000
1362	6¢ Waterfowl Conservation,						
	Oct. 24	.25	.05	1.75	(4)	.75	142,245,000
	Christmas Issue, Nov. 1						
1363	6¢ Angel Gabriel, from						
	"The Annunciation," by Jan van Eyck	.20	.05	2.75	(10)	.75	1,410,580,000
1364	6¢ American Indian, Nov. 4	.30	.05	1.35	(4)	.75	125,100,000
	Issues of 1969, Beautification of America Issue, Jan. 16						
1365	6¢ Capitol, Azaleas and Tulips	.90	.15	7.50	(4)	2.00	48,142,500
1366	6¢ Washington Monument,						
	Potomac River and Daffodils	.90	.15	7.50	(4)	2.00	48,142,500
1367	6¢ Poppies and Lupines						
	along Highway	.90	.15	7.50	(4)	2.00	48,142,500
1368	6¢ Blooming Crabapples						
	Lining Avenue	.90	.15	7.50	(4)	2.00	48,142,500
1368a	Block of four, #1365-1368	4.50	3.50			5.00	
1369	6¢ American Legion, Mar. 15	.20	.05	1.10	(4)	.75	148,770,000
	American Folklore Issue, Grandma Moses, May 1						
1370	6¢ "July Fourth," by Grandma Moses	.25	.05	1.35	(4)	.75	139,475,000
1371	6¢ Apollo 8, May 5	.30	.06	1.50	(4)	2.00	187,165,000
1372	6¢ W.C. Handy, May 17	.20	.05	1.00	(4)	.75	125,555,000

Web-Footed Friends

There are at least 146 species of waterfowl (#1362), a collective term for geese, ducks and swans. Waterfowl are so named because of their affinity for water where — thanks to their webbed feet — they paddle, dabble and dive for food.

1356

1357

1358

1359

1360

1361

1362

1363

1364

1365
1367

1366
1368

1369

1370

1371

1372

1373

1374

1375

1376
1378

1377
1379

1380

1381

1382

1383

1384

1384a

1385

1386

	1969 continued, Perf. 11	Un	U	PB/LP	#	FDC	Q
1373	6¢ California Settlement, July 16	.20	.05	1.00	(4)	.75	144,425,000
1374	6¢ John Wesley Powell, Aug. 1	.20	.05	1.00	(4)	.75	135,875,000
1375	6¢ Alabama Statehood, Aug. 2	.20	.05	1.00	(4)	.75	151,110,000
	Botanical Congress Issue, Aug. 23						
1376	6¢ Douglas Fir (Northwest)	1.10	.15	8.50	(4)	2.00	39,798,750
1377	6¢ Lady's Slipper (Northeast)	1.10	.15	8.50	(4)	2.00	39,798,750
1378	6¢ Ocotillo (Southwest)	1.10	.15	8.50	(4)	2.00	39,798,750
1379	6¢ Franklinia (Southeast)	1.10	.15	8.50	(4)	2.00	39,798,750
1379a	Block of four, #1376-1379	5.50	5.00			7.00	
	Perf. 10½x11						
1380	6¢ Dartmouth College Case, Sept. 22	.20	.05	1.35	(4)	.75	129,540,000
	Perf. 11						
1381	6¢ Professional Baseball, Sept. 24	.25	.05	1.75	(4)	1.50	130,925,000
1382	6¢ College Football, Sept. 26	.25	.05	1.75	(4)	1.50	139,055,000
1383	6¢ Dwight D. Eisenhower, Oct. 14	.20	.05	1.00	(4)	.75	150,611,200
	Christmas Issue, Nov. 3, Perf. 11x10½						
1384	6¢ Winter Sunday in Norway, Maine	.18	.05	2.25	(10)	.75	1,709,795,000
1384a	Precanceled	.60	.06				
1385	6¢ Hope for the Crippled, Nov. 20	.18	.05	1.00	(4)	.75	127,545,000
1386	6¢ William M. Harnett, Dec. 3	.18	.05	1.20	(4)	.75	145,788,800

Handicapped Can Achieve—And Do

Approximately 35 million people in the United States have disabilities (#1385) —physical or mental conditions that may affect their ability to lead normal lives. But statistics show that handicapped workers are at least as productive, if not more so, than those who have no disabilities. Steven Hawking is one example. Although he suffers from a form of severe degenerative paralysis, Hawking is one of the world's top mathematical physicists.

	Issues of 1970	Un	U	PB/LP	#	FDC	Q
	Natural History Issue, May 6, Perf. 11						
1387	6¢ American Bald Eagle	.22	.12	1.75	(4)	2.00	50,448,550
1388	6¢ African Elephant Herd	.22	.12	1.75	(4)	2.00	50,448,550
1389	6¢ Tlingit Chief						
	in Haida Ceremonial Canoe	.22	.12	1.75	(4)	2.00	50,448,550
1390	6¢ Brontosaurus, Stegosaurus and						
	Allosaurus from Jurassic Period	.22	.12	1.75	(4)	2.00	50,448,550
1390a	Block of four, #1387-1390	1.00	1.00			3.00	
1391	6¢ Maine Statehood, July 9	.18	.05	1.10	(4)	.75	171,850,000
	Perf. 11x10½						
1392	6¢ Wildlife Conservation, July 20	.18	.05	1.10	(4)	1.00	142,205,000
	Issues of 1970-74, Perf. 11x10½, 10½x11, 11						
1393	6¢ Eisenhower, Aug. 6, 1970	.12	.05	.60	(4)	.75	
1393a	Bklt. pane of 8	1.25	.50				
1393b	Bklt. pane of 5 + label	1.20	.35				
1393D	7¢ Franklin, Oct. 20, 1972	.14	.05	1.35	(4)	.75	
1394	8¢ Eisenhower, May 10, 1971	.16	.05	1.00	(4)	.75	
1395	8¢ deep claret Eisenhower (1393),						
	Single from booklet	.16	.05			.75	
1395a	Bklt. pane of 8, May 10, 1971	2.00	1.25				
1395b	Bklt. pane of 6	1.00	.75				
1395c	Bklt. pane of 4 + 2 labels,						
	Jan. 28, 1972	1.00	.50				
1395d	Bklt. pane of 7 + label	1.75	1.00				
1396	8¢ U.S. Postal Service, July 1, 1971	.25	.05	5.00	(12)	.75	
1397	14¢ Fiorello H. LaGuardia, 1972	.32	.05	2.35	(4)	.85	
1398	16¢ Ernie Pyle, May 7, 1971	.35	.05	2.35	(4)	.75	
1399	18¢ Dr. Elizabeth Blackwell,						
	Jan. 23, 1974	.40	.06	2.25	(4)	1.25	
1400	21¢ Amadeo P. Giannini,						
	June 27, 1973	.45	.06	2.25	(4)	1.00	
	Coil Stamps, Perf. 10 Vertically						
1401	6¢ dark blue gray Eisenhower						
	(1393), Aug. 6, 1970	.20	.05	1.00		.75	
1402	8¢ deep claret Eisenhower						
	(1395), May 10, 1971	.22	.05	1.00		.75	
1403-04 not assigned.							
	Issues of 1970, Perf. 11						
1405	6¢ Edgar Lee Masters, Aug. 22	.18	.05	1.00	(4)	.75	137,660,000
1406	6¢ Woman Suffrage, Aug. 26	.18	.05	1.00	(4)	.75	135,125,000
1407	6¢ South Carolina Settlement,						
	Sept. 12	.18	.05	1.00	(4)	.75	135,895,000
1408	6¢ Stone Mountain Memorial,						
	Sept. 19	.18	.05	1.00	(4)	.75	132,675,000
1409	6¢ Fort Snelling, Oct. 17	.18	.05	1.00	(4)	.75	134,795,000

AMERICAN BALD EAGLE | AFRICAN ELEPHANT HERD

1391

HAIDA CEREMONIAL CANOE | THE AGE OF REPTILES

1387   1388   1392
1389   1390

1393   1393D   1394   1396   1397

1398   1399   1400   1406

1405

1407   1408   1409

SAVE OUR SOIL — UNITED STATES · SIX CENTS

SAVE OUR CITIES — UNITED STATES · SIX CENTS

SAVE OUR WATER — UNITED STATES · SIX CENTS

SAVE OUR AIR — UNITED STATES · SIX CENTS

Christmas 6 us.

Christmas 6 us.

1414   1414a

1410
1412

1411
1413

1419

1420

1415
1417

1416
1418

1425

1421   1422   1423   1424

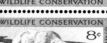

1426

1427 1428
1429 1430

160

	1970 continued	Un	U	PB/LP	#	FDC	Q
	Anti-Pollution Issue, Oct. 28, Perf. 11x10½						
1410	6¢ Save Our Soil-Globe and						
	Wheat Field	.45	.13	6.00	(10)	1.40	40,400,000
1411	6¢ Save Our Cities-Globe and						
	City Playground	.45	.13	6.00	(10)	1.40	40,400,000
1412	6¢ Save Our Water-Globe and						
	Bluegill Fish	.45	.13			1.40	40,400,000
1413	6¢ Save Our Air-Globe and						
	Seagull	.45	.13			1.40	40,400,000
1413a	Block of four, #1410-1413	2.50	2.00			4.25	
	Christmas Issue, Nov. 5, Perf. 10½x11						
1414	6¢ Nativity, by Lorenzo Lotto	.20	.05	2.25	(8)	1.40	638,730,000
1414a	Precanceled	.35	.08				358,245,000
	Perf 11x10½						
1415	6¢ Tin and Cast Iron Locomotive	.85	.10	8.50	(8)	1.40	122,313,750
1415a	Precanceled	2.00	.15				109,912,500
1416	6¢ Toy Horse on Wheels	.85	.10	8.50	(8)	1.40	122,313,750
1416a	Precanceled	2.00	.15				109,912,500
1417	6¢ Mechanical Tricycle	.85	.10			1.40	122,313,750
1417a	Precanceled	2.00	.15				109,912,500
1418	6¢ Doll Carriage	.85	.10			1.40	122,313,750
1418a	Precanceled	2.00	.15				109,912,500
1418b	Block of 4, #1415, 1418	4.50	3.50			3.50	
1418c	Block of 4, #1415a, 1418b	9.00	6.00				
	Perf. 11						
1419	6¢ United Nations, Nov. 20	.18	.05	1.25	(4)	.75	127,610,000
1420	6¢ Landing of the Pilgrims, Nov. 21	.18	.05	1.25	(4)	.75	129,785,000
	Disabled American Veterans and Servicemen Issue, Nov. 24						
1421	6¢ Disabled American Veterans						
	Emblem	.20	.10	3.00	(4)	.75	67,190,000
1421a	Attached pair, #1421-1422	.50	.65			1.20	
1422	6¢ U.S. Servicemen	.20	.10	3.00	(4)	.75	67,190,000
	Issues of 1971						
1423	6¢ American Wool Industry, Jan. 19	.18	.05	1.00	(4)	.75	135,305,000
1424	6¢ Gen. Douglas MacArthur,						
	Jan. 26	.18	.05	1.00	(4)	.75	134,840,000
1425	6¢ Blood Donor, Mar. 12	.18	.05	1.00	(4)	.75	130,975,000
	Perf. 11x10½						
1426	8¢ Missouri Statehood, May 8	.20	.05	3.50	(12)	.75	161,235,000
	Wildlife Conservation Issue, June 12, Perf. 11						
1427	8¢ Trout	.30	.10	1.75	(4)	1.75	43,920,000
1428	8¢ Alligator	.30	.10	1.75	(4)	1.75	43,920,000
1429	8¢ Polar Bear and Cubs	.30	.10	1.75	(4)	1.75	43,920,000
1430	8¢ California Condor	.30	.10	1.75	(4)	1.75	43,920,000
1430a	Block of four #1427-1430	1.30	1.00			3.00	

	1971 continued, Perf. 11	Un	U	PB/LP	#	FDC	Q
1431	8¢ Antarctic Treaty, June 23	.25	.05	1.50	(4)	.75	138,700,000
	American Bicentennial Issue, American Revolution, July 4						
1432	8¢ Bicentennial Commission Emblem	.50	.05	3.25	(4)	.75	138,165,000
1433	8¢ John Sloan, Aug. 2	.20	.05	1.50	(4)	.75	152,125,000
	Space Achievement Decade Issue, Aug. 2						
1434	8¢ Earth, Sun and Landing Craft						
	on Moon	.20	.10	1.75	(4)		88,147,500
1434a	Attached pair, #1434-1435	.50	.35			1.75	
1435	8¢ Lunar Rover and Astronauts	.20	.10	1.75	(4)		88,147,500
1436	8¢ Emily Dickinson, Aug. 28	.18	.05	1.25	(4)	.75	142,845,000
1437	8¢ San Juan, Puerto Rico, Sept. 12	.18	.05	1.25	(4)	.75	148,755,000
	Perf. 10½x11						
1438	8¢ Prevent Drug Abuse, Oct. 4	.18	.05	1.85	(6)	.75	139,080,000
1439	8¢ CARE, Oct. 27	.18	.05	2.10	(8)	.75	130,755,000
	Historic Preservation Issue, Oct. 29, Perf. 11						
1440	8¢ Decatur House,						
	Washington, D.C.	.25	.12	1.85	(4)	1.50	42,552,000
1441	8¢ Whaling Ship						
	Charles W. Morgan, Mystic,						
	Connecticut	.25	.12	1.85	(4)	1.50	42,552,000
1442	8¢ Cable Car, San Francisco	.25	.12	1.85	(4)	1.50	42,552,000
1443	8¢ San Xavier del Bac Mission,						
	Tucson, Arizona	.25	.12	1.85	(4)	1.50	42,552,000
1443a	Block of four, #1440-1443	1.20	1.20			3.00	
	Christmas Issue, Nov. 10, Perf. 10½x11						
1444	8¢ Adoration of the Shepherds,						
	by Giorgione	.18	.05	2.50	(12)	.75	1,074,350,000
1445	8¢ Partridge in a Pear Tree	.18	.05	2.50	(12)	.75	979,540,000
	Issues of 1972, Perf. 11						
1446	8¢ Sidney Lanier, Feb. 3	.18	.05	1.00	(4)	.75	137,355,000
	Perf. 10½x11						
1447	8¢ Peace Corps., Feb. 11	.18	.05	1.50	(6)	.75	150,400,000

"Army" Works for Peace

Established by President John F. Kennedy on March 1, 1961, the Peace Corps (#1447) seeks to help the poor people of other countries and to promote world peace. U.S. citizens over 18 years of age can volunteer for two years of Peace Corps duty.

8 U.S. ANTARCTIC TREATY 1961-1971

1431

AMERICAN REVOLUTION BICENTENNIAL 1776-1976

1432

John Sloan American Artist 1871-1951 United States 8 cents

1433

UNITED STATES IN SPACE··· A DECADE OF ACHIEVEMENT

1434   1435

Emily Dickinson American Poet

1436

SAN JUAN, PUERTO RICO 1521-1971

1437

Prevent drug abuse

United States Postage 8c

1438

CARE 1946-1971

1439

HISTORIC PRESERVATION   HISTORIC PRESERVATION

HISTORIC PRESERVATION   HISTORIC PRESERVATION

1440   1441
1442   1443

Christmas

Giorgione, ca. 1478-1510 National Gallery of Art 8c U.S.

444

ON THE FIRST DAY OF CHRISTMAS MY TRUE LOVE SENT TO ME

1445

8 CENTS SIDNEY LANIER American Poet

1446

Peace Corps 8c United States

1447

1448
1450

1449
1451

1452

1453

1454

1455

1456
1458

1457
1459

1460

1461

1462

1463

1464

1465

	1972 continued	Un	U	PB/LP	#	FDC	Q
	National Parks Centennial Issue, Cape Hatteras, Apr. 5, Perf. 11, (See also #C84)						
1448	2¢ Hull of Ship	.06	.06	1.60	(4)		172,730,000
1449	2¢ Cape Hatteras Lighthouse	.06	.06	1.60	(4)		172,730,000
1450	2¢ Laughing Gulls on Driftwood	.06	.06	1.60	(4)		172,730,000
1451	2¢ Laughing Gulls and Dune	.06	.06	1.60	(4)		172,730,000
1451a	Block of four, #1448-1451	.25	.30			1.25	
	Wolf Trap Farm, June 26						
1452	6¢ Performance at Shouse Pavilion	.16	.08	1.25	(4)	.75	104,090,000
	Yellowstone, Mar. 1						
1453	8¢ Old Faithful, Yellowstone	.18	.05	1.00	(4)	.75	164,096,000
	Mt. McKinley, July 28						
1454	15¢ View of Mt. McKinley in Alaska	.35	.22	2.75	(4)	.75	53,920,000

Note: Beginning with this issue, the USPS began to offer stamp collectors first day cancellations affixed to 8"x 10½" souvenir pages. The pages are similar to the stamp announcements that have appeared on Post Office bulletin boards beginning with Scott #1132.

		Un	U	PB/LP	#	FDC	Q
1455	8¢ Family Planning, Mar. 18	.16	.05	1.00	(4)	.75	153,025,000
	American Bicentennial Issue, Colonial American Craftsmen, July 4, Perf. 11x10½						
1456	8¢ Glassblower	.30	.08	1.75	(4)	1.00	50,472,500
1457	8¢ Silversmith	.30	.08	1.75	(4)	1.00	50,472,500
1458	8¢ Wigmaker	.30	.08	1.75	(4)	1.00	50,472,500
1459	8¢ Hatter	.30	.08	1.75	(4)	1.00	50,472,500
1459a	Block of four, #1456-1459	1.25	1.25			2.50	
	Olympic Games Issue, Aug. 17 (See also #C85)						
1460	6¢ Bicycling and Olympic Rings	.16	.12	2.25	(10)	.75	67,335,000
1461	8¢ Bobsledding and Olympic Rings	.16	.05	2.25	(10)	.85	179,675,000
1462	15¢ Running and Olympic Rings	.35	.18	4.50	(10)	1.00	46,340,000
1463	8¢ Parent Teachers Association,						
	Sept. 15	.16	.05	1.00	(4)	.75	180,155,000
	Wildlife Conservation Issue, Sept. 20, Perf. 11						
1464	8¢ Fur Seals	.25	.08	1.40	(4)	2.00	49,591,200
1465	8¢ Cardinal	.25	.08	1.40	(4)	2.00	49,591,200
1466	8¢ Brown Pelican	.25	.08	1.40	(4)	2.00	49,591,200
1467	8¢ Bighorn Sheep	.25	.08	1.40	(4)	2.00	49,591,200
1467a	Block of 4, #1464-1467	1.10	.85			3.00	

Note: With this issue the USPS introduced the "American Commemorative Series" Stamp Panels. Each panel contains a block of four mint stamps with text and background illustrations.

	1972 continued, Perf. 11x10½	Un	U	PB/LP	#	FDC	Q
1468	8¢ Mail Order Business, Sept. 27	.16	.05	2.75	(12)	.75	185,490,000
	Perf. 10½x11						
1469	8¢ Osteopathic Medicine, Oct. 9	.16	.05	1.35	(6)	.75	162,335,000
	American Folklore Issue, Tom Sawyer, Oct. 13, Perf. 11						
1470	8¢ Tom Sawyer Whitewashing a						
	Fence, by Norman Rockwell	.16	.05	1.00	(4)	.75	162,789,950
	Christmas Issue, Nov. 9, Perf. 10½x11						
1471	8¢ Angels from "Mary, Queen of						
	Heaven," by the Master						
	of the St. Lucy Legend	.16	.05	2.75	(12)	.75	1,003,475,000
1472	8¢ Santa Claus	.16	.05	2.75	(12)	.75	1,017,025,000
	Perf. 11						
1473	8¢ Pharmacy, Nov. 10	.16	.05	1.00	(4)	.75	165,895,000
1474	8¢ Stamp Collecting, Nov. 17	.16	.05	1.00	(4)	.75	166,508,000
	Issues of 1973, Perf. 11x10½						
1475	8¢ Love, Jan. 26	.16	.05	1.35	(6)	.75	330,055,000
	American Revolution Bicentennial Issues, Communications in Colonial Times, Perf. 11						
1476	8¢ Printer and Patriots Examining						
	Pamphlet, Feb. 16	.20	.05	1.35	(4)	.75	166,005,000
1477	8¢ Posting a Broadside, Apr. 13	.20	.05	1.35	(4)	.75	163,050,000
1478	8¢ Post Rider, June 22	.20	.05	1.35	(4)	.75	159,005,000
1479	8¢ Drummer, Sept. 28	.20	.05	1.35	(4)	.75	147,295,000
	Boston Tea Party, July 4						
1480	8¢ British Merchantman	.20	.10	1.35	(4)	1.75	49,068,750
1481	8¢ British Three-Master	.20	.10	1.35	(4)	1.75	49,068,750
1482	8¢ Boats and Ship's Hull	.20	.10	1.35	(4)	1.75	49,068,750
1483	8¢ Boat and Dock	.20	.10	1.35	(4)	1.75	49,068,750
1483a	Block of four, #1480-1483	.85	.80			3.75	
	American Arts Issue (See also #1485-1487)						
1484	8¢ George Gershwin and Scene						
	From "Porgy and Bess," Feb. 28	.16	.05	2.75	(12)	.75	139,152,000

Boys Will Be Boys...

*Created by humorist Mark Twain, Tom Sawyer (#1470) is the main character in **The Adventures of Tom Sawyer**, a novel published more than 110 years ago. Tom is particularly reknowned for his cleverness, which he displayed by tricking his friends into helping him whitewash a fence—a classic and humorous example of "old-fashioned American ingenuity."*

1468

1469

1470

1471

1472

1473

1474

1475

1476

1477

1478

1479

1480
1482

1481
1483

1484

1485 1486 1487

1488

U.S. POSTAL SERVICE 8¢   U.S. POSTAL SERVICE 8¢   U.S. POSTAL SERVICE 8¢   U.S. POSTAL SERVICE 8¢   U.S. POSTAL SERVICE 8¢

| Nearly 27 billion U.S. stamps are sold yearly to carry your letters to every corner of the world. | Mail is picked up from nearly a third of a million local collection boxes, as well as your mailbox. | More than 87 billion letters and packages are handled yearly—almost 300 million every delivery day. | The People in your Postal Service handle and deliver more than 500 million packages yearly. | Thousands of machines, buildings, and vehicles must be operated and maintained to keep your mail moving. |
| People Serving You | People Serving You | People Serving You | People Serving You | People Serving You |

1489   1490   1491   1492   1493

U.S. POSTAL SERVICE 8¢   U.S. POSTAL SERVICE 8¢   U.S. POSTAL SERVICE 8¢   U.S. POSTAL SERVICE 8¢   U.S. POSTAL SERVICE 8¢

| The skill of sorting mail manually is still vital to delivery of your mail. | Employees use modern, high-speed equipment to sort and process huge volumes of mail in central locations. | Thirteen billion pounds of mail are handled yearly by postal employees as they speed your letters and packages. | Our customers include 54 million urban and 12 million rural families, plus 9 million businesses. | Employees cover 4 million miles each delivery day to bring mail to your home or business. |
| People Serving You | People Serving You | People Serving You | People Serving You | People Serving You |

1494   1495   1496   1497   1498

	1973 continued	Un	U	PB/LP	#	FDC	Q
	American Arts Issue, Perf. 11 (See also #1484)						
1485	8¢ Robinson Jeffers, Man and Children						
	of Carmel with Burro, Aug. 13	.16	.05	2.75	(12)	.75	128,048,000
1486	8¢ Henry Ossawa Tanner,						
	Palette and Rainbow, Sept. 10	.16	.05	2.75	(12)	.75	146,008,000
1487	8¢ Willa Cather, Pioneer Family						
	and Covered Wagon, Sept. 20	.16	.05	2.75	(12)	.75	139,608,000
1488	8¢ Nicolaus Copernicus, Apr. 23	.16	.05	1.00	(4)	.75	159,475,000
	Postal Service Employees Issue, Apr. 30, Perf. 10½x11						
1489	8¢ Stamp Counter	.20	.12			1.10	48,602,000
1490	8¢ Mail Collection	.20	.12			1.10	48,602,000
1491	8¢ Letter-Facing on Conveyor	.20	.12			1.10	48,602,000
1492	8¢ Parcel Post Sorting	.20	.12			1.10	48,602,000
1493	8¢ Mail Canceling	.20	.12	2.25	(10)	1.10	48,602,000
1494	8¢ Manual Letter Routing	.20	.12			1.10	48,602,000
1495	8¢ Electronic Letter Routing	.20	.12			1.10	48,602,000
1496	8¢ Loading Mail on Truck	.20	.12			1.10	48,602,000
1497	8¢ Carrier Delivering Mail	.20	.12			1.10	48,602,000
1498	8¢ Rural Mail Delivery	.20	.12	2.25	(10)	1.10	48,602,000
1498a	Strip of 10, #1489-1498	2.25	2.00	4.50	(20)	6.00	

#1489-98 were the first United States stamps to have printing on the back. (See also #1559-62)

Neither Rain Nor Sleet...

The United States Postal Service operates some 40,000 postal facilities, employs more than 780,000 people and handles more than 150 billion pieces of mail a year. That's more than half the amount of mail handled by all other post offices in the world combined. Mail (#1489-98) has been a priority of the United States from the start: George Washington himself helped survey postal routes for more efficient mail service.

	1973 continued, Perf. 11	Un	U	PB/LP	#	FDC	Q
1499	8¢ Harry S. Truman, May 8	.16	.05	1.00	(4)	.75	157,052,800
	Progress in Electronics Issue, July 10 (See also #C86)						
1500	6¢ Marconi's Spark Coil and Gap	.12	.10	1.25	(4)	.75	53,005,000
1501	8¢ Transistors and						
	Printed Circuit Board	.16	.05	1.00	(4)	.75	159,775,000
1502	15¢ Microphone, Speaker,						
	Vacuum Tube, TV Camera Tube	.30	.20	3.00	(4)	.80	39,005,000
1503	8¢ Lyndon B. Johnson, Aug. 27	.16	.05	2.50	(12)	.75	152,624,000
	Issues of 1973-74, Rural America Issue						
1504	8¢ Angus and Longhorn Cattle,						
	by F.C. Murphy, Oct. 5, 1973	.16	.05	1.00	(4)	.75	145,840,000
1505	10¢ Chautauqua Tent and Buggies,						
	Aug. 6, 1974	.20	.05	1.00	(4)	.75	151,335,000
1506	10¢ Wheat Fields and Train,						
	Aug. 16, 1974	.20	.05	1.00	(4)	.75	141,085,000
	Issue of 1973, Christmas Issue, Nov. 7, Perf. 10½x11						
1507	8¢ Small Cowper Madonna,						
	by Raphael	.16	.05	2.10	(12)	.75	885,160,000
1508	8¢ Christmas Tree in Needlepoint	.16	.05	2.10	(12)	.75	939,835,000
	Issues of 1973-74 continued, Perf. 11x10½						
1509	10¢ 50-Star and 13-Star Flags,						
	Dec. 8, 1973	.20	.05	5.50	(20)	.75	
1510	10¢ Jefferson Memorial,						
	Dec. 14, 1973	.20	.05	1.00	(4)	.75	
1510b	Bklt. pane of 5 + label,						
	Dec. 14, 1973	1.50	*.30*				
1510c	Bklt. pane of 8, Dec. 14, 1973	1.60	*.30*				
1510d	Bklt. pane of 6, Aug. 5, 1974	2.50	*.30*				
1511	10¢ ZIP Code, Jan. 4, 1974	.20	.05	2.25	(8)	.75	
1512-1517 not assigned.							
	Coil Stamps, Perf. 10 Vertically						
1518	6.3¢ Liberty Bell, Oct. 1, 1974	.13	.07	.35		.75	
1519	10¢ red and blue Flags (1509),						
	Dec. 8, 1973	.25	.05	—		.75	
1520	10¢ blue Jefferson Memorial						
	(1510), Dec. 14, 1973	.20	.05	.50		.75	
1521-24 not assigned.							

1499

1500

1501

1502

1503

1504

1505

1506

1507

1508

1509

1510

1511

1518

1525

1526

1527

1528

1529

| 1530 | 1531 | 1532 | 1533 |
| 1534 | 1535 | 1536 | 1537 |

	Issues of 1974, Perf. 11	Un	U	PB/LP	#	FDC	Q
1525	10¢ Veterans of Foreign Wars, Mar. 11	.20	.05	1.25	(4)	.75	149,930,000
	Perf. 10½x11						
1526	10¢ Robert Frost, Mar. 26	.20	.05	1.00	(4)	.75	145,235,000
	Perf. 11						
1527	10¢ Expo '74 World's Fair, Apr. 18	.20	.05	2.60	(12)	.75	135,052,000
	Perf. 11x10½						
1528	10¢ Horse Racing, May 4	.20	.05	2.60	(12)	.75	156,750,000
	Perf. 11						
1529	10¢ Skylab I, May 14	.20	.05	1.00	(4)	1.25	164,670,000
	Universal Postal Union Issue, June 6						
1530	10¢ Michelangelo, from "School of Athens," by Raphael	.20	.18			1.10	23,769,600
1531	10¢ "Five Feminine Virtues," by Hokusai	.20	.18			1.10	23,769,600
1532	10¢ "Old Scraps," by John Fredrick Peto	.20	.18			1.10	23,769,600
1533	10¢ "The Lovely Reader," by Jean Etienne Liotard	.20	.18			1.10	23,769,600
1534	10¢ "Lady Writing Letter," by Gerard Terborch	.20	.18			1.10	23,769,600
1535	10¢ Inkwell and Quill, from "Boy with a Top," by Jean-Baptiste Simeon Chardin	.20	.18			1.10	23,769,600
1536	10¢ Mrs. John Douglas, by Thomas Gainsborough	.20	.18			1.10	23,769,600
1537	10¢ Don Antonio Noriega, by Francisco de Goya	.20	.18			1.10	23,769,600
1537a	Block or strip of 8, #1530-37	1.60	2.00	3.40	(16)	4.25	

Handle with Care

The Universal Postal Union's (UPU, #1530-1537) 150 member countries pledge to handle all mail with equal care. This statue of messengers circling the world stands at the UPU's headquarters in Bern, Switzerland, site of the first international postal congress. The UPU will hold its 20th Congress in Washington, D.C. in 1989. (See article, page 38.)

	1974 continued, Perf. 11	Un	U	PB/LP	#	FDC	Q
	Mineral Heritage Issue, June 13						
1538	10¢ Petrified Wood	.20	.10	1.50	(4)	1.50	41,803,200
1539	10¢ Tourmaline	.20	.10	1.50	(4)	1.50	41,803,200
1540	10¢ Amethyst	.20	.10	1.50	(4)	1.50	41,803,200
1541	10¢ Rhodochrosite	.20	.10	1.50	(4)	1.50	41,803,200
1541a	Block of 4, #1538-1541	.80	.80			3.00	
1542	10¢ First Kentucky Settlement-						
	Fort Harrod, June 15	.20	.05	1.20	(4)	.75	156,265,000
	American Bicentennial Issue, First Continental Congress, July 4						
1543	10¢ Carpenters' Hall	.20	.10	1.20	(4)	.90	48,896,250
1544	10¢ "We ask but for Peace,						
	Liberty and Safety"	.20	.10	1.20	(4)	.90	48,896,250
1545	10¢ "Deriving their Just Powers from						
	the Consent of the Governed"	.20	.10	1.20	(4)	.90	48,896,250
1546	10¢ Independence Hall	.20	.10	1.20	(4)	.90	48,896,250
1546a	Block of 4, #1543-1546	1.00	.80			2.75	
1547	10¢ Energy Conservation,						
	Sept. 22	.20	.05	1.00	(4)	.75	148,850,000
	American Folklore Issue, The Legend of Sleepy Hollow, Oct. 10						
1548	10¢ Headless Horseman and						
	Ichabod Crane	.20	.05	1.00	(4)	.75	157,270,000
1549	10¢ Retarded Children, Oct. 12	.20	.05	1.00	(4)	.75	150,245,000
	Christmas Issue						
1550	10¢ Angel from Pérussis Altarpiece,						
	Oct. 23	.20	.05	2.25	(10)	.75	835,180,000
1551	10¢ "The Road-Winter,"						
	by Currier and Ives, Oct. 23	.20	.05	2.60	(12)	.75	882,520,000
	Precanceled Self-Adhesive, Imperf.						
1552	10¢ Dove Weather Vane Atop						
	Mount Vernon, Nov. 15	.20	.08	5.50	(20)	.75	213,155,000

Americana Preserved

Lithographers Currier and Ives created a pictorial record of life in 19th-century America, publishing more than 7,000 titles between 1840 and 1890. Once inexpensive, these hand-colored prints now are very valuable. Currier and Ives scenes (#1551) continue to appear on Christmas cards to this day.

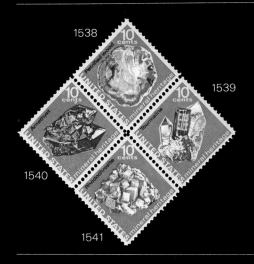

1538

1539

1540

1541

1542

1547

1548

1543
1545

1544
1546

1549

1550

1551

1552

Benjamin West

American artist
10 cents U.S. postage

1553

Paul Laurence
Dunbar

American poet

10 cents U.S. postage

1554

MOVIEMAKER US 10 C

D.W.GRIFFITH

1555

PIONEER ★ JUPITER

US
10c

1556

MARINER 10 ★ VENUS/MERCURY

US
10c

1557

collective bargaining
out of conflict...accord

UNITED
STATES

10c

1558

Contributors
To The
Cause

U.S.
8c

Sybil Ludington ★ *Youthful Heroine*

YOUTHFUL HEROINE
On the dark night of April 26, 1777,
16-year-old Sybil Ludington rode
her horse "Star" alone through the
Connecticut countryside rallying
her father's militia to repel a
raid by the British on Danbury.

1559

Contributors
To The
Cause

U.S.
10c

Salem Poor ★ *Gallant Soldier*

Contributors
To The
Cause

U.S.
10c

Haym Salomon ★ *Financial Hero*

Contributors
To The
Cause

U.S.
18c

Peter Francisco ★ *Fighter Extraordinary*

GALLANT SOLDIER
The conspicuously courageous
actions of black foot soldier
Salem Poor at the Battle of
Bunker Hill on June 17, 1775,
earned him citations for his
bravery and leadership ability.

FINANCIAL HERO
Businessman and broker Haym
Salomon was responsible for
raising most of the money
needed to finance the American
Revolution and later to save
the new nation from collapse.

FIGHTER EXTRAORDINARY
Peter Francisco's strength
and bravery made him a
legend around campfires.
He fought with distinction
at Brandywine, Yorktown
and Guilford Court House.

1560

1561

1562

Lexington & Concord 1775 by Sandham

US Bicentennial 10cents

1563

Bunker Hill 1775 by Trumbull
US Bicentennial 10c

1564

	Issues of 1975	Un	U	PB/LP	#	FDC	Q
	American Arts Issue, Perf. 10½x11						
1553	10¢ Benjamin West,						
	Self-Portrait, Feb. 10	.20	.05	2.20	(10)	.75	156,995,000
	Perf. 11						
1554	10¢ Paul Laurence Dunbar and						
	Lamp, May 1	.20	.05	2.20	(10)	.75	146,365,000
1555	10¢ D.W. Griffith and Motion-						
	Picture Camera, May 27	.20	.05	1.00	(4)	.75	148,805,000
	Space Issues						
1556	10¢ Pioneer 10 Passing Jupiter,						
	Feb. 28	.20	.05	1.00	(4)	1.25	173,685,000
1557	10¢ Mariner 10, Venus						
	and Mercury, Apr. 4	.20	.05	1.00	(4)	1.25	158,600,000
1558	10¢ Collective Bargaining,						
	Mar. 13	.20	.05	1.80	(8)	.75	153,355,000
	American Bicentennial Issues, Contributors to the Cause, Mar. 25, Perf. 11x10½						
1559	8¢ Sybil Ludington Riding Horse	.16	.13	2.00	(10)	.75	63,205,000
1560	10¢ Salem Poor Carrying Musket	.20	.05	2.50	(10)	.75	157,865,000
1561	10¢ Haym Salomon Figuring						
	Accounts	.20	.05	2.50	(10)	.75	166,810,000
1562	18¢ Peter Francisco Shouldering						
	Cannon	.36	.20	5.00	(10)	.75	44,825,000
	Battle of Lexington & Concord, Apr. 19, Perf. 11						
1563	10¢ "Birth of Liberty,"						
	by Henry Sandham	.20	.05	2.60	(12)	.75	144,028,000
	Battle of Bunker Hill, June 17						
1564	10¢ "Battle of Bunker Hill,"						
	by John Trumbull	.20	.05	2.60	(12)	.75	139,928,000

Probe Reveals Mercury's Craters

More than a year after leaving the Earth on November 3, 1973, U.S. space probe Mariner 10 transmitted data and photos from Venus. The first of the space probes to explore two planets, Mariner 10 (#1557) continued on to Mercury, where it sent back excellent photos of nearly half the planet's surface.

	1975 continued, Perf. 11	Un	U	PB/LP	#	FDC	Q
	American Bicentennial Issue, Military Uniforms, July 4						
1565	10¢ Soldier with Flintlock Musket,						
	Uniform Button	.20	.08	2.60	(12)	.90	44,963,750
1566	10¢ Sailor with Grappling Hook,						
	First Navy Jack, 1775	.20	.08			.90	44,963,750
1567	10¢ Marine with Musket,						
	Full-Rigged Ship	.20	.08	2.60	(12)	.90	44,963,750
1568	10¢ Militiaman with Musket and						
	Powder Horn	.20	.08			.90	44,963,750
1568a	Block of 4, #1565-1568	.80	.80			2.40	
	Apollo Soyuz Space Issue, July 15						
1569	10¢ Apollo and Soyuz after						
	Docking, and Earth	.20	.10	2.60	(12)	1.00	80,931,600
1569a	Pair, #1569-1570	.40	.25			3.00	
1570	10¢ Spacecraft before Docking,						
	Earth and Project Emblem	.20	.10	3.50	(16)	1.00	80,931,600
	Perf. 11x10½						
1571	10¢ International Women's Year,						
	Aug. 26	.20	.05	1.40	(6)	.75	145,640,000
	Postal Service Bicentennial Issue, Sept. 3						
1572	10¢ Stagecoach and Trailer Truck	.20	.08	2.60	(12)	.75	42,163,750
1573	10¢ Old and New Locomotives	.20	.08	2.60	(12)	.75	42,163,750
1574	10¢ Early Mail Plane and Jet	.20	.08			.75	42,163,750
1575	10¢ Satellite for Transmission						
	of Mailgrams	.20	.08			.75	42,163,750
1575a	Block of 4, #1572-1575	1.00	.80			2.40	
	Perf. 11						
1576	10¢ World Peace through Law,						
	Sept. 29	.20	.05	1.00	(4)	.75	146,615,000
	Banking and Commerce Issue, Oct. 6						
1577	10¢ Engine Turning, Indian Head						
	Penny and Morgan Silver Dollar	.20	.08	1.00	(4)	.75	73,098,000
1577a	Pair, #1577-1578	.40	.20			1.00	
1578	10¢ Seated Liberty Quarter,						
	$20 Gold Piece (Double Eagle) and						
	Engine Turning	.20	.08	1.00	(4)	.75	73,098,000

1565
1567

1566
1568

1569
1570

1571

1572
1574

1573
1575

1576

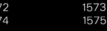

1577

1578

1579

1580

1581
1584

1582
1585

1597

1591
1593

1592
1594

1596
1599

1595a

1603
1605

1604
1606

1608
1611

1610
1612

	1975 continued, Perf. 11	Un	U	PB/LP	#	FDC	Q
	Christmas Issue, Oct. 14						
1579	(10¢) Madonna and Child, by						
	Domenico Ghirlandaio	.20	.05	2.60	(12)	.75	739,430,000
1580	(10¢) Christmas Card,						
	by Louis Prang, 1878	.20	.05	2.60	(12)	.75	878,690,000
	Issues of 1975-81, Americana Issue, Perf. 11 x 10½ (Designs 18½ x 22½ mm; #1590-90a, 17½ x 20 mm)						
1581	1¢ Inkwell & Quill, 1977	.05	.05	.25	(4)	.60	
1582	2¢ Speaker's Stand, 1977	.05	.05	.25	(4)	.60	
1583, 1586-89, 1600-02, 1607, 1609 not assigned.							
1584	3¢ Early Ballot Box, 1977	.06	.05	.30	(4)	.60	
1585	4¢ Books, Bookmark, Eyeglasses	.08	.05	.40	(4)	.60	
1590	9¢ Capitol Dome (1591),						
	Single from booklet (#1623a)	1.00	.20			1.00	
	Perf. 10						
1590a	Single (1591) from booklet						
	(1623b)	27.50	6.00				
1591	9¢ Capitol Dome, 1975	.18	.05	.90	(4)	.60	
1592	10¢ Contemplation of Justice, 1977	.20	.05	1.00	(4)	.60	
1593	11¢ Printing Press, 1975	.22	.05	1.10	(4)	.60	
1594	12¢ Torch, Apr. 8, 1981	.24	.05	1.20	(4)	.60	
1595	13¢ Liberty Bell						
	Single from booklet	.26	.05			.60	
1595a	Bklt. pane of 6, 1975	1.60	.50				
1595b	Bklt. pane of 7 + label	1.80	.50				
1595c	Bklt. pane of 8	2.10	.50				
1595d	Bklt. pane of 5 + label, 1976	1.30	.50				
	Perf. 11						
1596	13¢ Eagle and Shield, 1975	.26	.05	3.40	(12)	.60	
1597	15¢ Fort McHenry Flag, 1978	.30	.05	2.10	(6)	.65	
	Perf. 11x10½						
1598	15¢ Fort McHenry Flag (1597),						
	Single from booklet	.30	.05			.65	
1598a	Bklt. pane of 8, 1978	4.25	.60				
1599	16¢ Head of Liberty, 1978	.35	.05	2.25	(4)	.65	
1603	24¢ Old North Church, 1975	.60	.09	2.75	(4)	.75	
1604	28¢ Fort Nisqually, 1978	.70	.08	3.25	(4)	1.20	
1605	29¢ Sandy Hook Lighthouse, 1978	.70	.08	3.25	(4)	1.10	
1606	30¢ One-Room Schoolhouse, 1979	.75	.08	3.00	(4)	1.10	
1608	50¢ Whale Oil Lamp, 1979	1.00	.25	5.00	(4)	1.50	
1610	$1 Candle and Rushlight Holder,						
	July 2, 1979	2.00	.25	10.00	(4)	3.00	
1611	$2 Kerosene Table Lamp, 1978	4.00	.50	22.50	(4)	5.00	
1612	$5 Railroad Lantern, 1979	10.00	2.00	50.00	(4)	10.00	

#1590 is on white paper, #1591 is on gray paper.
For additional Americana Series, see #1613-19, 1623a-23d, 1811, 1813 and 1816.

	Issues of 1975-79	Un	U	PB/LP	#	FDC	Q
	Americana Issue, Coil Stamps, Perf. 10 Vertically						
1613	3.1¢ Guitar, Oct. 25, 1979	.20	.10	1.75		.60	
1614	7.7¢ Saxhorns, Nov. 20, 1976	.20	.08	1.00		.60	
1615	7.9¢ Drum, Apr. 23, 1976	.20	.08	1.10		.60	
1615C	8.4¢ Piano, July 13, 1978	.25	.08	2.00		.60	
1616	9¢ Capitol Dome (1591), 1976	.22	.05	.90		.60	
1617	10¢ Contemplation of Justice						
	(1592), Nov. 4, 1977	.20	.05	1.25		.60	
1618	13¢ Liberty Bell (1595), 1975	.26	.05	1.00		.65	
1618C	15¢ Ft. McHenry Flag (1597), 1978	.40	.05	—		.65	
1619	16¢ Head of Liberty (1599), 1978	.32	.05	1.50		.60	
1620-21, 1624 not assigned.							
	Perf. 11x10½						
1622	13¢ Flag over Independence						
	Hall, Nov. 15, 1975	.26	.05			.65	
1623	13¢ Flag over Capitol,						
	Single from booklet (1623a)	.26	.05			1.00	
1623a	Bklt. pane of 8,						
	(1 #1590 and 7 #1623), 1977	2.50	*.60*				
	Perf. 10						
1623b	13¢ Single from booklet	1.50	1.00				
1623c	Bklt. pane of 8,						
	(1 #1590 and 7 #1623b)	40.00	—				
	#1623, 1623b issued only in booklets						
	Perf. 11x10½						
1623d	Attached pair, #1590 and #1623	1.50					
	Perf. 10						
1623e	Attached pair, #1590a						
	and #1623b	30.00					
	Coil Stamp, Perf. 10 Vertically						
1625	13¢ Flag over Independence Hall						
	(1622), Nov. 15, 1975	.30	.05			.65	
	Issues of 1976, American Bicentennial Issues, The Spirit of '76, Jan. 1, Perf. 11						
1629	13¢ Drummer Boy	.26	.08			.65	
1630	13¢ Old Drummer	.26	.08			.65	
1631	13¢ Fifer	.26	.08			.65	
1631a	Strip of 3, #1629-1631	.78	.60	3.40	(12)	1.75	218,585,000
1632	13¢ Interphil 76, Jan. 17	.26	.05	1.30	(4)	.65	157,825,000
	State Flags, Feb. 23						
1633	13¢ Delaware	.45	.30			1.75	8,720,100
1634	13¢ Pennsylvania	.45	.30			1.75	8,720,100
1635	13¢ New Jersey	.45	.30			1.75	8,720,100
1636	13¢ Georgia	.45	.30			1.75	8,720,100
1637	13¢ Connecticut	.45	.30			1.75	8,720,100
1638	13¢ Massachusetts	.45	.30			1.75	8,720,100

1613

1614

1615

1615c

1622

1623a

1629   1630   1631

Interphil

1632

1633

1634

1635

1636

1637

1638

1639

1640

1641

1642

1643

1644

1645

1646

1647

1648

1649

1650

1651

1652

1653

1654

1655

1656

	1976 continued, Perf. 11	Un	U	PB/LP	#	FDC	Q
	American Bicentennial Issue continued, State Flags						
1639	13¢ Maryland	.45	.30			1.75	8,720,100
1640	13¢ South Carolina	.45	.30			1.75	8,720,100
1641	13¢ New Hampshire	.45	.30			1.75	8,720,100
1642	13¢ Virginia	.45	.30			1.75	8,720,100
1643	13¢ New York	.45	.30			1.75	8,720,100
1644	13¢ North Carolina	.45	.30			1.75	8,720,100
1645	13¢ Rhode Island	.45	.30			1.75	8,720,100
1646	13¢ Vermont	.45	.30			1.75	8,720,100
1647	13¢ Kentucky	.45	.30			1.75	8,720,100
1648	13¢ Tennessee	.45	.30			1.75	8,720,100
1649	13¢ Ohio	.45	.30			1.75	8,720,100
1650	13¢ Louisiana	.45	.30			1.75	8,720,100
1651	13¢ Indiana	.45	.30			1.75	8,720,100
1652	13¢ Mississippi	.45	.30			1.75	8,720,100
1653	13¢ Illinois	.45	.30			1.75	8,720,100
1654	13¢ Alabama	.45	.30			1.75	8,720,100
1655	13¢ Maine	.45	.30			1.75	8,720,100
1656	13¢ Missouri	.45	.30			1.75	8,720,100

200 Years of Statehood

Maryland, South Carolina, New Hampshire, Virginia and New York are among the states observing bicentennials in 1988. In honor of the 200-year celebration, the United States Postal Service issued a bicentennial statehood stamp for each.

South Carolina state flag

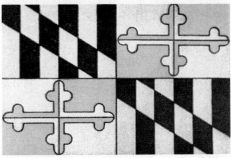

Maryland state flag

1976 continued, Perf. 11	Un	U	PB/LP	#	FDC	Q
American Bicentennial Issue continued, State Flags						
1657 13¢ Arkansas	.45	.30			1.75	8,720,100
1658 13¢ Michigan	.45	.30			1.75	8,720,100
1659 13¢ Florida	.45	.30			1.75	8,720,100
1660 13¢ Texas	.45	.30			1.75	8,720,100
1661 13¢ Iowa	.45	.30			1.75	8,720,100
1662 13¢ Wisconsin	.45	.30			1.75	8,720,100
1663 13¢ California	.45	.30			1.75	8,720,100
1664 13¢ Minnesota	.45	.30			1.75	8,720,100
1665 13¢ Oregon	.45	.30			1.75	8,720,100
1666 13¢ Kansas	.45	.30			1.75	8,720,100
1667 13¢ West Virginia	.45	.30			1.75	8,720,100
1668 13¢ Nevada	.45	.30			1.75	8,720,100
1669 13¢ Nebraska	.45	.30			1.75	8,720,100
1670 13¢ Colorado	.45	.30			1.75	8,720,100
1671 13¢ North Dakota	.45	.30			1.75	8,720,100
1672 13¢ South Dakota	.45	.30			1.75	8,720,100
1673 13¢ Montana	.45	.30			1.75	8,720,100
1674 13¢ Washington	.45	.30			1.75	8,720,100

"The Evergreen State"

Nicknamed the Evergreen State for its abundance of evergreen trees, Washington (#1674) boasts spectacular scenery, skiing and fishing. Among the state's chief products are lumber, salmon and apples. Spokane, shown here, is Washington's most populous eastern city.

13¢ USA — Arkansas — BICENTENNIAL ERA 1776-1976	13¢ USA — Michigan — BICENTENNIAL ERA 1776-1976	13¢ USA — Florida — BICENTENNIAL ERA 1776-1976
1657	1658	1659
13¢ USA — Texas — BICENTENNIAL ERA 1776-1976	13¢ USA — Iowa — BICENTENNIAL ERA 1776-1976	13¢ USA — Wisconsin — BICENTENNIAL ERA 1776-1976
1660	1661	1662
13¢ USA — California — CALIFORNIA REPUBLIC — BICENTENNIAL ERA 1776-1976	13¢ USA — Minnesota — BICENTENNIAL ERA 1776-1976	13¢ USA — Oregon — STATE OF OREGON 1859 — BICENTENNIAL ERA 1776-1976
1663	1664	1665

13¢ USA — Kansas — KANSAS — BICENTENNIAL ERA 1776-1976	13¢ USA — West Virginia — BICENTENNIAL ERA 1776-1976	13¢ USA — Nevada — BICENTENNIAL ERA 1776-1976
1666	1667	1668
13¢ USA — Nebraska — BICENTENNIAL ERA 1776-1976	13¢ USA — Colorado — BICENTENNIAL ERA 1776-1976	13¢ USA — North Dakota — BICENTENNIAL ERA 1776-1976
1669	1670	1671

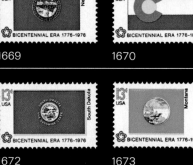

13¢ USA — South Dakota — BICENTENNIAL ERA 1776-1976	13¢ USA — Montana — BICENTENNIAL ERA 1776-1976	13¢ USA — Washington — BICENTENNIAL ERA 1776-1976
1672	1673	1674

1675   1676   1677

1678   1679   1680

1681   1682

Alexander Graham Bell 13c

Telephone Centennial USA

Commercial Aviation

USA 13c   1926-1976

CHEMISTRY

13c USA

1683   1684   1685

The Surrender of Lord Cornwallis at Yorktown
From a Painting by John Trumbull

1686

	1976 continued, Perf. 11	Un	U	PB/LP	#	FDC	Q
	American Bicentennial Issue continued, State Flags						
1675	13¢ Idaho	.45	.30			1.75	8,720,100
1676	13¢ Wyoming	.45	.30			1.75	8,720,100
1677	13¢ Utah	.45	.30			1.75	8,720,100
1678	13¢ Oklahoma	.45	.30			1.75	8,720,100
1679	13¢ New Mexico	.45	.30			1.75	8,720,100
1680	13¢ Arizona	.45	.30			1.75	8,720,100
1681	13¢ Alaska	.45	.30			1.75	8,720,100
1682	13¢ Hawaii	.45	.30			1.75	8,720,100
1682a	Pane of 50, #1633-1682	25.00	—	25.00 (50)		32.50	
1683	13¢ Telephone Centennial, Mar. 10	.26	.05	1.30 (4)		.65	158,915,000
1684	13¢ Commercial Aviation, Mar. 19	.26	.05	2.90 (10)		.65	156,960,000
1685	13¢ Chemistry, Apr. 6	.26	.05	3.40 (12)		.65	158,470,000
	American Bicentennial Issue, Souvenir Sheets, May 29						
	Sheets of 5 Stamps Each, Perf. 11						
1686	13¢ Surrender of Cornwallis at						
	Yorktown, by John Trumbull	4.50	—			6.00	1,990,000
	a. 13¢ Two American Officers	.65	.40				1,990,000
	b. 13¢ Gen. Benjamin Lincoln	.65	.40				1,990,000
	c. 13¢ George Washington	.65	.40				1,990,000
	d. 13¢ John Trumbull, Col. David Cobb,						
	General Friedrich						
	von Steuben, Marquis de Lafayette						
	and Thomas Nelson	.65	.40				1,990,000
	e. 13¢ Alexander Hamilton, John						
	Laurens and Walter Stewart	.65	.40				1,990,000

More than Laboratory Beakers and Flasks

The science of chemistry (#1685) has uncovered the basic laws of how matter in the universe is put together. And modern technology has put this understanding to good use in new drugs to combat and treat disease, stronger metals for home and industry and products that help farmers grow better and more abundant crops.

	1976 continued, Perf. 11	Un	U	PB/LP	#	FDC	Q
	American Bicentennial Issue continued, Souvenir Sheets, May 29						
1687	18¢ Declaration of Independence,						
	by John Trumbull	6.00	—			7.50	1,983,000
	a. 18¢ John Adams, Roger Sherman						
	and Robert R. Livingston	.80	.55				1,983,000
	b. 18¢ Thomas Jefferson and						
	Benjamin Franklin	.80	.55				1,983,000
	c. 18¢ Thomas Nelson, Jr., Francis						
	Lewis, John Witherspoon						
	and Samuel Huntington	.80	.55				1,983,000
	d. 18¢ John Hancock and						
	Charles Thomson	.80	.55				1,983,000
	e. 18¢ George Read,						
	John Dickinson and						
	Edward Rutledge	.80	.55				1,983,000
1688	24¢ Washington Crossing the						
	Delaware, by Emanuel Leutze/						
	Eastman Johnson	7.50	—			8.50	1,953,000
	a. 24¢ Boatsmen	1.00	.75				1,953,000
	b. 24¢ George Washington	1.00	.75				1,953,000
	c. 24¢ Flagbearer	1.00	.75				1,953,000
	d. 24¢ Men in Boat	1.00	.75				1,953,000
	e. 24¢ Steersman and						
	Men on Shore	1.00	.75				1,953,000
1689	31¢ Washington Reviewing Army						
	at Valley Forge, by William T. Trego	9.00	—			9.50	1,903,000
	a. 31¢ Two Officers	1.25	.90				1,903,000
	b. 31¢ George Washington	1.25	.90				1,903,000
	c. 31¢ Officer and Brown Horse	1.25	.90				1,903,000
	d. 31¢ White Horse and Officer	1.25	.90				1,903,000
	e. 31¢ Three Soldiers	1.25	.90				1,903,000

Washington's Surprise Attack

Commander-in-Chief George Washington chose the stormy night of Christmas 1776 to cross the Delaware River with his troops. Once across, they defeated the British at Princeton and Trenton, New Jersey. This historic event was immortalized in a painting by Emanuel Leutze (#1688).

The Declaration of Independence, 4 July 1776 at Philadelphia
From a Painting by John Trumbull

1687

Washington Crossing the Delaware
From a Painting by Emanuel Leutze / Eastman Johnson

1688

Washington Reviewing His Ragged Army at Valley Forge
From a Painting by William T. Trego

1689

1690

1691   1692   1693   1694

1699

1700

1695   1696
1697   1698

1701

1702

1703

1705

1704

	1976 continued, Perf. 11	Un	U	PB/LP	#	FDC	Q
	American Bicentennial Issues, Benjamin Franklin, June 1						
1690	13¢ Franklin and Map						
	of North America, 1776	.26	.05	1.30	(4)	.65	164,890,000
	Declaration of Independence, by John Trumbull, July 4						
1691	13¢ Delegates	.26	.08	5.50	(20)	.65	51,008,750
1692	13¢ Delegates and John Adams	.26	.08			.65	51,008,750
1693	13¢ Roger Sherman, Robert R.						
	Livingston, Thomas Jefferson and						
	Benjamin Franklin	.26	.08			.65	51,008,750
1694	13¢ John Hancock, Charles Thomson,						
	George Read, John Dickinson						
	and Edward Rutledge	.26	.08	5.50	(20)	.65	51,008,750
1694a	Strip of 4, #1691-1694	1.10	.75			2.00	
	Olympic Games Issue, July 16						
1695	13¢ Diver and Olympic Rings	.26	.08	3.40	(12)	.75	46,428,750
1696	13¢ Skier and Olympic Rings	.26	.08			.75	46,428,750
1697	13¢ Runner and Olympic Rings	.26	.08	3.40	(12)	.75	46,428,750
1698	13¢ Skater and Olympic Rings	.26	.08			.75	46,428,750
1698a	Block of 4, #1695-1698	1.10	1.00			2.00	
1699	13¢ Clara Maass, Aug. 18	.26	.06	3.40	(12)	.75	130,592,000
1700	13¢ Adolph S. Ochs, Sept. 18	.26	.05	1.30	(4)	.75	158,332,800
	Christmas Issue, Oct. 27						
1701	13¢ Nativity,						
	by John Singleton Copley	.26	.05	3.40	(12)	.65	809,955,000
1702	13¢ "Winter Pastime,"						
	by Nathaniel Currier	.26	.05	3.00	(10)	.65	481,685,000
1703	13¢ as 1702	.26	.05	5.70	(20)	.65	481,685,000

#1702 has overall tagging. Lettering at base is black and usually ½mm. below design. As a rule, no "snowflaking" in sky or pond. Pane of 50 has margins on 4 sides with slogans. #1703 has block tagging the size of the printed area. Lettering at base is gray black and usually ¾mm. below design. "Snowflaking" generally in sky and pond. Pane of 50 has margin only at right or left and no slogans.

	Issues of 1977, American Bicentennial Issue, Washington at Princeton, Jan. 3						
1704	13¢ Washington, Nassau Hall,						
	Hessian Prisoners and 13-star Flag,						
	by Charles Willson Peale	.26	.05	2.90	(10)	.65	150,328,000
1705	13¢ Sound Recording, Mar. 23	.26	.05	1.30	(4)	.65	176,830,000

	1977 continued, Perf. 11	Un	U	PB/LP	#	FDC	Q
	American Folk Art Issue, Pueblo Pottery, Apr. 13						
1706	13¢ Zia Pot	.26	.08	3.00	(10)	.75	48,994,000
1707	13¢ San Ildefonso Pot	.26	.08			.75	48,994,000
1708	13¢ Hopi Pot	.26	.08	5.00	(16)	.75	48,994,000
1709	13¢ Acoma Pot	.26	.08			.75	48,994,000
1709a	Block of 4, #1706-1709	1.05	1.00			2.00	
1710	13¢ Solo Transatlantic Flight,						
	May 20	.26	.05	3.65	(12)	.75	208,820,000
1711	13¢ Colorado Statehood, May 21	.26	.05	3.65	(12)	.65	192,250,000
	Butterflies Issue, June 6						
1712	13¢ Swallowtail	.26	.08	3.65	(12)	.75	54,957,500
1713	13¢ Checkerspot	.26	.08	3.65	(12)	.75	54,957,500
1714	13¢ Dogface	.26	.08			.75	54,957,500
1715	13¢ Orange-Tip	.26	.08			.75	54,957,500
1715a	Block of 4, #1712-1715	1.05	.90			2.00	
	American Bicentennial Issues, Lafayette's Landing In South Carolina, June 13						
1716	13¢ Marquis de Lafayette	.26	.05	1.30	(4)	.65	159,852,000
	Skilled Hands for Independence, July 4						
1717	13¢ Seamstress	.26	.08	3.65	(12)	.65	47,077,500
1718	13¢ Blacksmith	.26	.08	3.65	(12)	.65	47,077,500
1719	13¢ Wheelwright	.26	.08			.65	47,077,500
1720	13¢ Leatherworker	.26	.08			.65	47,077,500
1720a	Block of 4, #1717-1720	1.05	.90			1.75	
	Perf. 11x10½						
1721	13¢ Peace Bridge, Aug. 4	.26	.05	1.30	(4)	.65	163,625,000

1706 1707
1708 1709

1710

1711

1716

1712 1714
1713 1715

1717 1718
1719 1720

1721

Herkimer at Oriskany 1777 by Yohn
US Bicentennial 13 cents

1722

ENERGY CONSERVATION USA 13c
ENERGY DEVELOPMENT USA 13c

1723
1724

First Civil Settlement·Alta California·1777

1725

Drafting the Articles of Confederation
York Town, Pennsylvania 1777 13c USA

1726

1727

Surrender at Saratoga 1777 by Trumbull
US Bicentennial 13 cents

1728

VALLEY FORGE Christmas USA 13c

1729

Christmas USA 13

1730

Carl Sandburg
USA 13c

1731

Alaska 1778 Capt.ⁿ James Cook 13c USA
Capt.ⁿ James Cook 13c USA
Hawaii 1778

1732
1733

USA 13c

1734

A US Postage

1735

15c USA

1737

USA 15c Virginia 1720
USA 15c Rhode Island 1790
USA 15c Massachusetts 1793
USA 15c Illinois 1860
USA 15c Texas 1890

USA 15c Virginia 1720
USA 15c Rhode Island 1790
USA 15c Massachusetts 1793
USA 15c Illinois 1860
USA 15c Texas 1890

1738   1739   1740   1741   1742

	1977 continued, Perf. 11	Un	U	PB/LP	#	FDC	Q
	American Bicentennial Issue, Battle of Oriskany, Aug. 6						
1722	13¢ Herkimer at Oriskany,						
	by Frederick Yohn	.26	.05	3.10	(10)	.65	156,296,000
	Energy Issue, Oct. 20						
1723	13¢ Energy Conservation	.26	.08	3.65	(12)	.65	79,338,000
1723a	Attached pair, #1723-1724	.60	.35			1.00	
1724	13¢ Energy Development	.26	.08			.65	79,338,000
1725	13¢ First Civil Settlement-						
	Alta, California, Sept. 9	.26	.05	1.30	(4)	.65	154,495,000
	American Bicentennial Issue, Articles of Confederation, Sept. 30						
1726	13¢ Members of Continental						
	Congress in Conference	.26	.05	1.30	(4)	.65	168,050,000
1727	13¢ Talking Pictures, Oct. 6	.26	.05	1.30	(4)	.75	156,810,000
	American Bicentennial Issue, Surrender at Saratoga, Oct. 7						
1728	13¢ Surrender of Burgoyne,						
	by John Trumbull	.26	.05	3.10	(10)	.65	153,736,000
	Christmas Issue, Oct. 21						
1729	13¢ Washington at Valley Forge,						
	by J. C. Leyendecker	.35	.05	8.00	(20)	.65	882,260,000
1730	13¢ Rural Mailbox	.26	.05	3.10	(10)	.65	921,530,000
	Issues of 1978						
1731	13¢ Carl Sandburg, Jan. 6	.26	.05	1.30	(4)	.65	156,580,000
	Capt. Cook Issue, Jan. 20						
1732	13¢ Capt. James Cook-Alaska,						
	by Nathaniel Dance	.26	.08	1.30	(4)	.75	101,095,000
1732a	Attached pair, #1732-1733	.55	.30			1.50	
1733	13¢ *Resolution* and *Discovery*-Hawaii,						
	by John Webber	.26	.08	1.30	(4)	.75	101,095,000
1734	13¢ Indian Head Penny, Jan. 11	.26	.10	3.25	(4)	1.00	
1735	(15¢) A Stamp, May 22	.30	.05	1.50	(4)	.65	
	Perf. 11x10½						
1736	(15¢) orange Eagle (1735),						
	Single from booklet	.30	.05			.65	
1736a	Bklt. pane of 8, May 22	2.40	.60				
	Roses Booklet Issue, July 11, Perf. 10						
1737	15¢ Roses, Single from booklet	.30	.06			.65	
1737a	Bklt. pane of 8	2.40	.60				
	Issue of 1980, Windmills Booklet Issue, Feb. 7, Perf. 11						
1738	15¢ Virginia, 1720	.30	.05			.65	
1739	15¢ Rhode Island, 1790	.30	.05			.65	
1740	15¢ Massachusetts, 1793	.30	.05			.65	
1741	15¢ Illinois, 1860	.30	.05			.65	
1742	15¢ Texas, 1890	.30	.05			.65	
1742a	Bklt. pane of 10, #1738-42	4.00	.60				
	#1737-42 issued only in booklets. All stamps have one or two straight edges.						

1978 continued, Coil Stamp, Perf. 10 Vertically	Un	U	PB/LP	#	FDC	Q
1743 (15¢) orange Eagle (1735), May 22	.30	.05	1.00		.65	

Black Heritage Issue, Harriet Tubman, Feb. 1, Perf. 11

| 1744 13¢ Harriet Tubman and | | | | | | |
| Cart Carrying Slaves | .26 | .05 | 3.65 (12) | | 1.00 | 156,555,000 |

American Folk Art Issue, Quilts, Mar. 8

1745 13¢ Basket design, red & orange	.26	.08	3.65 (12)		.75	41,295,600
1746 13¢ Basket design, red	.26	.08	3.65 (12)		.75	41,295,600
1747 13¢ Basket design, orange	.26	.08			.75	41,295,600
1748 13¢ Basket design, brown	.26	.08			.75	41,295,600
1748a Block of 4, #1745-1748	1.05	.75			2.00	

American Dance Issue, Apr. 26

1749 13¢ Ballet	.26	.08	3.65 (12)		.75	39,399,600
1750 13¢ Theater	.26	.08	3.65 (12)		.75	39,399,600
1751 13¢ Folk	.26	.08			.75	39,399,600
1752 13¢ Modern	.26	.08			.75	39,399,600
1752a Block of 4, #1749-1752	1.05	.75			1.75	

American Bicentennial Issue, French Alliance, May 4

| 1753 13¢ King Louis XVI and Benjamin | | | | | | |
| Franklin, by Charles Gabriel Sauvage | .26 | .05 | 1.30 (4) | | .65 | 102,920,000 |

Perf. 10½x11

| 1754 13¢ Early Cancer Detection, May 18 | .26 | .05 | 1.30 (4) | | .65 | 152,355,000 |

Performing Arts Issues, Jimmie Rodgers, May 24, and George M. Cohan, July 3, Perf. 11

1755 13¢ Jimmie Rodgers						
with Locomotive, Guitar and						
Brakeman's Cap	.26	.05	3.65 (12)		.65	94,625,000
1756 15¢ George M. Cohan, "Yankee						
Doodle Dandy" and Stars	.30	.05	4.20 (12)		.65	151,570,000

20th-Century Dance

Modern dance (#1752) developed from a desire to break away from the classic traditions of ballet and to fully utilize the body as a means of artistic expression. Alvin Ailey, Twyla Tharp and Paul Taylor are among the foremost choreographers in contemporary modern dance, which first made its appearance in the early 20th century.

1744

1745
1747

1746
1748

1749

1750

1752

1751

1753

1754

1755

1756

1757a, b, c, d

1757e, f, g, h

1757

1758

1759

1760

1761

1762

1763

1764
1766

1765
1767

1768

1769

	1978 continued, Perf. 11	Un	U	PB/LP	#	FDC	Q
	CAPEX '78, Souvenir Sheet, June 10						
1757	13¢ Souvenir sheet of 8	2.10	2.10	2.75	(8)	3.00	15,170,400
1757a	13¢ Cardinal	.26	.10				
1757b	13¢ Mallard	.26	.10				
1757c	13¢ Canada Goose	.26	.10				
1757d	13¢ Blue Jay	.26	.10				
1757e	13¢ Moose	.26	.10				
1757f	13¢ Chipmunk	.26	.10				
1757g	13¢ Red Fox	.26	.10				
1757h	13¢ Raccoon	.26	.10				
1758	15¢ Photography, June 26	.30	.05	4.20	(12)	.65	163,200,000
1759	15¢ Viking Missions to Mars,						
	July 20	.30	.05	1.50	(4)	1.10	158,880,000
	Wildlife Conservation Issue, American Owls, Aug. 26						
1760	15¢ Great Gray Owl	.30	.08	1.50	(4)	.75	46,637,500
1761	15¢ Saw-Whet Owl	.30	.08	1.50	(4)	.75	46,637,500
1762	15¢ Barred Owl	.30	.08	1.50	(4)	.75	46,637,500
1763	15¢ Great Horned Owl	.30	.08	1.50	(4)	.75	46,637,500
1763a	Block of 4, #1760-1763	1.25	.85			2.00	
	American Trees Issue, Oct. 9						
1764	15¢ Giant Sequoia	.30	.08	4.20	(12)	.75	42,034,000
1765	15¢ White Pine	.30	.08	4.20	(12)	.75	42,034,000
1766	15¢ White Oak	.30	.08			.75	42,034,000
1767	15¢ Gray Birch	.30	.08			.75	42,034,000
1767a	Block of 4, #1764-1767	1.25	.85			2.00	
	Christmas Issue, Oct. 18						
1768	15¢ Madonna and Child with Cherubim,						
	by Andrea della Robbia	.30	.05	4.20	(12)	.65	963,370,000
1769	15¢ Child on Hobby Horse and						
	Christmas Trees	.30	.05	4.20	(12)	.65	916,800,000

Consider the Moose

The largest member of the deer family, the moose (#1757e) may weigh as much as 1,800 pounds, with antlers spanning six feet or more.

Moose inhabit the world's northern regions and are protected by law in Canada and the United States.

	Issues of 1979, Perf. 11	Un	U	PB/LP	#	FDC	Q
1770	15¢ Robert F. Kennedy, Jan. 12	.35	.05	1.50	(4)	.65	159,297,600
	Black Heritage Issue, Martin Luther King, Jr., Jan. 13						
1771	15¢ Martin Luther King, Jr.,						
	and Civil Rights Marchers	.35	.05	4.20	(12)	.65	166,435,000
1772	15¢ International Year of the Child,						
	Feb. 15	.30	.05	1.50	(4)	.65	162,535,000
	Literary Arts Issue, John Steinbeck, Feb. 27, Perf. 10½x11						
1773	15¢ John Steinbeck,						
	by Philippe Halsman	.30	.05	1.50	(4)	.65	155,000,000
1774	15¢ Albert Einstein, Mar. 4	.30	.05	1.50	(4)	.65	157,310,000
	American Folk Art Issue, Pennsylvania Toleware, Apr. 19, Perf. 11						
1775	15¢ Coffeepot	.30	.08	3.50	(10)	.75	43,524,000
1776	15¢ Tea Caddy	.30	.08			.75	43,524,000
1777	15¢ Sugar Bowl	.30	.08			.75	43,524,000
1778	15¢ Coffeepot	.30	.08			.75	43,524,000
1778a	Block or strip of 4, #1775-1778	1.25	.85			2.00	
	American Architecture Issue, June 4						
1779	15¢ Virginia Rotunda,						
	by Thomas Jefferson	.30	.08	1.75	(4)	.75	41,198,400
1780	15¢ Baltimore Cathedral,						
	by Benjamin Latrobe	.30	.08	1.75	(4)	.75	41,198,400
1781	15¢ Boston State House,						
	by Charles Bulfinch	.30	.08	1.75	(4)	.75	41,198,400
1782	15¢ Philadelphia Exchange,						
	by William Strickland	.30	.08	1.75	(4)	.75	41,198,400
1782a	Block of 4, #1779-1782	1.50	.85			2.00	
	Endangered Flora Issue, June 7						
1783	15¢ Persistent Trillium	.30	.08	4.20	(12)	.75	40,763,750
1784	15¢ Hawaiian Wild Broadbean	.30	.08			.75	40,763,750
1785	15¢ Contra Costa Wallflower	.30	.08	4.20	(12)	.75	40,763,750
1786	15¢ Antioch Dunes Evening Primrose	.30	.08			.75	40,763,750
1786a	Block of 4, #1783-1786	1.25	.85			2.00	
1787	15¢ Seeing Eye Dogs, June 15	.30	.05	6.50	(20)	.65	161,860,000

1770

1771

International Year of the Child

1772

1773

Einstein
USA 15c

1774

1775   1776
1777   1778

1779   1780
1781   1782

1783   1784
1785   1786

USA 15c

Seeing For Me

1787

1788 1789 1790

1791 1792
1793 1794

1799 1800

1795 1796
1797 1798

1801

1802

1803 1804

	1979 continued, Perf. 11	Un	U	PB/LP #	FDC	Q
1788	15¢ Special Olympics, Aug. 9	.30	.05	3.50 (10)	.65	165,775,000

American Bicentennial Issue, John Paul Jones, Sept. 23, Perf. 11x12

| 1789 | 15¢ John Paul Jones, | | | | | |
| | by Charles Willson Peale | .30 | .05 | 3.50 (10) | .65 | 160,000,000 |

Olympic Summer Games Issues, Sept. 5, Perf. 11 (see also #C97)

1790	10¢ Javelin Thrower	.25	.22	3.75 (12)	1.00	67,195,000
1791	15¢ Runner	.35	.08	4.75 (12)	.75	46,726,250
1792	15¢ Swimmer	.35	.08	4.75 (12)	.75	46,726,250
1793	15¢ Rowers	.35	.08		.75	46,726,250
1794	15¢ Equestrian Contestant	.35	.08		.75	46,726,250
1794a	Block of 4, #1791-1794	1.50	.85		2.00	

Issues of 1980, Olympic Winter Games Issue, Feb. 1, Perf. 11x10½

1795	15¢ Speed Skater	.45	.08	6.50 (12)	.75	52,073,750
1796	15¢ Downhill Skier	.45	.08	6.50 (12)	.75	52,073,750
1797	15¢ Ski Jumper	.45	.08		.75	52,073,750
1798	15¢ Hockey Goaltender	.45	.08		.75	52,073,750
1798a	Block of 4, #1795-1798	1.90	.85		2.00	

1979 continued, Christmas Issue, Oct. 18, Perf. 11

1799	15¢ Virgin and Child with Cherubim,					
	by Gerard David	.30	.05	4.25 (12)	.65	873,710,000
1800	15¢ Santa Claus,					
	Christmas Tree Ornament	.30	.05	4.25 (12)	.65	931,880,000

Performing Arts Issue, Will Rogers, Nov. 4

1801	15¢ Will Rogers Portrait and					
	Rogers as a Cowboy Humorist	.30	.05	4.25 (12)	.65	161,290,000
1802	15¢ Vietnam Veterans, Nov. 11	.30	.05	3.50 (10)	1.25	172,740,000

1980 continued, Performing Arts Issue, W.C. Fields, Jan. 29

| 1803 | 15¢ W.C. Fields Portrait | | | | | |
| | and Fields as a Juggler | .30 | .05 | 4.25 (12) | .65 | 168,995,000 |

Black Heritage Issue, Benjamin Banneker, Feb. 15

| 1804 | 15¢ Benjamin Banneker Portrait | | | | | |
| | and Banneker as Surveyor | .30 | .05 | 4.25 (12) | .65 | 160,000,000 |

	1980 continued	Un	U	PB/LP	#	FDC	Q
	Letter Writing Issue, Feb. 25, Perf. 11						
1805	15¢ Letters Preserve Memories	.35	.08	11.10	(36)	.65	38,933,000
1806	15¢ P.S. Write Soon	.35	.08			.65	38,933,000
1807	15¢ Letters Lift Spirits	.35	.08			.65	38,933,000
1808	15¢ P.S. Write Soon	.35	.08			.65	38,933,000
1809	15¢ Letters Shape Opinions	.35	.08			.65	38,933,000
1810	15¢ P.S. Write Soon	.35	.08	11.10	(36)	.65	
1810a	Vertical Strip of 6, #1805-1810	2.75	1.25			3.00	
	Issues of 1980-81, Americana Issue, Coil Stamps, Perf. 10 Vertically						
1811	1¢ Inkwell & Quill, May 6, 1980	.05	.05	.15		.60	
1813	3.5¢ Weaver Violins, June 23, 1980	.08	.05	.30		.60	
1816	12¢ Torch from Statue of Liberty,						
	Apr. 8, 1981	.24	.05	.75		.60	
	Issues of 1981, Perf. 11x10½						
1818	(18¢) B Stamp, Mar. 15	.36	.05	1.80	(4)	.75	
	Perf 10						
1819	(18¢) B Stamp (1818),						
	Single from booklet	.36	.05			.75	
1819a	Bklt. pane of 8, Mar. 15	4.50	1.50				
	Coil Stamp, Perf. 10 Vertically						
1820	(18¢) B Stamp (1818), Mar. 15	.45	.05	1.50		.75	
	1980 continued, Perf. 10½x11						
1821	15¢ Frances Perkins, April 10	.30	.05	1.50	(4)	.65	163,510,000
	Perf. 11						
1822	15¢ Dolley Madison, May 20	.30	.05	1.50	(4)	.65	256,620,000
1823	15¢ Emily Bissell, May 31	.30	.05	1.50	(4)	.65	95,695,000
1824	15¢ Helen Keller/Anne Sullivan,						
	June 27	.30	.05	1.50	(4)	.80	153,975,000
1825	15¢ Veterans Administration,						
	July 21	.30	.05	1.50	(4)	.65	160,000,000
	American Bicentennial Issue, General Bernardo de Galvez, July 23						
1826	15¢ General Bernardo de Galvez						
	and Revolutionary Flag at						
	Battle of Mobile	.30	.05	1.50	(4)	.65	103,855,000
	Coral Reefs Issue, Aug. 26						
1827	15¢ Brain Coral, Beaugregory Fish	.30	.08	4.50	(12)	.85	51,291,250
1828	15¢ Elkhorn Coral, Porkfish	.30	.08			.85	51,291,250
1829	15¢ Chalice Coral, Moorish Idol	.30	.08	4.50	(12)	.85	51,291,250
1830	15¢ Finger Coral, Sabertooth Blenny	.30	.08			.85	51,291,250
1830a	Block of 4, #1827-1830	1.20	.85			2.00	

1811   1813

1805   1807   1809
1806   1808   1810

1816   1818

1822

1821   1823

1824   1825   1826

1827   1828
1829   1830

1831

1832

1833

1834

1835

1836

1837

1842

1843

1838

1839

1840

1841

	1980 continued, Perf. 11	Un	U	PB/LP	#	FDC	Q
1831	15¢ Organized Labor, Sept. 1	.30	.05	4.50	(12)	.65	166,590,000
	Literary Arts Issue, Edith Wharton, Sept. 5, Perf. 10½x11						
1832	15¢ Edith Wharton Reading Letter	.30	.05	1.50	(4)	.65	163,275,000
	Perf. 11						
1833	15¢ Education, Sept. 12	.30	.05	2.25	(6)	.65	160,000,000
	American Folk Art Issue, Pacific Northwest Indian Masks, Sept. 25						
1834	15¢ Heiltsuk, Bella Bella Tribe	.30	.08			.75	38,101,000
1835	15¢ Chilkat Tlingit Tribe	.30	.08			.75	38,101,000
1836	15¢ Tlingit Tribe	.30	.08			.75	38,101,000
1837	15¢ Bella Coola Tribe	.30	.08			.75	38,101,000
1837a	Block of 4, #1834-1837	1.20	.85	3.50	(10)	2.00	
	American Architecture Issue, Oct. 9						
1838	15¢ Smithsonian Institution, by James Renwick	.30	.08			.75	38,756,000
1839	15¢ Trinity Church, by Henry Hobson Richardson	.30	.08			.75	38,756,000
1840	15¢ Pennsylvania Academy of Fine Arts, by Frank Furness	.30	.08			.75	38,756,000
1841	15¢ Lyndhurst, by Alexander Jefferson Davis	.30	.08			.75	38,756,000
1841a	Block of 4, #1838-1841	1.20	.85	1.50	(4)	2.00	
	Christmas Issue, Oct. 31						
1842	15¢ Madonna and Child, from Epiphany Window, Washington Cathedral	.30	.05	4.25	(12)	.65	693,250,000
1843	15¢ Wreath and Toys	.30	.05	6.50	(20)	.65	718,715,000

Teach Me

From parents to classrooms to libraries to television programs, education involves both teaching and learning. Although much education takes place outside of schools, teachers and institutions have the chief responsibility for providing organized instruction and setting the framework for learning (#1833).

	Issues of 1980-85	Un	U	PB/LP	#	FDC		Q
	Great Americans Issue, Perf. 11							
1844	1¢ Dorothea Dix, Sept. 23, 1983,	.05	.05	1.00	(20)	.60		
	Perf. 10½x11							
1845	2¢ Igor Stravinsky, Nov. 18, 1982	.05	.05	.25	(4)	.60		
1846	3¢ Henry Clay, July 13, 1983	.06	.05	.40	(4)	.60		
1847	4¢ Carl Schurz, June 3, 1983	.08	.05	.50	(4)	.60		
1848	5¢ Pearl Buck, June 25, 1983	.10	.05	.60	(4)	.60		
	Perf. 11							
1849	6¢ Walter Lippman, Sept. 19, 1985	.12	.05	2.75	(20)	.60		
1850	7¢ Abraham Baldwin, Jan. 25, 1985	.14	.05	3.00	(20)	.60		
1851	8¢ Henry Knox, July 25, 1985	.16	.05	.80	(4)	.60		
1852	9¢ Sylvanus Thayer, June 7, 1985	.18	.05	4.00	(20)	.60		
1853	10¢ Richard Russell, May 31, 1984	.20	.05	4.50	(20)	.65		
1854	11¢ Alden Partridge, Feb. 12, 1985	.22	.05	1.10	(4)	.65		
	Perf. 10½x11							
1855	13¢ Crazy Horse, Jan. 15, 1982	.26	.05	1.50	(4)	.65		
	Perf. 11							
1856	14¢ Sinclair Lewis, Mar. 21, 1985	.28	.05	7.00	(20)	.65		
	Perf. 10½x11							
1857	17¢ Rachel Carson, May 28, 1981	.34	.05	2.10	(4)	.75		
1858	18¢ George Mason, May 7, 1981	.36	.05	2.20	(4)	.75		
1859	19¢ Sequoyah, Dec. 27, 1980	.38	.07	2.00	(4)	.80		
1860	20¢ Ralph Bunche, Jan. 12, 1982	.40	.05	2.50	(4)	.75		
1861	20¢ Thomas H. Gallaudet,							
	June 10, 1983	.40	.05	2.50	(4)	.75		
	Perf. 11							
1862	20¢ Harry S. Truman, Jan. 26, 1984	.40	.05	8.50	(20)	.75		
1863	22¢ John J. Audubon, Apr. 23, 1985	.44	.05	9.25	(20)	.80		
1864	30¢ Frank C. Laubach,							
	Sept. 2, 1984	.60	.08	12.50	(20)	.85		
	Perf. 10½x11							
1865	35¢ Charles R. Drew, M.D.,							
	June 3, 1981	.70	.08	3.50	(4)	1.00		
1866	37¢ Robert Millikan, Jan. 26, 1982	.75	.05	3.75	(4)	1.00		
	Perf. 11							
1867	39¢ Grenville Clark, May 20, 1985	.80	.08	20.00	(20)	1.00		
1868	40¢ Lillian M. Gilbreth,							
	Feb. 24, 1984	.80	.10	17.50	(20)	1.00		
1869	50¢ Chester W. Nimitz,							
	Feb. 22, 1985	1.00	.10	5.00	(4)	1.25		

1844

1845

1846

1847

1848

1849

1850

1851

1852

1853

1854

1855

1856

1857

1858

1859

1860

1861

1862

1863

1864

1865

1866

1867

1868

1869

211

USA 15c
Everett Dirksen

1874

1875

1876
1878

1877
1879

1889a

1890

1891

1893a

	Issues of 1981, Perf. 11	Un	U	PB/LP	#	FDC	Q
1874	15¢ Everett Dirksen, Jan. 4	.30	.05	1.50	(4)	.65	160,155,000
	Black Heritage Issue, Whitney Moore Young, Jan. 30						
1875	15¢ Whitney Moore Young at Desk	.30	.05	1.50	(4)	.65	159,505,000
	Flower Issue, April 23						
1876	18¢ Rose	.36	.08			.75	52,658,250
1877	18¢ Camellia	.36	.08			.75	52,658,250
1878	18¢ Dahlia	.36	.08			.75	52,658,250
1879	18¢ Lily	.36	.08			.75	52,658,250
1879a	Block of 4, #1876-1879	1.90	.85	2.15	(4)	2.50	
	Wildlife Booklet Issue, May 14						
1880	18¢ Bighorn Sheep	.36	.05			.75	
1881	18¢ Puma	.36	.05			.75	
1882	18¢ Harbor Seal	.36	.05			.75	
1883	18¢ Bison	.36	.05			.75	
1884	18¢ Brown Bear	.36	.05			.75	
1885	18¢ Polar Bear	.36	.05			.75	
1886	18¢ Elk (Wapiti)	.36	.05			.75	
1887	18¢ Moose	.36	.05			.75	
1888	18¢ White-Tailed Deer	.36	.05			.75	
1889	18¢ Prong Horned Antelope	.36	.05			.75	
1889a	Bklt. pane of 10, #1880-1889	7.50					
	#1880-89 issued only in booklets. All stamps have one or two straight edges.						
	Flag and Anthem Issue, April 24						
1890	18¢ Flag and Anthem, "…for						
	amber waves of grain"	.36	.05	10.00	(20)	.75	
	Coil Stamp, Perf. 10 Vertically						
1891	18¢ Flag and Anthem,						
	"…from sea to shining sea"	.36	.05			.75	
	Perf. 11						
1892	6¢ USA Circle of Stars,						
	Single from booklet (1893a)	.50	.10			.75	
1893	18¢ Flag and Anthem, "…for						
	purple mountain majesties,"						
	Single from booklet (1893a)	.36	.05			.75	
1893a	Bklt. pane of 8,						
	(2 #1892 & 6 #1893)	3.50	—				
	#1892-93 issued only in booklets. All stamps have one or two straight edges.						

	1981 continued, Perf. 11	Un	U	PB/LP	#	FDC		Q
	Flag over Supreme Court Issue, Dec. 17 (except # 1896b, issued June 1, 1982)							
1894	20¢ Flag over Supreme Court	.40	.05	9.50	(20)	.75		
	Coil Stamp, Perf. 10 Vertically							
1895	20¢ Flag over Supreme Court (1894)	.40	.05	—		.75		
	Perf. 11x10½							
1896	20¢ Flag over Supreme Court							
	(1894), Single from booklet	.40	.05	—		.75		
1896a	Bklt. pane of 6	2.50						
1896b	Bklt. pane of 10 (1894)	4.25						
	Issues of 1981-84, Transportation Issue, Coil Stamps, Perf. 10 Vertically (See also #2123-36,							
	2225-26, 2228, 2231, 2255, 2259, 2264)							
1897	1¢ Omnibus 1880s, Aug. 19, 1983	.05	.05	.85	(3)	.60		
1897A	2¢ Locomotive 1870s,							
	May 20, 1982	.10	.05	.75	(3)	.60		
1898	3¢ Handcar 1880s, Mar. 25, 1983	.15	.05	1.00	(3)	.60		
1898A	4¢ Stagecoach 1890s,							
	Aug. 19, 1982	.12	.05	1.50	(3)	.60		
1899	5¢ Motorcycle 1913, Oct. 10, 1983	.15	.05	1.50	(3)	.60		
1900	5.2¢ Sleigh 1880s, Mar. 21, 1983	.20	.05	6.00	(3)	.60		
1901	5.9¢ Bicycle 1870s, Feb. 17, 1982	.20	.05	7.00	(3)	.60		
1902	7.4¢ Baby Buggy 1880s,							
	April 7, 1984	.20	.08	7.00	(3)	.65		
1903	9.3¢ Mail Wagon 1880s,							
	Dec. 15, 1981	.20	.08	8.00	(3)	.65		
1904	10.9¢ Hansom Cab 1890s,							
	Mar. 26, 1982	.25	.05	10.00	(3)	.65		
1905	11¢ RR Caboose 1890s,							
	Feb. 3, 1984	.25	.08	4.50	(3)	.65		
1906	17¢ Electric Auto 1917,							
	June 25, 1981	.34	.05	4.00	(3)	.75		
1907	18¢ Surrey 1890s, May 15, 1981	.36	.05	4.00	(3)	.75		
1908	20¢ Fire Pumper 1860s,							
	Dec. 10, 1981	.40	.05	4.50	(3)	.65		
	Issue of 1983, Aug. 12							
1909	$9.35 Express Mail,							
	Single from booklet	25.00	6.00	—		25.00		
1909a	Bklt. pane of 3	77.50	—					
	Issues of 1981, Perf. 11x10½							
1910	18¢ American Red Cross, May 1	.36	.05	1.80	(4)	.75		165,175,000
	Perf. 11							
1911	18¢ Savings and Loans, May 8	.36	.05	1.80	(4)	.75		107,240,000

USA 20c

1894

Omnibus 1880s
USA 1c

1897

Locomotive 1870s
USA 2c

1897A

Handcar 1880s
USA 3c

1898

Stagecoach 1890s
USA 4c

1898A

Motorcycle
1913
USA 5c

1899

Sleigh 1880s
USA 5.2c Nonprofit
Org

1900

Bicycle 1870s
USA 5.9c

1901

Baby Buggy 1880s
USA 7.4c

1902

Mail Wagon 1880s
USA 9.3c
Bulk Rate

1903

Hansom Cab 1890s
USA 10.9c

1904

RR Caboose 1890s
USA 11c
Bulk Rate

1905

Electric Auto 1917
USA 17c

1906

Surrey 1890s
USA 18c

1907

Fire Pumper
1860s
USA 20c

1908

USA $9.35

1909

The Gift of Self
USA 18c

American Red Cross
1881-1981

1910

SAVINGS AND LOANS
SAVE
USA 18c

1911

1912　　　1913　　　　1914　　　　1915
1916　　　1917　　　　1918　　　　1919

1920

1925

1921　　　1922
1923　　　1924

1926

Alcoholism
You can beat it!
USA 18c

1927

	1981 continued	Un	U	PB/LP	#	FDC	Q
	Space Achievement Issue, May 21, Perf 11						
1912	18¢ Exploring the Moon-						
	Moon Walk	.36	.10			.75	42,227,375
1913	18¢ Benefiting Mankind (upper right)-						
	Columbia Space Shuttle	.36	.10			.75	42,227,375
1914	18¢ Benefiting Mankind (upper left)	.36	.10			.75	42,227,375
1915	18¢ Understanding the Sun-Skylab	.36	.10			.75	42,227,375
1916	18¢ Probing the Planets-Pioneer II	.36	.10			.75	42,227,375
1917	18¢ Benefiting Mankind (lower right)-						
	Columbia Space Shuttle	.36	.10			.75	42,227,375
1918	18¢ Benefiting Mankind (lower left)	.36	.10			.75	42,227,375
1919	18¢ Comprehending the						
	Universe-Telescope	.36	.10			.75	42,227,375
1919a	Block of 8, #1912-1919	3.75	2.25	4.25	(8)	5.00	
1920	18¢ Professional Management,						
	June 18	.36	.05	1.80	(4)	.75	99,420,000
	Preservation of Wildlife Habitats Issue, June 26						
1921	18¢ Save Wetland Habitats-						
	Great Blue Heron	.36	.08			.75	46,732,500
1922	18¢ Save Grassland Habitats-						
	Badger	.36	.08			.75	46,732,500
1923	18¢ Save Mountain Habitats-						
	Grizzly Bear	.36	.08			.75	46,732,500
1924	18¢ Save Woodland Habitats-						
	Ruffled Grouse	.36	.08			.75	46,732,500
1924a	Block of 4, #1921-1924	1.90	.85	2.15	(4)	2.50	
1925	18¢ International Year of the						
	Disabled, June 29	.36	.05	1.80	(4)	.75	100,265,000
1926	18¢ Edna St. Vincent Millay,						
	July 10	.36	.05	1.80	(4)	.75	99,615,000
1927	18¢ Alcoholism, Aug. 19	.45	.05	30.00	(20)	.75	97,535,000

	1981 continued	Un	U	PB/LP	#	FDC	Q
	American Architecture Issue, Aug. 28, Perf. 11						
1928	18¢ NYU Library,						
	by Sanford White	.36	.08			.75	41,827,000
1929	18¢ Biltmore House,						
	by Richard Morris Hunt	.36	.08			.75	41,827,000
1930	18¢ Palace of the Arts,						
	by Bernard Maybeck	.36	.08			.75	41,827,000
1931	18¢ National Farmer's Bank,						
	by Louis Sullivan	.36	.08			.75	41,827,000
1931a	Block of 4, #1928-1931	1.50	.85	1.80	(4)	2.00	
	American Sports Issues, Babe Zaharias and Bobby Jones, Sept. 22, Perf. 10½x11						
1932	18¢ Babe Zaharias Holding Trophy	.36	.05	1.80	(4)	.75	101,625,000
1933	18¢ Bobby Jones Teeing Off	.36	.05	1.80	(4)	.75	99,170,000
	Perf. 11						
1934	18¢ Frederic Remington, Oct. 9	.36	.05	1.80	(4)	.75	101,155,000
1935	18¢ James Hoban, Oct. 13	.50	.25	3.00	(4)	.75	101,200,000
1936	20¢ James Hoban, Oct. 13	.40	.05	2.00	(4)	.75	167,360,000
	American Bicentennial Issue, Yorktown-Virginia Capes, Oct. 16						
1937	18¢ Battle of Yorktown 1781	.36	.06			.75	81,210,000
1938	18¢ Battle of the						
	Virginia Capes 1781	.36	.06			.75	81,210,000
1938a	Attached pair, #1937-1938	.90	.15	1.95	(4)	1.00	
	Christmas Issue, Oct. 28						
1939	20¢ Madonna and Child,						
	by Botticelli	.40	.05	2.00	(4)	.75	597,720,000
1940	20¢ Felt Bear on Sleigh	.40	.05	2.00	(4)	.75	792,600,000
1941	20¢ John Hanson, Nov. 5	.40	.05	2.00	(4)	.75	167,130,000

Wright at Architectural Forefront

One of America's most influential architects, Frank Lloyd Wright is one of several whose work has been honored by U.S. stamp issues (#1779-1782, 1838-1841, 1928-1931, 2019-2022). Wright's best-known designs include the Guggenheim Museum in New York City and the "Fallingwater" house (#2019) at Bear Run near Uniontown, Pennsylvania.

1928   1929

1930   1931

1932   1933

1934   1935   1936

1937   1938   1939

1940

1941

1946

1942   1943   1945
              1944

1950

1949a

1951

1952

	1981 continued	Un	U	PB/LP	#	FDC	Q
	Desert Plants Issue, Dec. 11, Perf. 11						
1942	20¢ Barrel Cactus	.40	.06			.75	47,890,000
1943	20¢ Agave	.40	.06			.75	47,890,000
1944	20¢ Beavertail Cactus	.40	.06			.75	47,890,000
1945	20¢ Saguaro	.40	.06			.75	47,890,000
1945a	Block of 4, #1942-1945	1.90	.85	2.30	(4)	2.50	
	Perf. 11x10½						
1946	(20¢) C Stamp, Oct. 11	.45	.05	2.00	(4)	.75	
	Coil Stamp, Perf. 10 Vertically						
1947	(20¢) C Stamp (1946), Oct. 11	.45	.05	1.00		.75	
	Perf. 11x10½						
1948	(20¢) C Stamp (1946),						
	Single from booklet	.45	.05			.75	
1948a	Bklt. pane of 10, Oct. 11	4.25	—				
	Issues of 1982, Bighorn Sheep Booklet Issue, Jan. 8, Perf. 11						
1949	20¢ Bighorn Sheep,						
	Single from booklet	.45	.05			.75	
1949a	Bklt. pane of 10	5.50	—				
	#1949 issued only in booklets. All stamps have one or two straight edges.						
1950	20¢ Franklin D. Roosevelt, Jan. 3	.40	.05	2.00	(4)	.75	163,939,200
	Perf. 11x10½						
1951	20¢ Love, Feb. 1	.45	.05	2.00	(4)	.75	
	Perf. 11						
1952	20¢ George Washington, Feb. 22	.45	.05	2.00	(4)	.75	180,700,000

"Desert Skyscraper"

The largest of the cacti, the saguaro (#1945) may grow as high as 50 feet and weigh up to 10 tons! At least four-fifths of its weight is water that is absorbed through a widespread system of roots. As the plant takes in water, its accordion-like surface expands. The saguaro grows only in the southwestern United States, and its blossom is the state flower of Arizona (#1955).

	1982 continued	Un	U	PB/LP	#	FDC	Q
	State Birds & Flowers Issue, Apr. 14, Perf. 10½x11						
1953	20¢ Alabama	.45	.25			1.00	13,339,900
1954	20¢ Alaska	.45	.25			1.00	13,339,900
1955	20¢ Arizona	.45	.25			1.00	13,339,900
1956	20¢ Arkansas	.45	.25			1.00	13,339,900
1957	20¢ California	.45	.25			1.00	13,339,900
1958	20¢ Colorado	.45	.25			1.00	13,339,900
1959	20¢ Connecticut	.45	.25			1.00	13,339,900
1960	20¢ Delaware	.45	.25			1.00	13,339,900
1961	20¢ Florida	.45	.25			1.00	13,339,900
1962	20¢ Georgia	.45	.25			1.00	13,339,900
1963	20¢ Hawaii	.45	.25			1.00	13,339,900
1964	20¢ Idaho	.45	.25			1.00	13,339,900
1965	20¢ Illinois	.45	.25			1.00	13,339,900
1966	20¢ Indiana	.45	.25			1.00	13,339,900
1967	20¢ Iowa	.45	.25			1.00	13,339,900
1968	20¢ Kansas	.45	.25			1.00	13,339,900
1969	20¢ Kentucky	.45	.25			1.00	13,339,900
1970	20¢ Louisiana	.45	.25			1.00	13,339,900
1971	20¢ Maine	.45	.25			1.00	13,339,900
1972	20¢ Maryland	.45	.25			1.00	13,339,900

Friendly Robin Is Connecticut Pick

American naturalist John Burroughs described the robin as "the most native and democratic" of American birds. Robins are naturally gregarious and typically live near people in open areas. A kind of thrush, the male has brownish-gray feathers on his head, upper body and tail, and he is easily recognized by orange-red breast feathers. The robin is the state bird of Wisconsin (#2001), Michigan (#1974) and Connecticut (#1959), the latter of which is celebrating its bicentennial in 1988.

Alabama USA 20c	Alaska USA 20c	Arizona USA 20c	Arkansas USA 20c	California USA 20c
 *Yellowhammer &* *Camellia*	*Willow Ptarmigan &* *Forget-Me-Not*	 *Cactus Wren &* *Saguaro Cactus Blossom*	 *Mockingbird &* *Apple Blossom*	 *California Quail &* *California Poppy*
1953	1954	1955	1956	1957

Colorado USA 20c	Connecticut USA 20c	Delaware USA 20c	Florida USA 20c	Georgia USA 20c
 *Lark Bunting &* *Rocky Mountain Columbine*	*Robin &* *Mountain Laurel*	 *Blue Hen Chicken &* *Peach Blossom*	 *Mockingbird &* *Orange Blossom*	 *Brown Thrasher &* *Cherokee Rose*
1958	1959	1960	1961	1962

Hawaii USA 20c	Idaho USA 20c	Illinois USA 20c	Indiana USA 20c	Iowa USA 20c
Hawaiian Goose & *Hibiscus*	*Mountain Bluebird &* *Syringa*	*Cardinal &* *Violet*	*Cardinal &* *Peony*	*Eastern Goldfinch &* *Wild Rose*
1963	1964	1965	1966	1967

Kansas USA 20c	Kentucky USA 20c	Louisiana USA 20c	Maine USA 20c	Maryland USA 20c
 *Western Meadowlark &* *Sunflower*	*Cardinal &* *Goldenrod*	 *Brown Pelican &* *Magnolia*	 *Chickadee &* *White Pine Cone and Tassel*	 *Baltimore Oriole &* *Black-Eyed Susan*
1968	1969	1970	1971	1972

Massachusetts
USA 20c
Black-Capped Chickadee & *Mayflower*

Michigan
USA 20c
Robin & *Apple Blossom*

Minnesota
USA 20c
Common Loon & *Showy Lady Slipper*

Mississippi
USA 20c
Mockingbird & *Magnolia*

Missouri
USA 20c
Eastern Bluebird & *Red Hawthorn*

1973

1974

1975

1976

1977

Montana
USA 20c
Western Meadowlark & *Bitterroot*

Nebraska
USA 20c
Western Meadowlark & *Goldenrod*

Nevada
USA 20c
Mountain Bluebird & *Sagebrush*

New Hampshire
USA 20c
Purple Finch & *Lilac*

New Jersey
USA 20c
American Goldfinch & *Violet*

1978

1979

1980

1981

1982

New Mexico
USA 20c
Roadrunner & *Yucca Flower*

New York
USA 20c
Eastern Bluebird & *Rose*

North Carolina
USA 20c
Cardinal & *Flowering Dogwood*

North Dakota
USA 20c
Western Meadowlark & *Wild Prairie Rose*

Ohio
USA 20c
Cardinal & *Red Carnation*

1983

1984

1985

1986

1987

Oklahoma
USA 20c
Scissor-tailed Flycatcher & *Mistletoe*

Oregon
USA 20c
Western Meadowlark & *Oregon Grape*

Pennsylvania
USA 20c
Ruffed Grouse & *Mountain Laurel*

Rhode Island
USA 20c
Rhode Island Red & *Violet*

South Carolina
USA 20c
Carolina Wren & *Carolina Jessamine*

1988

1989

1990

1991

1992

	1982 continued, Perf. 10½x11	Un	U	PB/LP	#	FDC	Q
	State Birds and Flowers Issue continued						
1973	20¢ Massachusetts	.45	.25			1.00	13,339,900
1974	20¢ Michigan	.45	.25			1.00	13,339,900
1975	20¢ Minnesota	.45	.25			1.00	13,339,900
1976	20¢ Mississippi	.45	.25			1.00	13,339,900
1977	20¢ Missouri	.45	.25			1.00	13,339,900
1978	20¢ Montana	.40	.25			1.00	13,339,900
1979	20¢ Nebraska	.40	.25			1.00	13,339,900
1980	20¢ Nevada	.45	.25			1.00	13,339,900
1981	20¢ New Hampshire	.45	.25			1.00	13,339,900
1982	20¢ New Jersey	.45	.25			1.00	13,339,900
1983	20¢ New Mexico	.45	.25			1.00	13,339,900
1984	20¢ New York	.45	.25			1.00	13,339,900
1985	20¢ North Carolina	.45	.25			1.00	13,339,900
1986	20¢ North Dakota	.45	.25			1.00	13,339,900
1987	20¢ Ohio	.45	.25			1.00	13,339,900
1988	20¢ Oklahoma	.45	.25			1.00	13,339,900
1989	20¢ Oregon	.45	.25			1.00	13,339,900
1990	20¢ Pennsylvania	.45	.25			1.00	13,339,900
1991	20¢ Rhode Island	.45	.25			1.00	13,339,900
1992	20¢ South Carolina	.45	.25			1.00	13,339,900

Harbinger of Spring

The clear, flute-like song of the western meadowlark (#1968, 1978, 1979, 1986, 1989) is one of spring's earliest, most tuneful melodies. Ranging from western Canada to Mexico, the western meadowlark, or Sturnella neglecta, is streaked with brown, has a yellow breast and is between 8 and 11 inches long. Females conceal their eggs in grass-domed nests that they build in fields. The western meadowlark is the state bird of Kansas, Montana, Nebraska, North Dakota and Oregon.

1982 continued, Perf. 10½×11	Un	U	PB/LP	#	FDC	Q
State Birds and Flowers Issue continued						
1993 20¢ South Dakota	.45	.25			1.00	13,339,900
1994 20¢ Tennessee	.45	.25			1.00	13,339,900
1995 20¢ Texas	.45	.25			1.00	13,339,900
1996 20¢ Utah	.45	.25			1.00	13,339,900
1997 20¢ Vermont	.45	.25			1.00	13,339,900
1998 20¢ Virginia	.45	.25			1.00	13,339,900
1999 20¢ Washington	.45	.25			1.00	13,339,900
2000 20¢ West Virginia	.45	.25			1.00	13,339,900
2001 20¢ Wisconsin	.45	.25			1.00	13,339,900
2002 20¢ Wyoming	.45	.25			1.00	13,339,900
2002b Sheet of 50	22.50	—				
Perf. 11						
2003 20¢ USA/The Netherlands, Apr. 20	.45	.05	10.00	(20)	.75	109,245,000
2004 20¢ Library of Congress, Apr. 21	.40	.05	2.00	(4)	.75	112,535,000
Coil Stamp, Perf. 10 Vertically						
2005 20¢ Consumer Education,						
Apr. 27	.50	.05	1.00		.75	
Knoxville World's Fair Issue, Apr. 29, Perf. 11						
2006 20¢ Solar Energy	.40	.08			.75	31,160,000
2007 20¢ Synthetic Fuels	.40	.08			.75	31,160,000
2008 20¢ Breeder Reactor	.40	.08			.75	31,160,000
2009 20¢ Fossil Fuels	.40	.08			.75	31,160,000
2009a Block of 4, #2006-2009	1.90	.85	2.30	(4)	2.50	
2010 20¢ Horatio Alger, Apr. 30	.40	.05	2.00	(4)	.75	107,605,000
2011 20¢ Aging Together, May 21	.40	.05	2.00	(4)	.75	173,160,000
Performing Arts Issue, The Barrymores, June 8						
2012 20¢ Portraits of John, Ethel						
and Lionel Barrymore	.40	.05	2.00	(4)	.75	107,285,000

Solar Energy Heats Up

Since the ancient Greeks designed their houses to capture the sun's heat in the winter, solar technology and architecture (#2006) have gradually improved. This house, designed by Steven J. Strong, draws all of its energy needs from the sun.

South Dakota
USA 20c
Ring-Necked Pheasant &
Pasqueflower

1993

Tennessee
USA 20c
Mockingbird & Iris

1994

Texas
USA 20c
Mockingbird &
Bluebonnet

1995

Utah
USA 20c
California Gull &
Sego Lily

1996

Vermont
USA 20c
Hermit Thrush & Red Clover

1997

Virginia
USA 20c
Cardinal &
Flowering Dogwood

1998

Washington
USA 20c
American Goldfinch &
Rhododendron

1999

West Virginia
USA 20c
Cardinal &
Rhododendron Maximum

2000

Wisconsin
USA 20c
Robin &
Wood Violet

2001

Wyoming
USA 20c
Western Meadowlark & Indian Paintbrush

2002

20c
1982·USA·THE·NETHERLANDS

2003

Library of Congress
USA 20c

2004

Wise shoppers
stretch dollars
Consumer
Education
USA 20c

2005

USA 20c
Solar energy   Knoxville World's Fair
USA 20c
Synthetic fuels   Knoxville World's Fair
USA 20c
Breeder reactor Knoxville World's Fair
USA 20c
Fossil fuels   Knoxville World's Fair

2006   2007
2008   2009

Horatio Alger
USA 20c

2010

THE BARRYMORES
Performing Arts USA 20c

2012

Aging
together
USA
20c

2011

2013

2014

2015

2016

2017

2019 2020

2018

2021 2022

2023

2024

2025

2026

2027 2028
2029 2030

	1982 continued, Perf. 11	Un	U	PB/LP	#	FDC	Q
2013	20¢ Dr. Mary Walker, June 10	.40	.05	2.00	(4)	.75	109,040,000
2014	20¢ International Peace Garden,						
	June 30	.40	.05	2.00	(4)	.75	183,270,000
2015	20¢ America's Libraries, July 13	.40	.05	2.00	(4)	.75	169,495,000
	Black Heritage Issue, Jackie Robinson, Aug. 2, Perf. 10½x11						
2016	20¢ Jackie Robinson Portrait, and						
	Robinson Stealing Home Plate	.45	.05	2.00	(4)	.75	164,235,000
	Perf. 11						
2017	20¢ Touro Synagogue, Aug. 22	.45	.05	10.00	(20)	.85	110,130,000
2018	20¢ Wolf Trap Farm Park,						
	Sept. 1	.40	.05	2.00	(4)	.75	110,995,000
	American Architecture Issue, Sept. 30						
2019	20¢ Fallingwater,						
	by Frank Lloyd Wright	.40	.08			.75	41,335,000
2020	20¢ Illinois Institute of Technology,						
	by Mies van der Rohe	.40	.08			.75	41,335,000
2021	20¢ Gropius House,						
	by Walter Gropius	.40	.08			.75	41,335,000
2022	20¢ Dulles Airport,						
	by Eeno Saarinen	.40	.08			.75	41,335,000
2022a	Block of 4, #2019-2022	1.90	.85	2.30	(4)	2.50	
2023	20¢ Francis of Assisi, Oct. 7	.40	.05	2.00	(4)	.75	174,180,000
2024	20¢ Ponce de Leon, Oct. 12	.45	.05	10.00	(20)	.75	110,261,000
	Christmas Issue						
2025	13¢ Puppy and Kitten, Nov. 3	.26	.05	1.30	(4)	.75	
2026	20¢ Madonna and Child,						
	by Tiepolo, Oct. 28	.40	.05	10.00	(20)	.75	703,295,000
	Seasons Greetings Issue, Oct. 28						
2027	20¢ Children Sledding	.40	.05			.75	197,220,000
2028	20¢ Children Building a Snowman	.40	.05			.75	197,220,000
2029	20¢ Children Skating	.40	.05			.75	197,220,000
2030	20¢ Children Trimming a Tree	.40	.05			.75	197,220,000
2030a	Block of 4, #2027-2030	1.90	.85	2.30	(4)	2.50	

	Issues of 1983, Perf. 11	Un	U	PB/LP	#	FDC	Q
2031	20¢ Science & Industry, Jan. 19	.40	.05	2.00	(4)	.75	118,555,000
	Balloons Issue, March 31						
2032	20¢ Intrepid, 1861	.40	.08			.75	
2033	20¢ Hot Air Ballooning	.40	.08			.75	
2034	20¢ Hot Air Ballooning	.40	.08			.75	
2035	20¢ Explorer II, 1935	.40	.08			.75	
2035a	Block of 4, #2032-2035	1.90	.85	2.30	(4)	2.50	226,128,000
2036	20¢ U.S./Sweden Treaty, Mar. 24	.40	.05	2.00	(4)	.75	118,225,000
2037	20¢ Civilian Conservation Corps, Apr. 5	.40	.05	2.00	(4)	.75	114,290,000
2038	20¢ Joseph Priestley, Apr. 13	.40	.05	2.00	(4)	.75	165,000,000
2039	20¢ Voluntarism, Apr. 20	.40	.05	10.00	(20)	.75	120,430,000
2040	20¢ Concord-German Immigration, Apr. 29	.40	.05	2.00	(4)	.75	117,025,000
2041	20¢ Brooklyn Bridge, May 5	.40	.05	2.00	(4)	.75	181,700,000
2042	20¢ TVA, May 18	.40	.05	10.00	(20)	.75	114,250,000
2043	20¢ Physical Fitness, May 14	.40	.05	10.00	(20)	.75	111,775,000

Sound Mind, Sound Body

Experts believe that physical fitness (#2043) is an important key to good health. Involving mental as well as bodily activity, physical fitness includes endurance, agility and the ability to engage in vigorous exercise. Fitness programs vary according to age and physical needs. In general, people who are physically fit exercise at least three times a week.

Science & Industry
USA 20c

2031

2032

2033
2034

2035

TREATY OF AMITY
AND COMMERCE
BETWEEN USA AND
SWEDEN 1783

2036

1933-1983
Civilian Conservation Corps USA 20c

2037

Joseph Priestley
USA 20c

2038

Volunteer
lend a hand

USA 20c

2039

Concord 1683   USA 20c

German
Immigration
Tricentennial

2040

Brooklyn Bridge
1883 1983
USA 20c

2041

Tennessee
Valley
Authority
USA 20c

2042

Physical Fitness

USA
20c

2043

2044

2045

2046 2047

2048
2050

2049
2051

2052

2053

2054

2055
2057

2056
2058

	1983 continued	Un	U	PB/LP	#	FDC	Q
	Black Heritage Issue, Scott Joplin, June 9, Perf. 11						
2044	20¢ Scott Joplin Portrait						
	and Joplin Playing the Piano	.40	.05	2.00	(4)	.80	115,200,000
2045	20¢ Medal of Honor, June 7	.40	.05	2.00	(4)	.80	108,820,000
	American Sports Issue, Babe Ruth, July 6, Perf. 10½x11						
2046	20¢ Babe Ruth Hitting a Home Run	.45	.05	2.00	(4)	.80	184,950,000
	Literary Arts Issue, Nathaniel Hawthorne, July 8, Perf. 11						
2047	20¢ Nathaniel Hawthorne,						
	by Cephus Giovanni Thompson	.40	.05	2.00	(4)	.80	110,925,000
	Olympic Summer Games Issue, July 28 (see also #2082-85, C101-112)						
2048	13¢ Discus Thrower	.26	.05			.80	98,856,250
2049	13¢ High Jumper	.26	.05			.80	98,856,250
2050	13¢ Archer	.26	.05			.80	98,856,250
2051	13¢ Boxers	.26	.05			.80	98,856,250
2051a	Block of 4, #2048-2051	1.50	.65	1.75	(4)	2.50	
	American Bicentennial Issue, Treaty of Paris, Sept. 2						
2052	20¢ Signing of Treaty of Paris						
	(John Adams, Benjamin Franklin and						
	John Jay observing David Hartley),						
	by Benjamin West	.40	.05	2.00	(4)	.75	104,340,000
2053	20¢ Civil Service, Sept. 9	.40	.05	10.00	(20)	.75	114,725,000
2054	20¢ Metropolitan Opera, Sept. 14	.40	.05	2.00	(4)	.75	112,525,000
	American Inventors Issue, Sept. 21						
2055	20¢ Charles Steinmetz and						
	Curve on Graph	.40	.08			.70	48,263,750
2056	20¢ Edwin Armstrong and						
	Frequency Modulator	.40	.08			.75	48,263,750
2057	20¢ Nikola Tesla and						
	Induction Motor	.40	.08			.75	48,263,750
2058	20¢ Philo T. Farnsworth and						
	First Television Camera	.40	.08			.75	48,263,750
2058a	Block of 4, #2055-2058	1.60	.85	2.00	(4)	2.50	

	1983 continued, Perf. 11	Un	U	PB/LP	#	FDC	Q
	Streetcars Issue, Oct. 8						
2059	20¢ First American Streetcar	.40	.08			.75	51,931,250
2060	20¢ Early Electric Streetcar	.40	.08			.75	51,931,250
2061	20¢ "Bobtail" Horsecar	.40	.08			.75	51,931,250
2062	20¢ St. Charles Streetcar	.40	.08			.75	51,931,250
2062a	Block of 4, #2059-2062	1.60	.85	2.00	(4)	2.50	
	Christmas Issue, Oct. 28						
2063	20¢ Niccolini-Cowper Madonna,						
	by Raphael	.40	.05	2.00	(4)	.75	715,975,000
2064	20¢ Santa Claus	.40	.05	10.00	(20)	.75	848,525,000
2065	20¢ Martin Luther, Nov. 11	.40	.05	2.00	(4)	.75	165,000,000
	Issues of 1984						
2066	20¢ Alaska Statehood, Jan. 3	.40	.05	2.00	(4)	.75	120,000,000
	Olympic Winter Games Issue, Jan. 6, Perf. 10½x11						
2067	20¢ Ice Dancers	.40	.08			.75	79,918,750
2068	20¢ Alpine Skiers	.40	.08			.75	79,918,750
2069	20¢ Nordic Skiers	.40	.08			.75	79,918,750
2070	20¢ Hockey Player	.40	.08			.75	79,918,750
2070a	Block of 4, #2067-2070	1.90	.85	2.30	(4)	2.50	
	Perf. 11						
2071	20¢ Federal Deposit Insurance						
	Corporation, Jan. 12	.40	.05	2.00	(4)	.75	103,975,000
	Perf. 11x10½						
2072	20¢ Love, Jan. 31	.40	.05	10.00	(20)	.75	554,675,000

Horses First Powered Streetcars

Pulled by horses, the original streetcar (#2059-2062) was a "horsecar." After the invention of the electric generator, electricity became, in the 1880s, the principal means of power for streetcars. In Chicago and many other cities, the streetcar was the main means of transportation. However, more and more people acquired automobiles until, by the 1930s, the importance of the streetcar had declined.

2063

2059
2061

2060
2062

2064

2065

2066

2071

2072

2067
2069

2068
2070

2073

2074

2075

2080

2076
2078

2077
2079

2081

2086

2087

2082
2084

2083
2085

1984 continued, Perf. 11	Un	U	PB/LP	#	FDC	Q
Black Heritage Issue, Carter G. Woodson, Feb. 1						
2073 20¢ Carter G. Woodson Holding History Book	.40	.05	2.00	(4)	.75	120,000,000
2074 20¢ Soil and Water Conservation, Feb. 6	.40	.05	2.00	(4)	.75	106,975,000
2075 20¢ Credit Union Act, Feb. 10	.40	·05	2.00	(4)	.75	107,325,000
Orchids Issue, Mar. 5						
2076 20¢ Wild Pink	.40	.08			.75	76,728,000
2077 20¢ Yellow Lady's-Slipper	.40	.08			.75	76,728,000
2078 20¢ Spreading Pogonia	.40	.08			.75	76,728,000
2079 20¢ Pacific Calypso	.40	.08			.75	76,728,000
2079a Block of 4, #2076-2079	1.60	.85	2.00	(4)	2.50	
2080 20¢ Hawaii Statehood, Mar. 12	.40	.05	2.00	(4)	.75	120,000,000
2081 20¢ National Archives, Apr. 16	.40	.05	2.00	(4)	.75	108,000,000
Olympic Summer Games Issue, May 4 (see also #2048-52, C101-112)						
2082 20¢ Diver	.40	.08			.75	78,337,500
2083 20¢ Long Jumper	.40	.08			.75	78,337,500
2084 20¢ Wrestlers	.40	.08			.75	78,337,500
2085 20¢ Kayaker	.40	.08			.75	78,337,500
2085a Block of 4, #2082-2085	1.90	.85	2.30	(4)	2.50	
2086 20¢ Louisiana World Exposition, May 11	.40	.05	2.00	(4)	.75	130,320,000
2087 20¢ Health Research, May 17	.40	.05	2.00	(4)	.75	120,000,000

Soil and Water Conservation

Teddy Roosevelt once said, "When the soil is gone, man must go." Water, in turn, is essential if crops are to grow. Watershed lakes, such as these in Tennessee, are one way of conserving land and water resources (#2074). Designed to reduce flooding, these small bodies of water help to preserve topsoil and to achieve a flow of clear water into rivers in watershed areas.

1984 continued, Perf. 11	Un	U	PB/LP	#	FDC	Q
Performing Arts Issue, May 23						
2088	20¢ Douglas Fairbanks Portrait and					
	Fairbanks in Swashbuckling					
	Pirate Role	.40	.05	10.00	(20)	.75	117,050,000
American Sports Issue, Jim Thorpe, May 24						
2089	20¢ Jim Thorpe on Football Field	.45	.05	2.00	(4)	.75	115,725,000
Performing Arts Issue, John McCormack, June 6						
2090	20¢ John McCormack Portrait and					
	McCormack in Tenor Role	.40	.05	2.00	(4)	.75	116,600,000
2091	20¢ St. Lawrence Seaway,					
	June 26	.40	.05	2.00	(4)	.75	120,000,000
2092	20¢ Migratory Bird Hunting &					
	Preservation Act, July 2	.40	.05	2.00	(4)	.75	123,575,000
2093	20¢ Roanoke Voyages, July 13	.40	.05	2.00	(4)	.75	120,000,000
Literary Arts Issue, Herman Melville, Aug. 1						
2094	20¢ Herman Melville,					
	by Joseph Eaton	.40	.05	2.00	(4)	.75	117,125,000
2095	20¢ Horace Moses, Aug. 6	.40	.05	10.00	(20)	.75	117,225,000
2096	20¢ Smokey the Bear, Aug. 13	.40	.05	2.00	(4)	.75	92,525,000
American Sports Issue, Roberto Clemente, Aug. 17						
2097	20¢ Roberto Clemente Wearing					
	Pittsburgh Pirates Cap,					
	Puerto Rican Flag in Background	.45	.05	2.00	(4)	.75	119,125,000
American Dogs Issue, Sept. 7						
2098	20¢ Beagle and Boston Terrier	.40	.08			.75	54,065,000
2099	20¢ Chesapeake Bay Retriever					
	and Cocker Spaniel	.40	.08			.75	54,065,000
2100	20¢ Alaskan Malamute and Collie	.40	.08			.75	54,065,000
2101	20¢ Black and Tan Coonhound					
	and American Foxhound	.40	.08			.75	54,065,000
2101a	Block of 4, #2098-2101	1.90	.85	2.30	(4)	2.50	

Young Entrepreneurs

A paper manufacturer named Horace A. Moses (#2095) founded Junior Achievement in 1919 to give young people practical training and experience in modern business methods. The organization functions as a practical "laboratory" where students learn how economic theories work, often by developing and marketing their own products.

Junior Achievement

DOUGLAS
FAIRBANKS

Performing Arts USA 20c

088

Jim Thorpe

USA
20c

2089

JOHN McCORMACK

Performing Arts USA 20c

2090

USA 20c   1959-1984 Saint
Lawrence
Seaway

2091

Preserving Wetlands
1984
1984

USA 20c

092

Roanoke Voyages
North
Carolina
1584

USA 20c

2093

Herman Melville

USA 20c

2094

Horace Moses
Founder, Junior Achievement
USA 20c

2095

SMOKEY

USA 20c

2096

Roberto
Clemente

P

USA 20c

2097

USA 20c

Beagle, Boston Terrier

USA 20c

Chesapeake Bay Retriever, Cocker Spaniel

USA 20c

Alaskan Malamute, Collie

USA 20c

Black and Tan Coonhound, American Foxhound

2102

2103

2104

2105

2106

2107

2108

2109

2110

2111

2114

2115b

	1984 continued, Perf. 11	Un	U	PB/LP	#	FDC	Q
2102	20¢ Crime Prevention, Sept. 26	.40	.05	2.00	(4)	.75	120,000,000
2103	20¢ Hispanic Americans, Oct. 31	.40	.05	2.00	(4)	.75	106,140,000
2104	20¢ Family Unity, Oct. 1	.40	.05	10.00	(20)	.75	117,625,000
2105	20¢ Eleanor Roosevelt, Oct. 11	.40	.05	2.00	(4)	.75	112,896,000
2106	20¢ A Nation of Readers, Oct. 16	.40	.05	2.00	(4)	.75	116,500,000
	Christmas Issue, Oct. 30						
2107	20¢ Madonna and Child,						
	by Fra Filippo Lippi	.40	.05	2.00	(4)	.75	751,300,000
2108	20¢ Santa Claus	.40	.05	2.00	(4)	.75	786,225,000
	Perf. 10½						
2109	20¢ Vietnam Veterans' Memorial,						
	Nov. 10	.40	.05	2.00	(4)	.75	105,300,000
	Issues of 1985, Performing Arts Issue, Jerome Kern, Jan. 23, Perf. 11						
2110	22¢ Jerome Kern Portrait and						
	Kern Studying Sheet Music	.44	.05	2.20	(4)	.80	124,500,000
2111	(22¢) D Stamp, Feb. 1	.44	.05	12.00	(20)	.80	
	Coil Stamp, Perf. 10 Vertically						
2112	(22¢) D Stamp (2111), Feb. 1	.44	.05			.80	
	Perf. 11						
2113	(22¢) D Stamp (2111),						
	Single from booklet	.44	.05			.80	
2113a	Bklt. pane of 10, Feb. 1	5.50	—				
	Flag over Capitol Issue, Mar. 29 (except #2115b, issued May 23, 1987)						
2114	22¢ Flag over Capitol	.44	.05	2.20	(4)	.80	
	Coil Stamp, Perf. 10 Vertically						
2115	22¢ Flag over Capitol (2114)	.44	.05			.80	
2115b	22¢ Flag over Capitol (2114),						
	Test on Pre-Phosphored Paper.						
	Paper is whiter and colors are						
	brighter than on #2115.	.44	.08	3.00	(3)		
	Perf. 10 Horizontally						
2116	22¢ Flag over Capitol (2114),						
	Single from booklet	.44	.05			.80	
2116a	Bklt. pane of 5	2.20	—				

#2116 issued only in booklets. Stamps are imperf. at sides or imperf. at sides and bottom.

	1985 continued, Perf. 10	Un	U	PB/LP	#	FDC	Q
	Seashells Booklet Issue, Apr. 4						
2117	22¢ Frilled Dogwinkle	.44	.05			.80	
2118	22¢ Reticulated Helmet	.44	.05			.80	
2119	22¢ New England Neptune	.44	.05			.80	
2120	22¢ Calico Scallop	.44	.05			.80	
2121	22¢ Lightning Whelk	.44	.05			.80	
2121a	Bklt. pane of 10, #2117-21	4.40	—				
	#2117-21 issued only in booklets						
	Perf. 10 Vertically						
2122	$10.75 Express Mail,						
	Single from booklet	22.00	—			30.00	
2122a	Bklt. pane of 3, Apr. 29	67.50	—				
	Issues of 1985-87, Transportation Issue						
2123	3.4¢ School Bus 1920s,						
	June 8, 1985	.08	.05	1.00	(3)	.70	
2124	4.9¢ Buckboard 1880s,						
	June 21, 1985	.10	.05	1.25	(3)	.70	
2125	5.5¢ Star Route Truck 1910s,						
	Nov. 3, 1986	.11	.05	1.90	(3)		
2126	6¢ Tricycle 1880s, May 6, 1985	.12	.05	1.75	(3)	.60	
2127	7.1¢ Tractor 1920s, Feb. 6, 1987	.15	.05	2.25	(3)	.70	
2128	8.3¢ Ambulance 1860s,						
	June 21, 1985	.18	.05	1.90	(3)	.70	
2129	8.5¢ Tow Truck, Jan. 24, 1987	.18	.05	2.75	(3)	.70	
2130	10.1¢ Oil Wagon 1890s,						
	Apr. 18, 1985	.22	.05	2.75	(3)	.75	
2131	11¢ Stutz Bearcat 1933,						
	June 11, 1985	.22	.05	2.50	(3)	.75	
2132	12¢ Stanley Steamer 1909,						
	Apr. 2, 1985	.24	.05	2.50	(3)	.75	
2133	12.5¢ Pushcart 1880s, Apr. 18, 1985	.25	.05	3.00	(3)	.75	
2134	14¢ Iceboat 1880s, Mar. 23, 1985	.28	.05	1.50	(3)	.80	
2135	17¢ Dog Sled 1920s, Aug. 20, 1986	.34	.05	3.50	(3)	.80	
2136	25¢ Bread Wagon 1880s,						
	Nov. 22, 1986	.50	.05	4.00	(3)		

USA
22
Frilled Dogwinkle

USA
22
Reticulated Helmet

USA
22
New England Neptune

USA
22
Calico Scallop

USA
22
Lightning Whelk

2121a

2122

School Bus 1920s
3.4 USA

2123

Buckboard 1880s
USA
4.9

2124

Star Route Truck
5.5 USA 1910s

2125

Tricycle 1880s
6 USA

2126

Tractor 1920s
7.1 USA

2127

Ambulance 1860s
8.3 USA

2128

TowTruck 1920s
8.5 USA

2129

Oil Wagon 1890s
10.1 USA

2130

Stutz Bearcat 1933
11 USA

2131

Stanley Steamer 1909
USA
12

2132

Pushcart 1880s
12.5
USA

2133

Iceboat 1880s
USA
14

2134

Dog Sled 1920s
17 USA

2135

Bread Wagon 1880s
25 USA

2136

2137

2138
2140

2139
2141

2142

2143

2144

2145

2146

F.A. Bartholdi, Statue of Liberty Sculptor

2147

2149

2150

2152

2153

	1985 continued, Perf. 11	Un	U	PB/LP	#	FDC	Q
	Black Heritage Issue, Mary McLeod Bethune, Mar. 5						
2137	22¢ Mary McLeod Bethune Portrait	.44	.05	2.20	(4)	.80	120,000,000
	American Folk Art Issue, Duck Decoys, Mar. 22						
2138	22¢ Broadbill Decoy	.44	.08			.80	75,000,000
2139	22¢ Mallard Decoy	.44	.08			.80	75,000,000
2140	22¢ Canvasback Decoy	.44	.08			.80	75,000,000
2141	22¢ Redhead Decoy	.44	.08			.80	75,000,000
2141a	Block of 4, #2138-2141	2.00	1.00	2.40	(4)	2.75	
2142	22¢ Winter Special Olympics,						
	Mar. 25	.44	.05	2.20	(4)	.80	120,580,000
2143	22¢ Love, Apr. 17	.44	.05	2.20	(4)	.80	729,700,000
2144	22¢ Rural Electrification						
	Administration, May 11	.44	.05	9.25	(20)	.80	124,750,000
2145	22¢ AMERIPEX 86, May 25	.44	.05	2.20	(4)	.80	203,496,000
2146	22¢ Abigail Adams, June 14	.44	.05	2.20	(4)	.80	126,325,000
2147	22¢ Frederic A. Bartholdi, July 18	.44	.05	2.20	(4)	.80	130,000,000
	Coil Stamps, Perf. 10 Vertically						
2149	18¢ George Washington,						
	Washington Monument, Nov. 6	.36	.08			.80	
2150	21.1¢ Sealed Envelopes, Oct. 22	.45	.08			.80	
	Perf. 11						
2152	22¢ Korean War Veterans, July 26	.44	.05	2.20	(4)	.80	119,975,000
2153	22¢ Social Security Act, Aug. 14	.44	.05	2.20	(4)	.80	120,000,000

Korean War Veterans

The Korean War was the first conflict in which U.S. troops (#2152) fought under the flag of the United Nations. Our country's fighting men were welcomed home via parades, such as this one in Seattle, Washington in 1951.

	1985 continued, Perf. 11	Un	U	PB/LP	#	FDC	Q
2154	22¢ World War I Veterans,						
	Aug. 26	.44	.05	2.20	(4)	.80	119,975,000
	American Horses Issue, Sept. 25						
2155	22¢ Quarter Horse	.44	.08			.80	36,985,000
2156	22¢ Morgan	.44	.08			.80	36,985,000
2157	22¢ Saddlebred	.44	.08			.80	36,985,000
2158	22¢ Appaloosa	.44	.08			.80	36,985,000
2158a	Block of 4, #2155-2158	2.00	1.00	2.40	(4)	2.75	
2159	22¢ Public Education, Oct. 1	.44	.05	2.20	(4)	.80	120,000,000
	International Youth Year Issue, Oct. 7						
2160	22¢ YMCA Youth Camping	.44	.08			.80	32,500,000
2161	22¢ Boy Scouts	.44	.08			.80	32,500,000
2162	22¢ Big Brothers/Big Sisters	.44	.08			.80	32,500,000
2163	22¢ Camp Fire	.44	.08			.80	32,500,000
2163a	Block of 4, #2160-2163	2.00	1.00	2.40	(4)	2.75	
2164	22¢ Help End Hunger, Oct. 15	.44	.05	2.20	(4)	.80	120,000,000
	Christmas Issue, Oct. 31						
2165	22¢ Genoa Madonna,						
	by Luca della Robbia	.44	.05	2.20	(4)	.80	759,200,000
2166	22¢ Poinsettia Plants	.44	.05	2.20	(4)	.80	757,600,000

Feeding the World

American donations of food and money to the needy across the world are part of an international effort to provide sufficient food and properly balanced diets for millions of hungry people (#2164).

2154

Quarter horse

Morgan

Saddlebred

Appaloosa

2155   2156
2157   2158

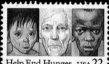

Public Education

2159

YMCA Youth Camping USA

Boy Scouts USA

Big Brothers/Big Sisters USA

Camp Fire USA

2160   2161
2162   2163

Help End Hunger USA 22

2164

CHRISTMAS

USA 22
Luca della Robbia, Detroit Institute of Arts

2165

Season's Greetings USA 22

2166

2167   2168   2169   2170

2171   2172   2176   2177   2179

2183   2191   2194   2195   2196

2198   2199   2200   2201

2202   2203   2204

	Issue of 1986, Perf. 11	Un	U	PB/LP	#	FDC	Q
2167	Arkansas Statehood, Jan. 3	.44	.05	2.25	(4)	.80	130,000,000
	Issues of 1986-87, Great Americans Issue						
2168	1¢ Margaret Mitchell, June 30, 1986	.05	.05	.25	(4)	.80	
2169	2¢ Mary Lyon, Feb. 28, 1987	.05	.05	.25	(4)	.80	
2170	3¢ Paul Dudley White, MD,						
	Sept. 15, 1986	.06	.05	.30	(4)	.80	
2171	4¢ Father Flanagan, July 14, 1986	.08	.05	.40	(4)	.80	
2172	5¢ Hugo L. Black, Feb. 27, 1987	.10	.05	.50	(4)	.80	
2173-75 not assigned.							
2176	10¢ Red Cloud, Aug 15, 1987	.20	.05	1.00	(4)	.80	
2177	14¢ Julia Ward Howe, Feb 12, 1987	.28	.05	1.40	(4)	.80	
2178 not assigned.							
2179	17¢ Belva Ann Lockwood,						
	June 18, 1986	.34	.06	1.75	(4)	.80	
2180-82 not assigned.							
2183	25¢ Jack London, Jan. 11, 1986	.50	.06	2.50	(4)	.85	
2184-90 not assigned.							
2191	56¢ John Harvard, Sept. 3, 1986	1.10	.08	5.50	(4)	1.25	
2192-93 not assigned.							
2194	$1 Bernard Revel, Sept. 23, 1986	2.00	.50	10.00	(4)	2.00	
2195	$2 William Jennings Bryan,						
	Mar. 19, 1986	4.00	.50	20.00	(4)	4.00	
2196	$5 Bret Harte, Aug. 25, 1987						
	Issues of 1986, United States-Sweden Stamp Collecting Booklet Issue, Jan. 23, Perf. 10 Vertically						
2198	22¢ Handstamped Cover	.44	.05			.80	16,999,200
2199	22¢ Boy Examining Stamp Collection	.44	.05			.80	16,999,200
2200	22¢ #836 Under Magnifying Glass	.44	.05			.80	16,999,200
2201	22¢ 1986 Presidents Miniature Sheet	.44	.05			.80	16,999,200
2201a	Bklt. pane of 4, #2198-2201	1.80					
	#2198-2201 issued only in booklets. Stamps are imperf. at top and bottom or imperf. at top,						
	bottom and one side.						
	Perf. 11						
2202	22¢ Love, Jan. 30	.44	.05	2.25	(4)	.80	947,450,000
	Black Heritage Issue, Sojourner Truth, Feb. 4						
2203	22¢ Sojourner Truth Portrait and						
	Truth Lecturing	.44	.05	2.25	(4)	.80	130,000,000
2204	22¢ Republic of Texas						
	150th Anniversary, Mar. 2	.44	.05	2.20	(4)	.80	136,500,000

	1986 continued	Un	U	PB/LP	#	FDC	Q
	Fish Booklet Issue, Mar. 21, Perf. 10 Horizontally						
2205	22¢ Muskellunge	.44	.05			.80	43,998,000
2206	22¢ Atlantic Cod	.44	.05			.80	43,998,000
2207	22¢ Largemouth Bass	.44	.05			.80	43,998,000
2208	22¢ Bluefin Tuna	.44	.05			.80	43,998,000
2209	22¢ Catfish	.44	.05			.80	43,998,000
2209c	Bklt. pane of 5, #2205-09	2.25					
	#2205-09 issued only in booklets. Stamps are imperf. at sides or imperf. at sides and bottom.						
	Perf. 11						
2210	22¢ Public Hospitals, Apr. 11	.44	.05	2.20	(4)	.80	130,000,000
	Performing Arts Issue, Duke Ellington, Apr. 29						
2211	22¢ Duke Ellington Portrait and						
	Piano Keys	.44	.05	2.20	(4)	.80	130,000,000
	AMERIPEX '86 Issue, Presidents Miniature Sheets, May 22						
2216	Sheet of 9	4.00				4.00	5,825,050
2216a	22¢ George Washington						
2216b	22¢ John Adams						
2216c	22¢ Thomas Jefferson						
2216d	22¢ James Madison						
2216e	22¢ James Monroe						
2216f	22¢ John Quincy Adams						
2216g	22¢ Andrew Jackson						
2216h	22¢ Martin Van Buren						
2216i	22¢ William H. Harrison						
	a-i, any single	.44	.20			.80	

And All That Ellington Jazz...

Edward Kennedy "Duke" Ellington (#2211) was one of the "greats" in American music. A jazz pianist and a prolific composer, he wrote a number of classic songs, including "Mood Indigo." His works often were innovative and extended the existing boundaries of jazz. Born in 1899 in Washington, D.C., Ellington formed a band before he was 20. Playing in Harlem nightclubs, the band quickly gained reknown. Ellington died in 1974, leaving a rich musical legacy.

22 USA
Muskellunge

2205

22 USA
Atlantic Cod

2206

Largemouth Bass
22 USA

2207

Bluefin Tuna
USA 22

2208

Catfish
USA 22

2209

Public Hospitals USA 22

2210

Duke Ellington
22 USA

2211

USA 22
George Washington 1789-1797

2216a

USA 22
John Adams 1797-1801

2216b

USA 22
Thomas Jefferson 1800-1809

2216c

USA 22
James Madison 1809-1817

2216d

USA 22
James Monroe 1817-1825

2216e

USA 22
John Quincy Adams 1825-1829

2216f

USA 22
Andrew Jackson 1829-1837

2216g

USA 22
Martin Van Buren 1837-1841

2216h

USA 22
William Henry Harrison 1841-1841

2216i

USA 22
John Tyler 1841-1845

2217a

USA 22
James K. Polk 1845-1849

2217b

USA 22
Zachary Taylor 1849-1850

2217c

USA 22
Millard Fillmore 1850-1853

2217d

USA 22
Franklin Pierce 1853-1857

2217e

USA 22
James Buchanan 1857-1861

2217f

USA 22
Abraham Lincoln 1861-1865

2217g

USA 22
Andrew Johnson 1865-1869

2217h

USA 22
Ulysses S. Grant 1869-1877

2217i

USA 22
Rutherford B. Hayes 1877-1881

2218a

USA 22
James A. Garfield 1881-1881

2218b

USA 22
Chester A. Arthur 1881-1885

2218c

USA 22
Grover Cleveland 1885-89, 1893-97

2218d

USA 22
Benjamin Harrison 1889-1893

2218e

USA 22
William McKinley 1897-1901

2218f

USA 22
Theodore Roosevelt 1901-1909

2218g

USA 22
William H. Taft 1909-1913

2218h

USA 22
Woodrow Wilson 1913-1921

2218i

	1986 continued, Perf. 11	Un	U	PB/LP	#	FDC	Q
	AMERIPEX '86 Issue continued, Presidents Miniature Sheets, May 22						
2217	Sheet of 9	4.00				4.00	5,825,050
2217a	22¢ John Tyler						
2217b	22¢ James Polk						
2217c	22¢ Zachary Taylor						
2217d	22¢ Millard Fillmore						
2217e	22¢ Franklin Pierce						
2217f	22¢ James Buchanan						
2217g	22¢ Abraham Lincoln						
2217h	22¢ Andrew Johnson						
2217i	22¢ Ulysses S. Grant						
	a-i, any single	.44	.20			.80	
2218	Sheet of 9	4.00				4.00	5,825,050
2218a	22¢ Rutherford B. Hayes						
2218b	22¢ James A. Garfield						
2218c	22¢ Chester A. Arthur						
2218d	22¢ Grover Cleveland						
2218e	22¢ Benjamin Harrison						
2218f	22¢ William McKinley						
2218g	22¢ Theodore Roosevelt						
2218h	22¢ William H. Taft						
2218i	22¢ Woodrow Wilson						
	a-i, any single	.44	.20			.80	

Lincoln Looms Large in U.S. History

The 16th President of the United States, Abraham Lincoln (#2217g) was elected to that office in 1860 and again in 1864. Lincoln guided the country through the Civil War and in 1863 issued the Emancipation Proclamation, freeing the slaves. In the same year he delivered his famed Gettysburg Address, an expression of his feelings concerning the war. Born in 1809, Lincoln was assassinated in 1865 by the actor John Wilkes Booth.

	1986 continued, Perf. 11	Un	U	PB/LP	#	FDC	Q
	AMERIPEX '86 Issue continued, Presidents Miniature Sheets, May 22						
2219	Sheet of 9	4.00				4.00	5,825,050
2219a	22¢ Warren G. Harding						
2219b	22¢ Calvin Coolidge						
2219c	22¢ Herbert Hoover						
2219d	22¢ Franklin D. Roosevelt						
2219e	22¢ White House						
2219f	22¢ Harry S. Truman						
2219g	22¢ Dwight D. Eisenhower						
2219h	22¢ John F. Kennedy						
2219i	22¢ Lyndon B. Johnson						
	a-i, any single	.44	.20			.80	
	Polar Explorers Issue, May 28						
2220	22¢ Elisha Kent Kane	.44	.05			.80	32,500,000
2221	22¢ Adolphus W. Greely	.44	.05			.80	32,500,000
2222	22¢ Vilhjalmur Stefansson	.44	.05			.80	32,500,000
2223	22¢ Robert E. Peary, Matthew Henson	.44	.05			.80	32,500,000
2223a	Block of 4, #2220-23	1.80	1.00			2.75	
2224	22¢ Statue of Liberty, July 4	.44	.05	2.20	(4)	.80	220,725,000
	Issues of 1986-87, Transportation Issue, Coil Stamps, Perf. 10 Vertically						
2225	1¢ Reengraved Omnibus 1880s,						
	Nov. 26, 1986	.05	.05	.80	(3)		
2226	2¢ Reengraved Locomotive,						
	Mar. 6, 1987	.05	.05	.85	(3)	.70	
2227 not assigned.							
2228	4¢ Reengraved Stagecoach 1890s,						
	Aug. 1986	.08	.05				
2231	8.3¢ Reengraved Ambulance 1860s,						
	(precancel), Aug. 29, 1986		.16	3.50	(3)		
2232-34 not assigned.							

On #2228, "Stagecoach 1890s" is 17 mm long; on #1898A, it is 19½ mm long. On #2231, "Ambulance 1860s" is 18 mm long; on #2128, it is 18½ mm long.

Letting Freedom Ring

Given to the people of the United States by France in 1884 as a symbol of friendship between the two nations, the Statue of Liberty (#2224) was erected in 1886 in New York Harbor to welcome those seeking freedom.

2219a   2219b   2219c   2219d   2219e

2219f   2219g   2219h   2219i

2220
2222

2221
2223

2224

2225   2226

2239

2235	2236
2237	2238

2240	2241
2242	2243

2244

2245

2246

2247

2248

2249

2250

2251

	1986 continued	Un	U	PB/LP	#	FDC	Q
	American Folk Art Issue, Navajo Blankets, Sept. 4, Perf. 11						
2235	22¢ Navajo Blanket, black-and-white						
	lines dominate	.44	.08			.80	60,131,250
2236	22¢ Navajo Blanket, black and white						
	diamonds dominate	.44	.08			.80	60,131,250
2237	22¢ Navajo Blanket, white diamonds						
	dominate	.44	.08			.80	60,131,250
2238	22¢ Navajo Blanket, black-and-white						
	bordered patterns dominate	.44	.08			.80	60,131,250
2238a	Block of 4, #2235-38	1.80	1.00	2.20	(4)	2.75	
	Literary Arts Issue, T.S. Eliot, Sept. 26						
2239	22¢ T.S. Eliot Portrait	.44	.05	2.20	(4)	.80	131,700,000
	American Folk Art Issue, Wood-Carved Figurines, Oct. 1						
2240	22¢ Highlander Figure	.44	.08			.80	60,000,000
2241	22¢ Ship Figurehead	.44	.08			.80	60,000,000
2242	22¢ Nautical Figure	.44	.08			.80	60,000,000
2243	22¢ Cigar-Store Figure	.44	.08			.80	60,000,000
2243a	Block of 4, #2240-43	1.80	1.00	2.20	(4)	2.75	
	Christmas Issue, Oct. 24						
2244	22¢ Madonna and Child,						
	by Perugino	.44	.05	2.20	(4)	.80	690,100,000
2245	22¢ Village Scene	.44	.05	2.20	(4)	.80	882,150,000
	Issues of 1987, Perf. 11						
2246	22¢ Michigan Statehood, Jan. 26	.44	.05	2.20	(4)	.80	
2247	22¢ Pan American Games, Jan. 29	.44	.05	2.20	(4)	.80	
	Perf 11½x11						
2248	22¢ Love, Jan. 30	.44	.05	2.20	(4)	.80	
	Black Heritage Issue, Jean Baptiste Point Du Sable, Feb. 20, Perf. 11						
2249	22¢ Chicago Settlement and						
	Portrait of Du Sable	.44	.05	2.20	(4)	.80	
	Performing Arts Issue, Enrico Caruso, Feb. 27						
2250	22¢ Caruso as the Duke of						
	Mantua in *Rigoletti*	.44	.05	2.20	(4)	.80	
2251	22¢ Girl Scouts, Mar. 12	.44	.05	2.20	(4)	.80	

	1987 continued	Un	U	PB/LP	#	FDC		Q
	Transportation Issue, Coil Stamps, Perf. 10 Vertically							
2255	5¢ Milk Wagon, Sept. 25	.10	.05	1.75	(3)	.70		
2259	10¢ Canal Boat, Apr. 11	.20	.05	3.00	(3)	.75		
2264	17.5¢ Racing Car, Sept. 25	.35	.05	3.50	(3)	.80		
	Special Occasions Issue, Apr. 20, Perf. 10 on 1, 2 or 3 sides							
2267	22¢ Congratulations!	.44	.05			.80		
2268	22¢ Get Well!	.44	.05			.80		
2269	22¢ Thank You!	.44	.05			.80		
2270	22¢ Love You, Dad!	.44	.05			.80		
2271	22¢ Best Wishes!	.44	.05			.80		
2272	22¢ Happy Birthday!	.44	.05			.80		
2273	22¢ Love You, Mother!	.44	.05			.80		
2274	22¢ Keep In Touch!	.44	.05			.80		
2274a	Bklt. pane of 10, #2268-2271,							
	2273-2274, 2 of each							
	#2267, 2272	4.50						
	Perf. 11							
2275	United Way, Apr. 28	.44	.05	2.20	(4)	.80		
2276	Flag with Fireworks, May 9	.44	.05	2.20	(4)	.80		
	American Wildlife Issue, June 13							
2286	22¢ Barn Swallow	.44	.05			.80		
2287	22¢ Monarch	.44	.05			.80		
2288	22¢ Bighorn Sheep	.44	.05			.80		
2289	22¢ Broad-tailed Hummingbird	.44	.05			.80		
2290	22¢ Cottontail	.44	.05			.80		

Monarchs Fly South for the Winter

Of the more than 90,000 different butterflies and moths, the monarch (#2287) is one of the best-known species. Monarchs lay their eggs on the milkweed plant and, for that reason, sometimes are called milkweed butterflies. Swarms of monarchs migrate each year to the Gulf of Mexico region, where they spend the winter.

Milk Wagon 1900s
5 USA
DAIRY

2255

Canal Boat 1880s
10 USA

2259

Racing Car 1911
USA
17.5

2264

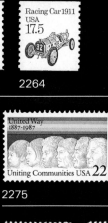

2275

2276

2286

2287

2288

2289

2290

2274 a

Osprey	Mountain Lion	Luna Moth	Mule Deer	Gray Squirrel
2291	2292	2293	2294	2295
Armadillo	Eastern Chipmunk	Moose	Black Bear	Tiger Swallowtail
2296	2297	2298	2299	2300
Bobwhite	Ringtail	Red-winged Blackbird	American Lobster	Black-tailed Jack Rabbit
2301	2302	2303	2304	2305
Scarlet Tanager	Woodchuck	Roseate Spoonbill	Bald Eagle	Alaskan Brown Bear
2306	2307	2308	2309	2310

	1987 continued, Perf. 11	Un	U	PB/LP	#	FDC	Q
2291	22¢ Osprey	.44	.05			.80	
2292	22¢ Mountain Lion	.44	.05			.80	
2293	22¢ Luna Moth	.44	.05			.80	
2294	22¢ Mule Deer	.44	.05			.80	
2295	22¢ Gray Squirrel	.44	.05			.80	
2296	22¢ Armadillo	.44	.05			.80	
2297	22¢ Eastern Chipmunk	.44	.05			.80	
2298	22¢ Moose	.44	.05			.80	
2299	22¢ Black Bear	.44	.05			.80	
2300	22¢ Tiger Swallowtail	.44	.05			.80	
2301	22¢ Bobwhite	.44	.05			.80	
2302	22¢ Ringtail	.44	.05			.80	
2303	22¢ Red-winged Blackbird	.44	.05			.80	
2304	22¢ American Lobster	.44	.05			.80	
2305	22¢ Black-tailed Jack Rabbit	.44	.05			.80	
2306	22¢ Scarlet Tanager	.44	.05			.80	
2307	22¢ Woodchuck	.44	.05			.80	
2308	22¢ Roseate Spoonbill	.44	.05			.80	
2309	22¢ Bald Eagle	.44	.05			.80	
2310	22¢ Alaskan Brown Bear	.44	.05			.80	

	1987 continued, Perf. 11	Un	U	PB/LP	#	FDC	Q
2311	22¢ Iiwi	.44	.05			.80	
2312	22¢ Badger	.44	.05			.80	
2313	22¢ Pronghorn	.44	.05			.80	
2314	22¢ River Otter	.44	.05			.80	
2315	22¢ Ladybug	.44	.05			.80	
2316	22¢ Beaver	.44	.05			.80	
2317	22¢ White-tailed Deer	.44	.05			.80	
2318	22¢ Blue Jay	.44	.05			.80	
2319	22¢ Pika	.44	.05			.80	
2320	22¢ Bison	.44	.05			.80	
2321	22¢ Snowy Egret	.44	.05			.80	
2322	22¢ Gray Wolf	.44	.05			.80	
2323	22¢ Mountain Goat	.44	.05			.80	
2324	22¢ Deer Mouse	.44	.05			.80	
2325	22¢ Black-tailed Prairie Dog	.44	.05			.80	
2326	22¢ Box Turtle	.44	.05			.80	
2327	22¢ Wolverine	.44	.05			.80	
2328	22¢ American Elk	.44	.05			.80	
2329	22¢ California Sea Lion	.44	.05			.80	
2330	22¢ Mockingbird	.44	.05			.80	

Elk or Wapiti

The American elk (#2328) once roamed much of North America. Known to the Shawnee Indians as wapiti, *the animal was renamed elk by the early colonists. At one time severely depleted by hunters, American elk are now being reintroduced into areas of the United States where they had completely disappeared.*

Inui	Badger	Pronghorn	River Otter	Ladybug
2311	2312	2313	2314	2315

Beaver	White-tailed Deer	Blue Jay	Pika	Bison
2316	2317	2318	2319	2320

Snowy Egret	Gray Wolf	Mountain Goat	Deer Mouse	Black-tailed Prairie Dog
2321	2322	2323	2324	2325

Box Turtle	Wolverine	American Elk	California Sea Lion	Mockingbird
2326	2327	2328	2329	2330

22 USA Raccoon 2331

22 USA Bobcat 2332

22 USA Black-footed Ferret 2333

22 USA Canada Goose 2334

22 USA Red Fox 2335

Dec 7, 1787 USA Delaware 22 — 2336

22 USA Pennsylvania Dec 12, 1787 — 2337

Dec 18, 1787 USA New Jersey 22 — 2338

Friendship with Morocco 1787-1987 USA 22 — 2349

William Faulkner USA 22 — 2350

Lacemaking USA 22
Lacemaking USA 22
Lacemaking USA 22
Lacemaking USA 22

2351 2352
2353 2354

The Bicentennial of the Constitution of the United States of America 1787-1987 USA 22

We the people of the United States, in order to form a more perfect Union... Preamble, U.S. Constitution USA 22

Establish justice, insure domestic tranquility, provide for the common defense, promote the general welfare... Preamble, U.S. Constitution USA 22

And secure the blessings of liberty to ourselves and our posterity... Preamble, U.S. Constitution USA 22

Do ordain and establish this Constitution for the United States of America. Preamble, U.S. Constitution USA 22

2359a

	1987 continued, Perf. 11	Un	U	PB/LP	#	FDC	Q
2331	22¢ Raccoon	.44	.05			.80	
2332	22¢ Bobcat	.44	.05			.80	
2333	22¢ Black-footed Ferret	.44	.05			.80	
2334	22¢ Canada Goose	.44	.05			.80	
2335	22¢ Red Fox	.44	.05			.80	
2335a	Pane of 50, #2286-2335	22.00					
2336	22¢ Delaware Statehood, July 4	.44	.05			.80	
2337	22¢ Pennsylvania Statehood,						
	Aug. 26	.44	.05			.80	
2338	22¢ New Jersey Statehood,						
	Sept. 11	.44	.05			.80	
2349	22¢ Friendship with Morocco,						
	July 17	.44	.05			.80	
	Literary Arts Issue, William Faulkner, Aug. 3						
2350	22¢ Portrait of Faulkner	.44	.05	2.20	(4)	.80	
	American Folk Art Issue, Lacemaking, Aug. 14						
2351	22¢ Squash Blossoms	.44	.08				
2352	22¢ Floral Piece	.44	.08				
2353	22¢ Floral Piece	.44	.08				
2354	22¢ Dogwood Blossoms	.44	.08				
2354a	Block of 4, #2351-2354	1.80	1.00	2.20	(4)		
	Drafting of the U.S. Constitution Issue, Aug. 28, Perf. 10 Horizontally						
2355	22¢ "The Bicentennial..."	.44	.08			.80	
2356	22¢ "We the people..."	.44	.08			.80	
2357	22¢ "Establish justice..."	.44	.08			.80	
2358	22¢ "And secure..."	.44	.08			.80	
2359	22¢ "Do ordain..."	.44	.08			.80	
2359a	Booklet pane of 5, #2355-2359	2.25					

Friends for Two Centuries

Ratified on July 18, 1787, the Treaty of Peace and Friendship with Morocco ranks as

the longest continuing friendship treaty between the United States and any nation (#2349). A North African country on the Strait of Gibraltar, Morocco has a population of more than 20 million, approximately 70 percent of whom either farm or herd sheep, goats or cattle.

	1987 continued, Perf. 11	Un	U	PB/LP	#	FDC	Q
2360	22¢ Signing of the U.S. Constitution,						
	Sept. 17	.44	.05	2.20	(4)		
2361	22¢ Certified Public Accountants,						
	Sept. 21	.44	.05	2.20	(4)		
	Locomotives Issue, Oct. 1, Perf. 10 Horizontally						
2362	22¢ Stourbridge Lion, 1829	.44	.08			.80	
2363	22¢ Best Friend of Charleston,						
	1830	.44	.08			.80	
2364	22¢ John Bull, 1831	.44	.08			.80	
2365	22¢ Brother Jonathan, 1832	.44	.08			.80	
2366	22¢ Gowan & Marx, 1839	.44	.08			.80	
2366a	Booklet pane of 5, #2362-2366	2.25					
	Christmas Issue, Oct. 23, Perf. 11						
2367	22¢ Madonna, by Moroni	.44	.05	2.20	(4)		
2368	22¢ Christmas Ornaments	.44	.05	2.20	(4)		

We the People

On May 14, 1787, 55 delegates met in Philadelphia and drew up the U.S. Constitution (#2355-2360), known as the law of the land, to provide a strong yet flexible framework of government.

2360

2361

2366a

2367

2368

Georgia Statehood (22¢, #2339)
Date of Issue: January 6, 1988
Place of Issue: Atlanta, Georgia
Designer: Greg Harlin
Printing: Gravure
Georgia was the first Southern state to ratify the
U.S. Constitution.

Connecticut Statehood (22¢, #2340)
Date of Issue: January 9, 1988
Place of Issue: Hartford, Connecticut
Designer: Christopher Calle
Printing: Offset/Intaglio
The Connecticut Compromise granted every state
an equal vote in the Senate.

Olympic Winter Games (22¢, #2369)
Date of Issue: January 10, 1988
Place of Issue: Anchorage, Alaska
Designer: Bart Forbes
Printing: Gravure
The world's greatest cold-weather athletes
competed this past February in Calgary.

Australia Bicentennial (22¢, #2370)
Date of Issue: January 26, 1988
Place of Issue: Washington, D.C.
Designer: Roland Harvey
Printing: Gravure
Part of a joint issuance, this stamp commemorates
the 200th anniversary of the founding of Australia.

James Weldon Johnson (22¢, #2371)
Date of Issue: February 2, 1988
Place of Issue: Nashville, Tennessee
Designer: Thomas Blackshear
Printing: Gravure
Johnson wrote "Lift Every Voice and Sing," often called the Negro National Anthem.

Cats (22¢, #2372-75)
Date of Issue:
    February 5, 1988
Place of Issue:
    New York, New York
Designer: John Dawson
Printing: Gravure
First domesticated in 2500 B.C., more than 57 million of these independent, playful pets now occupy human habitats in the United States. These stamps depict eight breeds popular among cat fanciers across the nation.

Massachusetts Statehood (22¢, #2341)
Date of Issue: February 6, 1988
Place of Issue: Boston, Massachusetts
Designer: Richard Sheaff
Printing: Intaglio
Several U.S. Constitution elements derive from the Bay State's own constitution.

Maryland Statehood (22¢, #2342)
Date of Issue: February 15, 1988
Place of Issue: Annapolis, Maryland
Designer: Stephen Hustvedt
Printing: Offset/Intaglio
Maryland's State House, built in 1772, is the oldest still in legislative use.

Knute Rockne (22¢, #2376)
Date of Issue: March 9, 1988
Place of Issue: Notre Dame, Indiana
Designers: Peter Cocci, Thomas Hipschen
Printing: Offset/Intaglio
The legendary Rockne coached Notre Dame's
football team to six national titles.

South Carolina Statehood (25¢, #2343)
Date of Issue: May 23, 1988
Place of Issue: Columbia, South Carolina
Designer: Bob Timberlake
Printing: Gravure
A palmetto, the state tree, graces the stamp honoring
South Carolina Statehood.

Francis Ouimet (25¢, #2377)
Date of Issue: June 13, 1988
Place of Issue: Brookline, Massachusetts
Designer: M. Gregory Rudd
Printing: Gravure
"America's first golfing hero," amateur Francis
Ouimet captured the U.S. Open in 1913.

New Hampshire (25¢, #2344)
Date of Issue: June 21, 1988
Place of Issue: Concord, New Hampshire
Designer: Thomas Szumowski
Printing: Gravure
When New Hampshire ratified the Constitution,
it became the law of the land.

Virginia Statehood (25¢, #2345)
Date of Issue: June 25, 1988
Place of Issue: Williamsburg, Virginia
Designer: Pierre Mion
Printing: Offset/Intaglio
Virginia delegates were highly influential in the development of the Constitution.

Love (25¢, #2378)
Date of Issue: July 4, 1988
Place of Issue: Pasadena, California
Designer: Richard Sheaff
Printing: Gravure
As in the past, the seventh love stamp should be a popular choice for mailers of valentines, wedding invitations and general correspondence.

New York Statehood (25¢, #2346)
Date of Issue: July 26, 1988
Place of Issue: Albany, New York
Designer: Bradbury Thompson
Printing: Offset/Intaglio
The Federalist Papers helped persuade New York to ratify the Constitution.

Love (45¢, #2379)
Date of Issue: August 8, 1988
Place of Issue: Shreveport, Louisiana
Designer: Richard Sheaff
Printing: Gravure
This stamp was designed particularly for wedding invitations weighing two ounces or more.

Summer Olympics (25¢, #2380)
Date of Issue: August 19, 1988
Place of Issue: Colorado Springs, Colorado
Designer: Bart Forbes
Printing: Gravure
The Postal Service paid tribute to the Olympic Summer Games in Seoul, Korea.

1928 Locomobile

1929 Pierce-Arrow

1931 Cord

1932 Packard

1935 Duesenberg

Classic Cars (25¢, #2381-85)
Date of Issue: August 25, 1988
Place of Issue: Detroit, Michigan
Designer: Ken Dallison
Printing: Offset/Intaglio
Many classic cars, famous for their simple lines and careful attention to lavish details, are cherished and admired by young and old even today.

Nathaniel Palmer

Lt. Charles Wilkes

Richard E. Byrd

Lincoln Ellsworth

Antarctic Explorers
(25¢, #2386-89)
Date of Issue:
September 14, 1988
Place of Issue:
Washington, D.C.
Designer: Dennis Lyall
Printing: Gravure
Four daring men of vision and their crews opened the doors to Antarctica, one of the most mysterious regions of the world.

Carousel Animals (25¢, #2390-93)

Date of Issue: October 1, 1988
Place of Issue: Sandusky, Ohio
Designer: Paul Calle
Printing: Offset/Intaglio

Fanciful ideas dreamt in youth and embodied in the craftsmanship of early American carousel animals, with their ornate features and dazzling carved beauty, have captured the imaginations of millions of people.

Design not available at press time.

Special Occasions (25¢, #2397-2400)

Date of Issue: October 19, 1988
Place of Issue: Undetermined
Designer: Harold Zelenko
Printing: Gravure

"Love You," "Thinking of You," "Best Wishes" and "Happy Birthday" are the messages on these stamps, which will be issued in booklets containing four panes of three stamps each.

Christmas Traditional (25¢, #2395)

Date of Issue: October 20, 1988
Place of Issue: Washington, D.C.
Designer: Bradbury Thompson
Printing: Offset/Intaglio

The Madonna and Child, from a classic painting by the Italian master Botticelli, continues a tradition of such Christmas depictions.

Christmas Contemporary (25¢, #2396)

Date of Issue: October 20, 1988
Place of Issue: Berlin, New Hampshire
Designer: Joan Landis
Printing: Gravure

The snow scene designs of this stamp and the Christmas traditional stamp are the first U.S. issues to be printed 75 stamps to a full pane.

1988 Issues
Definitives and Airmails

Conestoga Wagon (3¢, #2253)
Date of Issue: February 29, 1988
Place of Issue: Conestoga, Pennsylvania
Designer: Richard Schlecht
Printing: Intaglio

First used to carry goods between Lancaster County and Philadelphia in Pennsylvania, these vehicles later hauled freight to new Western settlements.

First-Class E Stamp (nondenominated, #2282)
Date of Issue: March 22, 1988
Place of Issue: Washington, D.C.
Designer: Robert McCall
Printing: Gravure

The colorful, nondenominated E stamp was issued to accommodate the increase in the First-Class letter rate from 22¢ to 25¢.

New Sweden (44¢, #C117)
Date of Issue: March 29, 1988
Place of Issue: Wilmington, Delaware
Designer: Göran Österland
Printing: Offset/Intaglio

This stamp celebrated the 350th anniversary of the first Swedish and Finnish settlement in America. The colony grew to more than 1,000 people.

Pheasant (25¢, #2283, booklet panes of 10)
Date of Issue: April 29, 1988
Place of Issue: Rapid City, South Dakota
Designer: Chuck Ripper
Printing: Gravure

First brought to the United States from Asia in the 1800s and now a popular game bird, the ring-necked pheasant is the state bird of South Dakota.

Jack London (25¢, #2183a, b)
Date of Issue: May 3, 1988
Place of Issue: San Francisco, California
Designer: Richard Sparks
Printing: Intaglio

This design, honoring one of America's finest adventure novelists, was reissued in panes of 6 and 10 to meet the demand for booklets.

Flag with Clouds (25¢, #2278)
Date of Issue: May 6, 1988
Place of Issue: Boxborough, Massachusetts
Designer: Peter Cocci
Printing: Gravure

This stamp continues a 25-year tradition of having at least one issue with a flag design always available to Postal Service customers.

Samuel P. Langley (45¢, #C118)
Date of Issue: May 14, 1988
Place of Issue: San Diego, California
Designer: Kenneth Dallison
Printing: Offset/Intaglio

Samuel P. Langley's experiments in mechanical flight provided groundwork and inspiration for the Wright brothers, Glenn Curtiss and other early aviation pioneers.

Flag over Yosemite (25¢, #2280)
Date of Issue: May 20, 1988
Place of Issue: Yosemite, California
Designer: Peter Cocci
Printing: Intaglio

The freedom symbolized by Old Glory is complemented on this stamp by the nearly 100 years of refuge and sanctuary provided by Yosemite National Park.

Owl and Grosbeak (25¢, #2284-85,
                              booklet panes of 10)
Date of Issue: May 28, 1988
Place of Issue: Arlington, Virginia
Designer: Chuck Ripper
Printing: Gravure
These booklet-format stamps portray two colorful members of the bird kingdom—the saw-whet owl and the rose-breasted grosbeak of the finch family.

Buffalo Bill Cody (15¢, #2178)

Date of Issue: June 6, 1988
Place of Issue: Cody, Wyoming
Designer: Jack Rosenthal
Printing: Intaglio

Cody, an American frontiersman and showman, was largely responsible for romanticizing the cowboy West via the exhibitions he staged.

Harvey Cushing, M.D. (45¢, #2188)

Date of Issue: June 17, 1988
Place of Issue: Cleveland, Ohio
Designer: Bradbury Thompson
Printing: Intaglio

Called the "father of neurosurgery," Dr. Cushing and his work have been credited with greatly reducing the brain surgery mortality rate.

Igor Sikorsky (36¢, #C119)

Date of Issue: June 23, 1988
Place of Issue: Stratford, Connecticut
Designer: Ren Wicks
Printing: Gravure/Intaglio

This aeronautical engineer, a Russian emigrant, was a pioneer in the design of American helicopters and multi-engine planes.

Oil Wagon (10.1¢, #2130c)

Date of Issue: June 27, 1988
Place of Issue: Washington, D.C.
Designer: James Schleyer
Printing: Intaglio

During the 19th century, horse-drawn oil wagons were a common sight, primarily delivering home heating oil and stove and lantern fuel.

Popcorn Wagon (16.7¢, #2263)

Date of Issue: July 7, 1988
Place of Issue: Chicago, Illinois
Designer: Lou Nolan
Printing: Intaglio

The popcorn wagon, developed in 1885, cooked the delicious snack fresh for customers on the streets of America's cities for more than 50 years.

Tugboat (15¢, #2262)
Date of Issue: July 12, 1988
Place of Issue: Long Beach, California
Designer: Richard Schlecht
Printing: Intaglio

Tugboats assist larger ships with docking and sailing; tow barges; rescue ships in distress, and help vessels avoid collisions.

Coal Car (13.2¢, #2261)
Date of Issue: July 19, 1988
Place of Issue: Pittsburgh, Pennsylvania
Designer: Richard Schlecht
Printing: Intaglio

The development of coal cars, particularly in the early 20th century, greatly aided the removal and transportation of coal.

Honeybee (25¢, #2281)
Date of Issue: July 22, 1988
Place of Issue: Omaha, Nebraska
Designer: Chuck Ripper
Printing: Offset/Intaglio

Honeybees live in highly organized colonies consisting of a single queen, several thousand workers and, usually, a few male drones.

Wheel Chair (8.4¢, #2258)
Date of Issue: August 12, 1988
Place of Issue: Tucson, Arizona
Designer: Christopher Calle
Printing: Intaglio

Significant progress in American wheel chairs was made in the 1920s and 1930s with the development of lightweight and folding chairs.

Railroad Mail Car (21¢, #2266A)
Date of Issue: August 16, 1988
Place of Issue: Santa Fe, New Mexico
Designer: David Stone
Printing: Intaglio

Use of railroad mail cars allowed for the time-efficient processing, sorting and routing of mail while it was en route to its destination.

Carreta (7.6¢, #2257)
Date of Issue: August 30, 1988
Place of Issue: San Jose, California
Designer: Richard Schlecht
Printing: Intaglio

An innovation of Spanish explorers, the carreta is believed to be the first vehicle introduced on the North American continent.

Elevator (5.3¢, #2256)
Date of Issue: September 16, 1988
Place of Issue: New York, New York
Designer: Lou Nolan
Printing: Intaglio

Elisha Graves Otis' safety system ensured the use of elevators by millions of passengers in stores, hotels and residential structures.

Fire Engine (20.5¢, #2266)
Date of Issue: September 28, 1988
Place of Issue: San Angelo, Texas
Designer: Christopher Calle
Printing: Intaglio

Steam fire engines, requiring fewer firefighters, came into prominent use in the early 1900s and made paid fire departments more feasible.

Express Mail ($8.75, #2394)
Date of Issue: October 4, 1988
Place of Issue: Terre Haute, Indiana
Designer: Ned Seidler
Printing: Offset/Intaglio

This Express Mail stamp reflects the reduced rate for overnight delivery.

---

*Design not available
at press time.*

Chester Carlson (21¢, #2180)
Date of Issue: October 21, 1988
Place of Issue: Rochester, New York
Designer: Susan Sanford
Printing: Intaglio
Chester Carlson invented a copying process, xerography, which led to an incalculable increase in the availability of information worldwide.

Design not available at press time.

Tandem Bicycle (24.1¢, #2266B)
Date of Issue: October 26, 1988
Place of Issue: Redmond, Washington
Designer: Christopher Calle
Printing: Intaglio

Early tandems were used as "sociables," when a gentleman took a lady for an excursion, and for great speed by sharing the effort of pedaling.

Design not available at press time.

Cable Car (20¢, #2265)
Date of Issue: October 28, 1988
Place of Issue: San Francisco, California
Designer: Dan Romano
Printing: Intaglio

By 1877, the cable car was in use on steep hills in 20 American cities and on numerous mining and passenger railroads around the country.

Design not available at press time.

Police Patrol Wagon (13¢, #2260)
Date of Issue: October 29, 1988
Place of Issue: Anaheim, California
Designer: Joe Brockert
Printing: Intaglio

The patrol wagon, introduced in Chicago in 1879, significantly improved response time and reduced costs for police departments.

Design not available at press time.

Gen. 'Hap' Arnold (65¢, #2192)
Date of Issue: November 5, 1988
Place of Issue: Gladwyne, Pennsylvania
Designer: Christopher Calle
Printing: Intaglio

Arnold, considered the "father of the modern Air Force," was the only person to serve as both general of the Army and of the Air Force.

Design not available at press time.

Mary Cassatt (23¢, #2182)
Date of Issue: November 4, 1988
Place of Issue: Philadelphia, Pennsylvania
Designer: Dennis Lyall
Printing: Intaglio

Cassatt, one of America's finest painters, generally portrayed women and children in the common activities of daily life.

Airmail and Special Delivery Stamps

1918-1933

C1

C2

C3

C3a

C4

C5

C6

C7

C10

C11

C12

C13

C14

C15

C18

	Airmail Stamps	Un	U	PB/LP	#	FDC	Q
	For prepayment of postage on all mailable matter sent by airmail. All unwatermarked.						
	Issues of 1918, Perf. 11						
C1	6¢ Curtiss Jenny, Dec. 10	100.00	45.00	1,200.00	(6)	*17,500.00*	3,395,854
C2	16¢ Curtiss Jenny, July 11	150.00	52.50	2,250.00	(6)	*22,500.00*	3,793,887
C3	24¢ Curtiss Jenny, May 13	145.00	65.00	775.00	(4)	*27,500.00*	2,134,888
C3a	Center Inverted	*115,000.00*					
	Issues of 1923						
C4	8¢ Airplane Radiator and Wooden						
	Propeller, Aug. 15	40.00	20.00	600.00	(6)	350.00	6,414,576
C5	16¢ Air Service Emblem, Aug. 17	145.00	50.00	3,250.00	(6)	750.00	5,309,275
C6	24¢ De Havilland Biplane, Aug. 21	165.00	40.00	4,250.00	(6)	900.00	5,285,775
	Issues of 1926-27						
C7	10¢ Map of U.S. and						
	Two Mail Planes, Feb. 13, 1926	4.50	.50	55.00	(6)	65.00	42,092,800
C8	15¢ olive brown (C7), Sept. 18, 1926	5.50	2.75	65.00	(6)	75.00	15,597,307
C9	20¢ yellow green (C7),						
	Jan. 25, 1927	14.00	2.25	165.00	(6)	115.00	17,616,350
	Issues of 1927-28						
C10	10¢ Lindbergh's "Spirit of						
	St. Louis," June 18, 1927	11.00	3.00	200.00	(6)	25.00	20,379,179
C10a	Bklt. pane of 3, May 26, 1928	110.00	60.00				
	#C1-10 inclusive also were available for ordinary postage.						
	Issue of 1928						
C11	5¢ Beacon on Rocky Mountains,						
	July 25	6.00	.65	65.00	(6)	50.00	106,887,675
	Issues of 1930						
C12	5¢ Winged Globe, Feb. 10	15.00	.45	250.00	(6)	20.00	97,641,200
	Graf Zeppelin Issue, Apr. 19						
C13	65¢ Zeppelin over Atlantic Ocean	450.00	275.00	3,850.00	(6)	1,850.00	93,536
C14	$1.30 Zeppelin Between						
	Continents	1,000.00	550.00	8,250.00	(6)	1,400.00	72,428
C15	$2.60 Zeppelin Passing Globe	1,600.00	800.00	13,000.00	(6)	2,000.00	61,296
	Issued for use on mail carried on the first Europe Pan-American round-trip flight of Graf Zeppelin, May 1930.						
	Issues of 1931-32, Perf. 10½x11						
C16	5¢ violet (C12), Aug. 19, 1931	10.00	.50	135.00	(4)	200.00	57,340,050
C17	8¢ olive bistre (C12), Sept. 26, 1932	4.00	.30	45.00	(4)	20.00	76,648,803
	Issue of 1933, Century of Progress Issue, Oct. 2, Perf. 11						
C18	50¢ Zeppelin, Federal Building						
	at Chicago Exposition and						
	Hangar at Friedrichshafen	115.00	95.00	1,100.00	(6)	250.00	324,070
	Issue of 1934, Perf. 10½x11						
C19	6¢ dull orange (C12), June 30	4.25	.12	27.50	(4)	*200.00*	302,205,100

	Issue of 1935-37, Perf. 11	Un	U	PB/LP	#	FDC	Q
	Trans-Pacific Issue						
C20	25¢ China Clipper over Pacific,						
	Nov. 22, 1935	1.50	1.25	20.00	(6)	40.00	10,205,400
C21	20¢ China Clipper over Pacific,						
	Feb. 15, 1937	12.50	2.25	150.00	(6)	40.00	12,794,600
C22	50¢ carm. (C21), Feb. 15, 1937	12.00	2.25	140.00	(6)	40.00	9,285,300
	Issue of 1938						
C23	6¢ Eagle Holding Shield, Olive						
	Branch and Arrows, May 14	.50	.06	11.00	(4)	15.00	349,946,500
	Issue of 1939, Trans-Atlantic Issue, May 16						
C24	30¢ Winged Globe	14.00	1.50	200.00	(6)	45.00	19,768,150
	Issues of 1941-44, Perf. 11x10½						
C25	6¢ Twin-Motor Transport Plane, 1941	.15	.05	1.00	(4)	2.25	4,476,527,700
C25a	Bklt. pane of 3, May 18, 1943	6.50	*1.00*				
	Singles of #C25a are imperf. at sides or imperf. at sides and bottom.						
C26	8¢ olive grn. (C25), Mar. 21, 1944	.20	.05	1.25	(4)	3.75	1,744,876,650
C27	10¢ vio. (C25), Aug. 15, 1941	1.65	.20	12.50	(4)	7.00	67,117,400
C28	15¢ brn. carm. (C25),						
	Aug. 19, 1941	3.75	.35	19.00	(4)	10.00	78,434,800
C29	20¢ brt. grn. (C25), Aug. 27, 1941	2.75	.30	16.50	(4)	10.00	42,359,850
C30	30¢ bl. (C25), Sept. 25, 1941	3.50	.30	17.50	(4)	16.00	59,880,850
C31	50¢ or. (C25), Oct. 29, 1941	16.00	4.00	100.00	(4)	40.00	11,160,600
	Issue of 1946						
C32	5¢ DC-4 Skymaster, Sept. 25	.15	.05	.75	(4)	2.00	864,753,100
	Issues of 1947, Perf. 10½x11						
C33	5¢ DC-4 Skymaster, Mar. 26	.12	.05	.75	(4)	2.00	971,903,700
	Perf. 11x10½						
C34	10¢ Pan American Union Building,						
	Washington, D.C. and Martin 2-0-2,						
	Aug. 30	.30	.06	2.25	(4)	2.00	207,976,550
C35	15¢ Statue of Liberty, N.Y. Skyline						
	and Lockheed Constellation, Aug. 20	.35	.05	2.50	(4)	2.75	756,186,350
C36	25¢ San Francisco-Oakland Bay Bridge						
	and Boeing Stratocruiser, July 30	1.60	.12	8.00	(4)	3.50	132,956,100
	Issues of 1948, Coil Stamp, Perf. 10 Horizontally						
C37	5¢ carmine (C33), Jan. 15	2.00	1.10	13.50		2.00	
	Perf. 11x10½						
C38	5¢ New York City, July 31	.18	.18	20.00	(4)	1.75	38,449,100
	Issues of 1949, Perf. 10½x11						
C39	6¢ carmine (C33), Jan. 18	.18	.05	.90	(4)	1.50	5,070,095,200
C39a	Bklt. pane of 6, Nov. 18	12.00	*5.00*				
	Perf. 11x10½						
C40	6¢ Alexandria, Virginia, May 11	.16	.10	.85	(4)	1.25	75,085,000
	Coil Stamp, Perf. 10 Horizontally						
C41	6¢ carmine (C33), Aug. 25	4.50	.05	20.00		1.25	

C20

C21

C23

C24

C25

C32

C33

C34

C35

C36

C38

C40

C42

C43

C44

C45

C46

C47

C48

C49

C50

C51

C53

C54

C55

C56

C57

C58

C59

C60

	1949 continued, Perf. 11x10½	Un	U	PB/LP	#	FDC	Q
	Universal Postal Union Issue						
C42	10¢ Post Office Dept. Bldg., Nov. 18	.35	.35	3.25	(4)	1.75	21,061,300
C43	15¢ Globe and Doves Carrying						
	Messages, Oct. 7	.50	.50	2.75	(4)	2.25	36,613,100
C44	25¢ Boeing Stratocruiser						
	and Globe, Nov. 30	.85	.85	11.00	(4)	2.75	16,217,100
C45	6¢ Wright Brothers, Dec. 17	.16	.10	.85	(4)	3.75	80,405,000
	Issue of 1952						
C46	80¢ Diamond Head, Honolulu,						
	Hawaii, Mar. 26	11.00	1.50	55.00	(4)	17.50	18,876,800
	Issue of 1953						
C47	6¢ Powered Flight, May 29	.16	.10	.85	(4)	1.50	78,415,000
	Issue of 1954						
C48	4¢ Eagle in Flight, Sept. 3	.12	.08	5.00	(4)	.75	50,483,600
	Issue of 1957						
C49	6¢ Air Force, Aug. 1	.16	.10	1.25	(4)	1.75	63,185,000
	Issues of 1958						
C50	5¢ rose red (C48), July 31	.22	.15	5.00	(4)	.80	72,480,000
	Perf. 10½x11						
C51	7¢ Jet Airliner, July 31	.22	.05	1.30	(4)	.75	532,410,300
C51a	Bklt. pane of 6, July 31	15.00	6.50				1,326,960,000
	Coil Stamp, Perf. 10 Horizontally						
C52	7¢ blue (C51), July 31	4.50	.20	22.50		.90	157,035,000
	Issues of 1959, Perf. 11x10½						
C53	7¢ Alaska Statehood, Jan. 3	.25	.12	1.50	(4)	.65	90,055,200
	Perf. 11						
C54	7¢ Balloon Jupiter, Aug. 17	.25	.12	1.50	(4)	1.10	79,290,000
	Perf. 11x10½						
C55	7¢ Hawaii Statehood, Aug. 21	.25	.12	1.50	(4)	1.00	84,815,000
	Perf. 11						
C56	10¢ Pan American Games, Aug. 27	.40	.40	5.00	(4)	.90	38,770,000
	Issue of 1959-60						
C57	10¢ Liberty Bell, June 10, 1960	3.00	1.00	15.00	(4)	1.50	39,960,000
C58	15¢ Statue of Liberty,						
	Nov. 20, 1959	.75	.06	4.00	(4)	1.10	
C59	25¢ Abraham Lincoln,						
	Apr. 22, 1960	.75	.06	4.00	(4)	1.50	
	Issues of 1960, Perf. 10½x11						
C60	7¢ Jet Airliner, Aug. 12	.30	.05	1.50	(4)	.70	289,460,000
C60a	Bklt. pane of 6, Aug. 19	20.00	7.00				
	Coil Stamp, Perf. 10 Horizontally						
C61	7¢ carmine (C60), Oct. 22	8.00	.25	50.00		1.00	87,140,000

	Issues of 1961, Perf. 11	Un	U	PB/LP	#	FDC	Q
C62	13¢ Liberty Bell, June 28	.65	.10	7.00	(4)	.80	
C63	15¢ Statue of Liberty, Jan. 13	.40	.08	2.25	(4)	1.00	
	#C63 has a gutter between the two parts of the design; #C58 does not.						
	Issues of 1962, Perf. 10½x11						
C64	8¢ Jetliner over Capitol, Dec. 5	.22	.05	1.10	(4)	.60	
C64b	Bklt. pane of 5 + label	7.50	*1.25*				
	Coil Stamp, Perf. 10 Horizontally						
C65	8¢ carmine (C64), Dec. 5	.50	.08	4.00		.80	
	Issues of 1963, Perf. 11						
C66	15¢ Montgomery Blair, May 3	1.30	.75	7.00	(4)	1.35	42,245,000
	Perf. 11x10½						
C67	6¢ Bald Eagle, July 12	.20	.15	3.50	(4)	.50	
	Perf. 11						
C68	8¢ Amelia Earhart, July 24	.30	.15	3.00	(4)	2.50	63,890,000
	Issue of 1964						
C69	8¢ Robert H. Goddard, Oct. 5	.90	.15	5.00	(4)	2.50	65,170,000
	Issues of 1967						
C70	8¢ Alaska Purchase, Mar. 30	.45	.20	4.00	(4)	.70	64,710,000
C71	20¢ "Columbia Jays," by Audubon,						
	Apr. 26 (see also #1241)	1.50	.15	8.50	(4)	2.00	165,430,000
	Issues of 1968, Perf. 11x10½						
C72	10¢ 50-Star Runway, Jan. 5	.30	.05	2.25	(4)	.60	
C72b	Bklt. pane of 8, Jan. 5	4.00	*.75*				
C72c	Bklt. pane of 5 + label, Jan. 6	2.50	*.75*				
	Coil Stamp, Perf. 10 Vertically						
C73	10¢ carmine (C72), Jan. 5	.65	.05	4.50		.60	
	Perf. 11						
C74	10¢ U.S. Air Mail Service, May 15	.60	.15	5.00	(4)	1.50	74,180,000
C75	20¢ USA and Jet, Nov. 22	.85	.06	5.00	(4)	1.10	
	Issue of 1969						
C76	10¢ Moon Landing, Sept. 9	.30	.15	2.50	(4)	3.50	152,364,800
	Issues of 1971-73, Perf. 10½x11, 11x10½						
C77	9¢ Plane, May 15, 1971	.22	.15	2.00	(4)	.50	
C78	11¢ Silhouette of Jet, May 7, 1971	.30	.05	1.75	(4)	.50	
C78a	Bklt. pane of 4 + 2 labels,						
	May 7, 1971	1.50	*.40*				
C79	13¢ Winged Airmail Envelope,						
	Nov. 16, 1973	.32	.10	1.65	(4)	.55	
C79a	Bklt. pane of 5 + label,						
	Dec. 27, 1973	1.35	*.70*				
	Perf. 11						
C80	17¢ Statue of Liberty, July 13, 1971	.55	.15	2.75	(4)	.60	
	Perf. 11x10½						
C81	21¢ USA and Jet, May 21, 1971	.55	.10	2.75	(4)	.75	

C62

C63

C64

C66

C67

C68

C69

C70

C71

C72

C74

C75

C76

C77

National Parks Centennial
City of Refuge · Hawaii

C84

C85

C86

C87

C88

C89

C90

C91
C92

C93
C94

C95
C96

C97

C98

	1971-73 continued, Coil Stamps, **Perf. 10 Vertically**	Un	U	PB/LP	#	FDC	Q
C82	11¢ Silhouette of Jet (C78),						
	May 7, 1971	.40	.06	2.25		.50	
C83	13¢ red (C79), Dec. 27, 1973	.40	.10	2.10		.50	
	Issues of 1972, National Parks Centennial Issue, May 3, Perf. 11 (see also #1448-54)						
C84	11¢ Kii Statue and Temple at						
	City of Refuge Historical National Park,						
	Honaunau, Hawaii	.30	.15	2.00	(4)	.65	78,210,000
	Olympic Games Issue, Aug. 17, Perf. 11x10½ (see also #1460-62)						
C85	11¢ Skiers and Olympic Rings	.30	.15	3.50	(10)	.50	96,240,000
	Issue of 1973, Progress in Electronics Issue, July 10, Perf. 11 (see also #1500-02)						
C86	11¢ De Forest Audions	.30	.15	1.75	(4)	.50	58,705,000
	Issues of 1974						
C87	18¢ Statue of Liberty, Jan. 11	.45	.45	2.50	(4)	.65	
C88	26¢ Mount Rushmore National						
	Memorial, Jan. 2	.60	.15	3.00	(4)	.85	
	Issues of Jan. 2, 1976						
C89	25¢ Plane and Globes	.60	.18	3.25	(4)	.85	
C90	31¢ Plane, Globes and Flag	.62	.10	3.25	(4)	.85	
	Issues of 1978, Wright Brothers Issue, Sept. 23						
C91	31¢ Orville and Wilbur Wright						
	and Flyer A	.90	.15			1.15	157,445,000
C92	31¢ Wright Brothers,						
	Flyer A and Shed	.90	.15			1.15	157,445,000
C92a	Attached pair, #C91-C92	1.85	.65	4.50	(4)	2.30	
	Issues of 1979, Octave Chanute Issue, March 29						
C93	21¢ Chanute and Biplane Hang-Glider	1.25	.32			1.00	29,012,500
C94	21¢ Biplane Hang-Glider and Chanute	1.25	.32			1.00	29,012,500
C94a	Attached pair, #C93-C94	2.60	.75	7.50	(4)	2.00	
	Wiley Post Issue, Nov. 20						
C95	25¢ Wiley Post and "Winnie Mae"	1.50	.35			1.00	32,005,000
C96	25¢ NR-105-W, Post in Pressurized						
	Suit and Portrait	1.50	.35			1.00	32,005,000
C96a	Attached pair, #C95-C96	3.10	.85	8.00	(4)	2.00	
	Olympic Summer Games Issue, Nov. 1 (see also #1790-94)						
C97	31¢ High Jumper	.90	.30	12.00	(12)	1.15	47,200,000
	Issues of 1980						
C98	40¢ Philip Mazzei, Oct. 13	.90	.30	12.00	(12)	1.35	80,935,000
C99	28¢ Blanche Stuart Scott, Dec. 30	.70	.15	9.25	(12)	1.10	20,190,000
C100	35¢ Glenn Curtiss, Dec. 30	.75	.15	10.00	(12)	1.25	22,945,000

	Issues of 1983	Un	U	PB/LP	#	FDC	Q
	Olympic Summer Games Issue, June 17, Perf. 11 (see also #2048-51 and 2082-85)						
C101	28¢ Gymnast	.56	.28			1.10	42,893,750
C102	28¢ Hurdler	.56	.28			1.10	42,893,750
C103	28¢ Basketball Player	.56	.28			1.10	42,893,750
C104	28¢ Soccer Player	.56	.28	3.25	(4)	1.10	42,893,750
C104a	Block of 4, #C101-C104	2.75	1.75			3.75	
	Olympic Summer Games Issue, April 8 (see also #2048-51 and 2082-85)						
C105	40¢ Shotputter	.80	.40			1.35	66,573,750
C106	40¢ Gymnast	.80	.40			1.35	66,573,750
C107	40¢ Swimmer	.80	.40			1.35	66,573,750
C108	40¢ Weightlifter	.80	.40	4.25	(4)	1.35	66,573,750
C108a	Block of 4, #C105-C108	3.75	2.00			5.00	
	Olympic Summer Games Issue, Nov. 4 (see also #2048-51 and 2082-85)						
C109	35¢ Fencer	.70	.35			1.25	42,587,500
C110	35¢ Bicyclist	.70	.35			1.25	42,587,500
C111	35¢ Volleyball Players	.70	.35			1.25	42,587,500
C112	35¢ Pole Vaulter	.70	.35	3.75	(4)	1.25	42,587,500
C112a	Block of 4, #C109-C112	3.25	1.85			4.50	
	Issues of 1985						
C113	33¢ Alfred V. Verville, Feb. 13	.66	.20	3.50	(4)	1.25	151,450,000
C114	39¢ Lawrence & Elmer Sperry,						
	Feb. 13	.78	.20	4.00	(4)	1.35	157,975,000
C115	44¢ Transpacific Airmail, Feb. 15	.88	.20	4.50	(4)	1.35	209,025,000
C116	44¢ Junipero Serra, Aug. 22	1.00	.20	4.50	(4)	1.35	164,350,000
	Airmail Special Delivery Stamps						
	Issue of 1934						
CE1	16¢ dark blue Great Seal						
	of the United States, Aug. 30	.75	.85	20.00	(6)	3.50	
	For imperforate variety see #771.						
	Issue of 1936						
CE2	16¢ carmine and blue Great Seal						
	of the United States, Feb. 10	.40	.25	8.50	(4)	17.50	

C105
C107

C106
C108

C101
C103

C102
C104

C109
C111

C110
C112

C113

C114

C115

CE1

C116

CE2

E1

E3

E4

E6

E7

E12

E13

E14

E15

E17

E18

E20

E21

E22

E23

	Special Delivery Stamps	Un	U	PB/LP	#	FDC	Q
	Issue of 1885, Oct. 1, Unwmkd., Perf. 12						
E1	10¢ Messenger Running	275.00	30.00	*12,000.00*	(8)	*8,000.00*	
	Issue of 1888, Sept. 6						
E2	10¢ blue (E3)	275.00	7.50	*12,000.00*	(8)		
	Issue of 1893, Jan. 24						
E3	10¢ Messenger Running	175.00	14.00	*7,250.00*	(8)		
	Issue of 1894, Line under "Ten Cents," Oct. 10						
E4	10¢ Messenger Running	750.00	17.50	*14,500.00*	(6)		
	Issue of 1895, Aug. 16, Wmkd. (191)						
E5	10¢ blue (E4)	135.00	2.50	*4,500.00*	(6)		
	Issue of 1902, Dec. 9						
E6	10¢ Messenger on Bicycle	90.00	2.50	*2,750.00*	(6)		
	Issue of 1908, Dec. 12						
E7	10¢ Mercury Helmet and Olive Branch	60.00	27.50	925.00	(6)		
	Issue of 1911, Jan., Wmkd. (190)						
E8	10¢ ultramarine (E6)	90.00	4.00	*2,750.00*	(6)		
	Issue of 1914, Sept., Perf. 10						
E9	10¢ ultramarine (E6)	175.00	5.25	*5,000.00*	(6)		
	Issue of 1916, Oct. 19, Unwmkd.						
E10	10¢ ultramarine (E6)	325.00	21.00	6,250.00	(6)		
	Issue of 1917, May 2, Perf. 11						
E11	10¢ ultramarine (E6)	15.00	.30	200.00	(6)		
	Issue of 1922, July 12						
E12	10¢ Postman and Motorcycle	22.50	.15	375.00	(6)	550.00	
	Issues of 1925						
E13	15¢ Postman and Motorcycle, Apr. 11	24.00	.65	250.00	(6)	250.00	
E14	20¢ Post Office Truck, Apr. 25	3.00	1.75	37.50	(6)	125.00	
	Issue of 1927, Nov. 29, Perf. 11x10½						
E15	10¢ Postman and Motorcycle	.70	.05	5.25	(4)	90.00	
	Issue of 1931, Aug. 13						
E16	15¢ orange (E12)	.80	.08	6.50	(4)	125.00	
	Issues of 1944, Oct. 30						
E17	13¢ Postman and Motorcycle	.65	.06	4.00	(4)	12.00	
E18	17¢ Postman and Motorcycle	5.00	2.25	28.50	(4)	12.00	
	Issue of 1951, Nov. 30						
E19	20¢ black (E14)	2.00	.12	12.00	(4)	5.00	
	Issues of 1954-57						
E20	20¢ Delivery of Letter, Oct. 13, 1954	.60	.08	4.00	(4)	3.00	
E21	30¢ Delivery of Letter, Sept. 3, 1957	.90	.05	5.00	(4)	2.25	
	Issues of 1969-71, Perf. 11						
E22	45¢ Arrows, Nov. 21, 1969	2.25	.20	11.50	(4)	3.50	
E23	60¢ Arrows, May 10, 1971	1.20	.12	5.50	(4)	3.50	

Registration, Certified Mail and Postage Due Stamps

F1

FA1

J2

J19

J25

J33

J69

J78

J88

J98

J101

Registration Stamp

Issued for the prepayment of registry; not usable for postage. Sale discontinued May 28, 1913.

	Issue of 1911, Wmkd. (190), Perf. 12	Un	U	PB/LP	#	FDC	Q
F1	10¢ Bald Eagle, Dec. 1	75.00	4.50	*1,850.00*	(6)	*8,000.00*	

Certified Mail Stamp

For use on First-Class mail for which no indemnity value was claimed, but for which proof of mailing and proof of delivery were available at less cost than registered mail.

	Issue of 1955, Perf. 10½x11						
FA1	15¢ Letter Carrier, June 6	.50	.30	6.25	(4)	3.25	54,460,300

Postage Due Stamps

For affixing by a postal clerk to any mail to denote amount to be collected from addressee because of insufficient prepayment of postage.

**Issues of 1879,
Printed by American Bank Note Co.,
Design of J2, Perf. 12, Unwmkd.**

		Un	U
J1	1¢ brown	30.00	5.00
J2	2¢ Figure of Value	175.00	4.00
J3	3¢ brown	20.00	2.50
J4	5¢ brown	275.00	25.00
J5	10¢ brown, Sept. 19	325.00	12.50
J6	30¢ brown, Sept. 19	165.00	20.00
J7	50¢ brown, Sept. 19	210.00	30.00

Special Printing, Soft, Porous Paper

J8	1¢ deep brown	*5,750.00*	—
J9	2¢ deep brown	*3,750.00*	—
J10	3¢ deep brown	*3,500.00*	—
J11	5¢ deep brown	*3,000.00*	—
J12	10¢ deep brown	*1,850.00*	—
J13	30¢ deep brown	*1,850.00*	—
J14	50¢ deep brown	*2,000.00*	—

**Issues of 1884-89,
Design of J19**

		Un	U
J15	1¢ red brown	25.00	2.50
J16	2¢ red brown	32.50	2.50
J17	3¢ red brown	475.00	100.00
J18	5¢ red brown	225.00	12.50
J19	10¢ Figure of Value,		
	Mar. 15, 1887	185.00	7.00
J20	30¢ red brown	95.00	22.50
J21	50¢ red brown	900.00	125.00

Issues of 1891, Design of J25

J22	1¢ bright claret	10.00	.50
J23	2¢ bright claret	12.50	.45
J24	3¢ bright claret	27.50	4.00
J25	5¢ Figure of Value	30.00	4.00
J26	10¢ bright claret	60.00	10.00
J27	30¢ bright claret	225.00	85.00
J28	50¢ bright claret	250.00	85.00

**Issues of 1894,
Printed by the Bureau of Engraving and
Printing, Design of J33, Perf. 12**

J29	1¢ vermilion	500.00	100.00
J30	2¢ vermilion	225.00	50.00

	Issues of 1894-95, Design of J33, Perf. 12, Unwmkd.	Un	U	PB/LP	#	FDC	Q
J31	1¢ deep claret, Aug. 14, 1894	17.50	3.00	375.00	(6)		
J32	2¢ deep claret, July 20, 1894	15.00	1.75	325.00	(6)		
J33	3¢ Figure of Value, Apr. 27, 1895	75.00	20.00	850.00	(6)		
J34	5¢ deep claret, Apr. 27, 1895	80.00	22.50	950.00	(6)		
J35	10¢ deep rose, Sept. 24, 1894	85.00	17.50	950.00	(6)		
J36	30¢ deep claret, Apr. 27, 1895	185.00	50.00				
J37	50¢ deep claret, Apr. 27, 1895	450.00	120.00				
	Issues of 1895-97, Design of J33, Wmkd. (191)						
J38	1¢ deep claret, Aug. 29, 1895	5.00	.30	190.00	(6)		
J39	2¢ deep claret, Sept. 14, 1895	5.00	.20	190.00	(6)		
J40	3¢ deep claret, Oct. 30, 1895	32.50	1.00	425.00	(6)		
J41	5¢ deep claret, Oct. 15, 1895	35.00	1.00	450.00	(6)		
J42	10¢ deep claret, Sept. 14, 1895	37.50	2.00	550.00	(6)		
J43	30¢ deep claret, Aug. 21, 1897	250.00	22.50	3,750.00	(6)		
J44	50¢ deep claret, Mar. 17, 1896	185.00	20.00	2,250.00	(6)		
	Issues of 1910-12, Design of J33, Wmkd. (190)						
J45	1¢ deep claret, Aug. 30, 1910	17.50	2.00	400.00	(6)		
J46	2¢ deep claret, Nov. 25, 1910	17.50	.15	350.00	(6)		
J47	3¢ deep claret, Aug. 31, 1910	325.00	17.50	3,850.00	(6)		
J48	5¢ deep claret, Aug. 31, 1910	55.00	3.50	600.00	(6)		
J49	10¢ deep claret, Aug. 31, 1910	70.00	7.50	1,150.00	(6)		
J50	50¢ deep claret, Sept. 23, 1912	575.00	75.00	6,500.00	(6)		
	Issues of 1914-15, Design of J33, Perf. 10						
J52	1¢ carmine lake	35.00	7.50	550.00	(6)		
J53	2¢ carmine lake	27.50	.20	350.00	(6)		
J54	3¢ carmine lake	375.00	20.00	4,500.00	(6)		
J55	5¢ carmine lake	22.50	1.50	285.00	(6)		
J56	10¢ carmine lake	37.50	1.00	675.00	(6)		
J57	30¢ carmine lake	125.00	12.00	2,100.00	(6)		
J58	50¢ carmine lake	*5,000.00*	375.00	*36,000.00*	(6)		
	Issues of 1916, Design of J33, Unwmkd.						
J59	1¢ rose	900.00	150.00	7,750.00	(6)		
J60	2¢ rose	80.00	8.00	800.00	(6)		
	Issues of 1917, Design of J33, Perf. 11						
J61	1¢ carmine rose	1.75	.08	40.00	(6)		
J62	2¢ carmine rose	1.50	.05	35.00	(6)		
J63	3¢ carmine rose	8.50	.08	100.00	(6)		
J64	5¢ carmine	8.50	.08	95.00	(6)		
J65	10¢ carmine rose	12.50	.20	125.00	(6)		
J66	30¢ carmine rose	55.00	.40	525.00	(6)		
J67	50¢ carmine rose	70.00	.12	750.00	(6)		

	Issue of 1925, Design of J33	Un	U	PB/LP	#	FDC	Q
J68	½¢ dull red, Apr. 13	.50	.06	11.00	(6)		
	Issues of 1930-31, Design of J69						
J69	½¢ Figure of Value	3.50	.70	35.00	(6)		
J70	1¢ carmine	2.50	.15	27.50	(6)		
J71	2¢ carmine	3.50	.15	40.00	(6)		
J72	3¢ carmine	27.50	1.00	250.00	(6)		
J73	5¢ carmine	22.50	1.50	225.00	(6)		
J74	10¢ carmine	47.50	.50	450.00	(6)		
J75	30¢ carmine	125.00	1.00	1,000.00	(6)		
J76	50¢ carmine	160.00	.30	1,250.00	(6)		
	Design of J78						
J77	$1 carmine	30.00	.06	275.00	(6)		
J78	$5 "FIVE" on $	40.00	.12	375.00	(6)		
	Issues of 1931-56, Design of J69, Perf. 11x10½						
J79	½¢ dull carmine	1.25	.08	22.50	(4)		
J80	1¢ dull carmine	.15	.05	2.00	(4)		
J81	2¢ dull carmine	.15	.05	2.00	(4)		
J82	3¢ dull carmine	.25	.05	3.00	(4)		
J83	5¢ dull carmine	.35	.05	4.00	(4)		
J84	10¢ dull carmine	1.10	.05	8.50	(4)		
J85	30¢ dull carmine	8.50	.08	45.00	(4)		
J86	50¢ dull carmine	9.50	.06	57.50	(4)		
	Design of J78, Perf. 10½x11						
J87	$1 scarlet	40.00	.20	300.00	(4)		
	Issues of 1959, June 19, Design of J88 and J98, Perf. 11x10½						
J88	½¢ Figure of Value	1.25	.85	125.00	(4)		
J89	1¢ carmine rose	.05	.05	.50	(4)		
J90	2¢ carmine rose	.06	.05	.60	(4)		
J91	3¢ carmine rose	.07	.05	.70	(4)		
J92	4¢ carmine rose	.08	.05	1.25	(4)		
J93	5¢ carmine rose	.10	.05	.75	(4)		
J94	6¢ carmine rose	.12	.05	1.40	(4)		
J95	7¢ carmine rose	.14	.06	1.60	(4)		
J96	8¢ carmine rose	.16	.05	1.75	(4)		
J97	10¢ carmine rose	.20	.05	1.25	(4)		
J98	30¢ Figure of Value	.70	.05	5.50	(4)		
J99	50¢ carmine rose	1.10	.05	6.50	(4)		
	Design of J101						
J100	$1 carmine rose	2.00	.05	10.00	(4)		
J101	$5 Outline Figure of Value	8.00	.15	40.00	(4)		
	Issues of 1978-85, Design of J88 and J98						
J102	11¢ carmine rose, Jan. 2, 1978	.22	.05	1.10	(4)		
J103	13¢ carmine rose, Jan. 2, 1978	.26	.05	1.30	(4)		
J104	17¢ carmine rose, June 10, 1985	.34	.05	1.70	(4)		

Penalty Mail, Parcel Post and Special Handling Stamps

1983-1985

O127

O128

O129

O129A

O130

O132

O133

O135

O136

O138

O139

Issues of 1983-85
Penalty Mail Issues, Perf. 11 x 10½, Unwmkd.

Beginning July 1, 1873, Official Mail stamps were provided to the various departments of the federal government for the prepayment of postage on official matter. On July 5, 1884, these stamps were declared obsolete.

Stamps for use by government departments were reinstituted in 1983. Now known as Penalty Mail stamps, they help provide a better accounting of actual mail costs for official departments and agencies, etc.

		Un	U
O127	1¢, Jan. 12, 1983	.05	—
O128	4¢, Jan. 12, 1983	.08	—
O129	13¢, Jan. 12, 1983	.26	—
O129A	14¢, May 15, 1985	.28	—
O130	17¢, Jan. 12, 1983	.34	—
O132	1.00, Jan. 12, 1983	2.00	—
O133	5.00, Jan. 12, 1983	10.00	—
Coil Stamps, Perf. 10 Vertically			
O135	20¢, Jan. 12, 1983	1.00	.40
O136	22¢, May 15, 1985	.44	—

O137 not assigned.

Perf. 11			
O138	(14¢) D Stamp, Feb. 4, 1985	.50	—
Coil Stamp, Perf. 10 Vertically			
O139	(22¢) D Stamp, Feb. 4, 1985	1.75	—

Parcel Post Stamps

Issued for the prepayment of postage on parcel post packages only.

Beginning July 1, 1913 these stamps were valid for all postal purposes.

Issue of 1912-13, Perf. 12, Wmkd. (190)

		Un	U
Q1	1¢ Post Office Clerk,		
	Nov. 27, 1912	4.00	.90
Q2	2¢ City Carrier,		
	Nov. 27, 1912	4.50	.70
Q3	3¢ Railway Postal Clerk,		
	Apr. 5, 1913	10.00	5.00
Q4	4¢ Rural Carrier,		
	Dec. 12, 1912	25.00	2.00
Q5	5¢ Mail Train,		
	Nov. 27, 1912	25.00	1.25
Q6	10¢ Steamship and		
	Mail Tender,		
	Dec. 9, 1912	40.00	1.75
Q7	15¢ Automobile		
	Service, Dec. 16, 1912	65.00	9.00
Q8	20¢ Aeroplane Carrying		
	Mail, Dec. 16, 1912	140.00	17.50
Q9	25¢ Manufacturing,		
	Nov. 27, 1912	80.00	4.50
Q10	50¢ Dairying,		
	Mar. 15, 1913	210.00	35.00
Q11	75¢ Harvesting,		
	Dec. 18, 1912	80.00	30.00
Q12	$1 Fruit Growing,		
	Jan. 3, 1913	400.00	20.00

Special Handling Stamps

For use on parcel post packages to secure the same expeditious handling accorded to First-class mail matter.

Issue of 1925-29, Perf. 11

QE1	10¢ Special Handling,		
	June 25, 1928	1.50	.90
QE2	15¢ Special Handling,		
	June 25, 1928	1.65	.90
QE3	20¢ Special Handling,		
	June 25, 1928	2.00	1.75
QE4	25¢ Special Handling,		
	1929	20.00	7.50
QE4a	25¢ deep green,		
	April 11, 1925	25.00	4.50

Parcel Post Postage Due Stamps

For affixing by a postal clerk to any parcel post package to denote the amount to be collected from the addressee because of insufficient prepayment of postage.

Beginning July 1, 1913 these stamps were valid for use as regular postage due stamps.

Issues of 1912, Design of JQ1 and JQ5, Perf. 12, Wkmd. (190)

JQ1	1¢ Figure of Value,		
	Nov. 27	9.00	3.00
JQ2	2¢ dark green,		
	Dec. 9	80.00	15.00
JQ3	5¢ dark green,		
	Nov. 27	11.50	3.50
JQ4	10¢ dark green,		
	Dec. 12	150.00	35.00
JQ5	25¢ Figure of Value,		
	Dec. 16	85.00	3.50

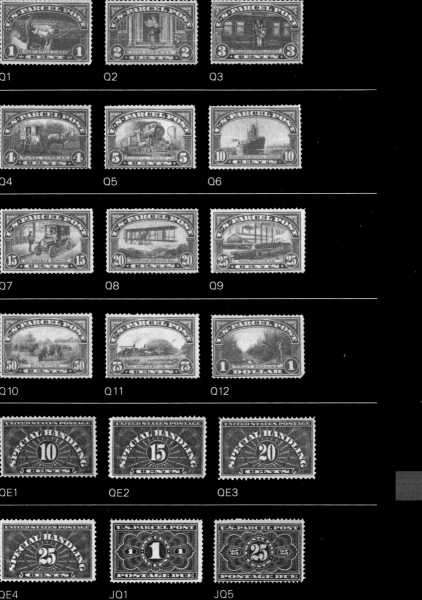

Q1

Q2

Q3

Q4

Q5

Q6

Q7

Q8

Q9

Q10

Q11

Q12

QE1

QE2

QE3

QE4

JQ1

JQ5

A Great Way to Collect... and to Learn

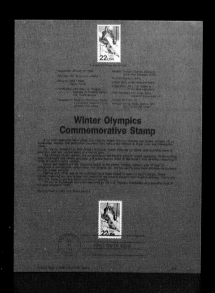

Colorful Keepsakes of 1988 U.S. Issues

The U.S. Postal Service's Souvenir Page Program is an informative, inexpensive way to obtain all the year's stamp issues. These display pages are printed in a limited quantity for every definitive, commemorative and special U.S. stamp issued in a given year, including airmails, coil stamps and booklet panes.

Each Souvenir Page includes the featured stamp, postmarked with its "FIRST DAY OF ISSUE" cancellation and mounted on an 8″ by 10½″ page. A black-and-white enlargement of the stamp and its technical specifications (designer, engraver, date of issue, printing information, etc.) precede a lively, historical narrative about its subject and issuance. Subscribers also receive monthly letters with information on upcoming issues, new designs and other postal products—and the average cost is only $1.00 per page.

Money-back Guarantee!

If you are ever dissatisfied, return your Souvenir Pages within 30 days of receipt for a *full* refund. For more information and an order form, use the postage-paid request card following page 312 or write to:

USPS Guide
Souvenir Page Program
Philatelic Sales Division
United States Postal Service
Washington, D.C. 20265-9980

Souvenir Pages

With First Day Cancellations

The Postal Service offers Souvenir Pages for new stamps. The series began with a page for the Yellowstone Park Centennial stamp issued March 1, 1972. The pages feature one or more stamps tied by the first day cancel, along with technical data and information on the subject of the issue. More than just collectors' items, Souvenir Pages make wonderful show and conversation pieces. Souvenir Pages are issued in limited editions.

1972

1	Yellowstone Park, FDC with Eagle 1971 watermark	$200.00
1a	Same with Parsons wmk.	$200.00
1b	Same without any wmk.	$200.00
1c	Yellowstone Park with Washington, DC first day cancel and Eagle 1971 wmk.	$750.00
1d	Same without any wmk.	$600.00
1A	Family Planning (ASDA) with Eagle 1971 wmk.	$750.00
1Aa	Same without any wmk.	$600.00
2	Cape Hatteras, with Eagle 1971 wmk.	$200.00
2a	Same with Parsons wmk.	$200.00
2b	Same without any wmk.	$200.00
3	Fiorello LaGuardia, with Eagle 1971 wmk.	$200.00
3a	Same with Parsons wmk.	$300.00
3b	Same without any wmk.	$200.00
4	City of Refuge, with 1971 Eagle wmk.	$200.00
4a	Same with Parsons wmk.	$200.00
4b	Same without any wmk.	$200.00
5	Wolf Trap Farm, with 1971 Eagle wmk. (No star before (GPO #)	$50.00
5a	Same with 1972 Eagle wmk.	$70.00
5b	Wolf Trap Farm with Parsons wmk. and Star before GPO#	$60.00
6	Colonial Craftsmen	$40.00
7	Mount McKinley	$50.00
8	Olympic Games	$25.00
8E	Olympic Games with broken red circle on 6¢ stamp	$800.00
9	PTA	$15.00
10	Wildlife Conservation	$20.00
11	Mail Order	$15.00
11E	Mail Order with double-tailed cat on stamp	$300.00

12	Osteopathic Medicine	$15.00
13	Tom Sawyer	$15.00
14	Benjamin Franklin	$15.00
15	Christmas	$20.00
16	Pharmacy	$12.00
17	Stamp Collecting	$12.00

1973

18	Eugene O'Neill coil, with 1972 Eagle wmk. and U.S. GPO # 1972-0-491-478	$25.00
18E	Same with 1973 Eagle wmk. and U.S. GPO # 1973-0-509-757	$600.00
19	Love	$20.00
20	Pamphleteers	$12.00
21	George Gershwin	$12.00
22	Posting a Broadside	$10.00
22E	Same with 1971 Eagle wmk.	$400.00
23	Copernicus	$10.00
24	Postal Service Employees	$12.00
25	Harry S. Truman	$10.00
26	Post Rider	$10.00
27	Amadeo Gianninni	$10.00
28	Boston Tea Party	$12.00
29	Progress in Electronics	$12.00
30	Robinson Jeffers	$7.00
31	Lyndon B. Johnson	$7.00
32	Henry O. Tanner	$7.00
33	Willa Cather	$7.00
34	Colonial Drummer	$8.00
35	Cattle	$7.00
36	Christmas	$12.00
37	13¢ Winged Envelope airmail sheet stamp	$5.00
38	10¢ Crossed Flags	$5.00
39	Jefferson Memorial	$5.00
40	13¢ Winged Envelope airmail coil	$5.00

1974

41	Mount Rushmore airmail	$5.00
41a	Mount Rushmore with wmk.	$40.00
42	ZIP Code	$5.00
42E	ZIP Code, date error	$600.00
43	Statue of Liberty airmail	$5.00
43a	Statue of Liberty with wmk.	$50.00
44	Elizabeth Blackwell	$5.00

45	VFW	$5.00
46	Robert Frost	$5.00
47	EXPO '74	$5.00
48	Horse Racing	$5.00
49	Skylab with wmk.	$8.00
49a	Skylab without wmk.	$30.00
50	Universal Postal Union	$10.00
51	Mineral Heritage	$8.00
52	First Kentucky Settlement	$5.00
53	First Continental Congress	$8.00
54	Chautauqua	$5.00
55	Kansas Wheat	$5.00
56	Energy Conservation	$5.00
57	6.3¢ Liberty Bell coil	$5.00
58	Sleepy Hollow	$5.00
59	Retarded Children	$5.00
60	Christmas	$9.00

1975

61	Benjamin West	$5.00
62	Pioneer/Jupiter	$8.00
63	Collective Bargaining	$5.00
64	8¢ Sybil Ludington	$5.00
65	Salem Poor	$5.00
66	Haym Salomon	$5.00
67	18¢ Peter Francisco	$5.00
68	Mariner 10	$8.00
69	Lexington & Concord	$5.00
70	Paul Laurence Dunbar	$5.00
71	D.W. Griffith	$5.00
72	Bunker Hill	$5.00
73	Military Uniforms	$9.00
74	Apollo Soyuz	$9.00
75	International Women's Year	$5.00
76	Postal Service Bicentennial	$8.00
77	World Peace Through Law	$5.00
78	Banking and Commerce	$5.00
79	Christmas	$6.00
80	3¢ Francis Parkman	$4.00
81	11¢ Freedom of the Press	$4.00
82	24¢ Old North Church	$4.00
83	Flag over Independence Hall	$4.00

#	Item	Price
84	9¢ Freedom to Assemble	$4.00
85	Liberty Bell coil	$4.00
86	American Eagle and Shield	$4.00

1976

#	Item	Price
87	Spirit of '76	$7.00
87E	Spirit of '76 with error cancellation	$800.00
88	25¢ & 31¢ Plane and Globes airmails	$5.00
89	Interphil 76	$5.00
90	Fifty State Flag Series, (5 pages)	$60.00
91	9¢ Freedom to Assemble coil	$4.00
92	Telephone	$4.00
93	Commercial Aviation	$4.00
94	Chemistry	$4.00
95	7.9¢ Drum coil	$4.00
96	Benjamin Franklin	$4.00
97	Bicentennial SS, (4 pages)	$60.00
97E	31¢ Souvenir Sheet with missing 31¢ values	$800.00
98	Declaration of Independence	$8.00
99	Olympics	$9.00
100	Clara Maass	$4.00
101	Adolph S. Ochs	$4.00
102	Christmas	$6.00
103	7.7¢ Saxhorns coil	$4.00

1977

#	Item	Price
104	Washington at Princeton	$4.00
105	$1 Flag over Capitol booklet, perf. 10	$30.00
106	Sound Recording	$4.00
107	Pueblo Pottery	$5.00
108	Lindbergh Flight	$5.00
109	Colorado Statehood	$4.00
110	Butterflies	$5.00
111	Lafayette	$4.00
112	Skilled Hands	$5.00
113	Peace Bridge	$4.00
114	Battle of Oriskany	$4.00
115	Alta, CA, First Civil Settlement	$4.00
116	Articles of Confederation	$4.00
117	Talking Pictures	$4.00
118	Surrender at Saratoga	$4.00
119	Energy	$4.00
120	Christmas, Mailbox	$4.00
121	Christmas, Valley Forge	$4.00
122	10¢ Petition for Redress coil	$4.00
123	10¢ Petition for Redress sheet stamp	$4.00
124	1¢, 2¢, 3¢, 4¢ Americana Issues	$4.00

1978

#	Item	Price
125	Carl Sandburg	$4.00
126	Indian Head Penny	$4.00
127	Captain Cook, Anchorage cancel	$5.00
128	Captain Cook, Honolulu cancel	$5.00
129	Harriet Tubman	$4.00
130	Quilts	$5.00

#	Item	Price
131	16¢ Statue of Liberty	$4.00
132	29¢ Lighthouse	$4.00
133	Dance	$5.00
134	French Alliance	$4.00
135	Early Cancer Detection	$4.00
136	A Stamps	$4.00
137	Jimmie Rodgers	$4.00
138	CAPEX '78, SS	$8.00
139	Oliver Wendell Holmes	$4.00
140	Photography	$4.00
141	Fort McHenry Flag	$4.00
142	George M. Cohan	$4.00
143	Rose booklet single	$4.00
144	8.4¢ Piano coil	$4.00
145	Viking Missions	$5.00
146	28¢ Remote Outpost	$4.00
147	Owls	$5.00
148	Wright Brothers airmails	$5.00
149	Trees	$5.00
150	Christmas, Hobby Horse	$4.00
151	Christmas, Madonna	$4.00
152	$2 Kerosene Lamp	$10.00

1979

#	Item	Price
153	Robert F. Kennedy	$4.00
154	Martin Luther King, Jr.	$4.00
155	Year of the Child	$4.00
156	John Steinbeck	$4.00
157	Albert Einstein	$4.00
158	Octave Chanute airmails	$5.00
159	Pennsylvania Toleware	$5.00
160	Architecture	$5.00
161	Endangered Flora	$5.00
162	Seeing Eye Dogs	$4.00
163	$1 Candle	$9.00
164	Special Olympics	$4.00
165	$5 Lantern	$20.00
166	30¢ Schoolhouse	$6.00
167	10¢ Olympics	$5.00
168	50¢ Lamp	$6.00
169	John Paul Jones	$4.00
170	15¢ Olympics	$8.00
171	Christmas, Madonna	$4.00
172	Christmas, Santa Claus	$4.00
173	3.1¢ Guitar coil	$5.00
174	31¢ Olympics airmails	$8.00
175	Will Rogers	$4.00
176	Vietnam Veterans	$4.00
177	Wiley Post airmails	$5.00

1980

#	Item	Price
178	W. C. Fields	$4.00
179	Winter Olympics	$8.00
180	Windmills booklet	$8.00
181	Benjamin Banneker	$3.50
182	Letter Writing	$5.00
183	1¢ Ability to Write	$3.50
184	Frances Perkins	$3.50
185	Dolley Madison	$3.50
186	Emily Bissell	$3.50
187	3.5¢ Violins coil	$5.00
188	Helen Keller/ Anne Sullivan	$3.50

#	Item	Price
189	Veterans Administration	$3.50
190	General Galvez	$3.50
191	Coral Reefs	$4.50
192	Organized Labor	$3.50
193	Edith Wharton	$3.50
194	Education	$3.50
195	Indian Masks	$4.50
196	Architecture	$4.50
197	Philip Mazzei airmail	$4.00
198	Christmas, Madonna	$4.00
199	Christmas, Wreath and Toys	$4.00
200	Sequoyah	$3.50
201	Blanche Scott airmail	$3.50
202	Glenn Curtiss airmail	$3.50

1981

#	Item	Price
203	Everett Dirksen	$3.50
204	Whitney M. Young	$3.50
205	B sheet and coil	$3.50
206	B booklet	$4.50
207	12¢ Freedom of Conscience sheet and coil	$3.50
208	Flowers	$4.00
209	Flag and Anthem sheet and coil	$3.50
210	Flag and Anthem booklet	$4.50
211	Red Cross	$3.50
212	George Mason	$3.50
213	Savings and Loans	$3.50
214	Wildlife Booklet	$6.00
215	Surrey coil	$4.50
216	Space Achievement	$10.00
217	Rachel Carson	$3.50
218	35¢ Charles Drew, MD	$3.50
219	Professional Management	$3.50
220	17¢ Electric Auto coil	$4.50
221	Wildlife Habitats	$4.00
222	Year of Disabled	$3.50
223	Edna St. Vincent Millay	$3.50
224	Alcoholism	$3.50
225	Architecture	$4.00
226	Babe Zaharias	$3.50
227	Bobby Jones	$3.50
228	Frederic Remington	$3.50
229	C sheet and coil	$3.50
230	C booklet	$5.00
231	18¢/20¢ Hoban	$3.50
232	Yorktown, Virginia Capes	$3.50
233	Christmas, Bear on Sleigh	$3.50
234	Christmas, Madonna	$3.50
235	John Hanson	$3.50
236	Fire Pumper coil	$4.00
237	Desert Plants	$4.00
238	9.3¢ Mail Wagon coil	$4.50
239	Flag over Supreme Court sheet and coil	$3.50
240	Flag over Supreme Court booklet	$4.50

1982

#	Item	Price
241	Sheep booklet	$5.00
242	Ralph Bunche	$3.00

243	13¢ Crazy Horse $3.00	**297A**	$9.35 Eagle booklet
244	37¢ Robert Millikan $3.00		pane of 3 $300.00
245	Franklin Roosevelt $3.00	**298**	1¢ Omnibus coil $3.00
246	Love $3.00	**299**	Treaty of Paris $2.50
247	5.9¢ Bicycle coil $4.00	**300**	Civil Service $2.50
248	George	**301**	Metropolitan
	Washington $3.00		Opera $2.50
249	10.9¢ Hansom Cab	**302**	Inventors $3.50
	coil $4.00	**303**	1¢ Dorothea Dix $2.50
250	Birds & Flowers Series,	**304**	Streetcars $3.50
	(5 pages) $50.00	**305**	5¢ Motorcycle coil $3.00
250a	Birds & Flowers with	**306**	Christmas,
	all 10½ x 11 perfs.$75.00		Santa Claus $2.50
250b	Birds & Flowers with	**307**	Christmas,
	all 11 x 11 perfs. $75.00		Madonna $2.50
251	U.S./Netherlands $3.00	**308**	35¢ Olympics
252	Library of Congress $3.00		airmails $4.50
253	Consumer Education	**309**	Martin Luther $2.50
	coil $3.00	**310**	Flag over Supreme Court
254	Knoxville World's		booklet $5.00
	Fair $3.50		**1984**
255	Horatio Alger $3.00	**311**	Alaska Statehood $2.50
256	2¢ Locomotive coil $4.00	**312**	Winter Olympics $4.00
257	Aging Together $3.00	**313**	FDIC $2.50
258	The Barrymores $3.00	**314**	Harry S. Truman $2.50
259	Dr. Mary Walker $3.00	**315**	Love $2.50
260	Peace Garden $3.00	**316**	Carter G. Woodson $2.50
261	America's Libraries $3.00	**317**	11¢ RR Caboose coil $4.00
262	Jackie Robinson $20.00	**318**	Soil and Water
263	4¢ Stagecoach coil $3.00		Conservation $2.50
264	Touro Synagogue $3.00	**319**	Credit Union Act $2.50
265	Wolf Trap	**320**	40¢ Lillian M.
	Farm Park $3.00		Gilbreth $2.50
266	Architecture $3.50	**321**	Orchids $4.00
267	Francis of Assisi $3.00	**322**	Hawaii Statehood $2.50
268	Ponce de Leon $3.00	**323**	7.4¢ Baby Buggy
269	Christmas, Seasons		coil $4.00
	Greetings $4.00	**324**	National Archives $2.50
270	Christmas,	**325**	20¢ Olympics $4.00
	Madonna $3.00	**326**	Louisiana World
271	13¢ Kitten and		Exposition $2.50
	Puppy $3.00	**327**	Health Research $2.50
272	2¢ Igor Stravinsky $3.00	**328**	Douglas Fairbanks $2.50
	1983	**329**	Jim Thorpe $6.00
273	Penalty Mail,	**330**	10¢ Richard Russell $2.50
	(7 stamps, 5 pgs.) $30.00	**331**	John McCormack $2.50
274	Science & Industry $2.50	**332**	St. Lawrence
275	5.2¢ Sleigh coil $4.00		Seaway $2.50
276	Sweden/USA	**333**	Migratory Bird Hunting
	Treaty $2.50		and Conservation
277	3¢ Handcar coil $4.00		Stamp Act $3.00
278	Balloons $4.00	**334**	Roanoke Voyages $2.50
279	Civilian Conservation	**335**	Herman Melville $2.50
	Corps $2.50	**336**	Horace Moses $2.50
280	40¢ Olympics	**337**	Smokey Bear $4.00
	airmail $5.00	**338**	Roberto Clemente $5.00
281	Joseph Priestley $2.50	**339**	30¢ Frank Laubach $2.50
282	Voluntarism $2.50	**340**	Dogs $3.50
283	Concord/German	**341**	Crime Prevention $2.50
	Immigration $2.50	**342**	Family Unity $2.50
284	Physical Fitness $2.50	**343**	Eleanor Roosevelt $2.50
285	Brooklyn Bridge $2.50	**344**	Nation of Readers $2.50
286	TVA $2.50	**345**	Christmas,
287	4¢ Carl Schurz $2.50		Santa Claus $2.50
288	Medal of Honor $2.50	**346**	Christmas,
289	Scott Joplin $2.50		Madonna $2.50
290	Thomas H.	**347**	Hispanic
	Gallaudet $2.50		Americans $2.50
291	28¢ Olympics	**348**	Vietnam Veterans
	airmails $4.00		Memorial $2.50
292	Pearl Buck $2.50		**1985**
293	Babe Ruth $6.00	**349**	Jerome Kern $3.00
294	Nathaniel	**350**	Abraham Baldwin $3.00
	Hawthorne $2.50	**351**	D sheet and coil $3.00
295	3¢ Henry Clay $2.50	**352**	D booklet $6.00
296	13¢ Olympics $4.00	**353**	D Penalty Mail
297	$9.35 Eagle booklet		sheet and coil $3.00
	single $200.00		

354	Alden Partridge $2.50
355	Alfred Verville
	airmail $3.00
356	Lawrence & Elmer
	Sperry airmail $3.00
357	Transpacific
	airmail $3.00
358	50¢ Chester Nimitz $3.00
359	Mary McLeod
	Bethune $2.50
360	39¢ Grenville Clark $2.50
361	6¢ Sinclair Lewis $2.50
362	Duck Decoys $4.00
363	14¢ Iceboat coil $4.00
364	Winter Special
	Olympics $2.50
365	Flag over Capitol
	sheet and coil $3.00
366	Flag over Capitol
	booklet $5.00
367	12¢ Stanley Steamer
	coil $4.00
368	Seashells booklet $6.00
369	Love $2.50
370	10.1¢ Oil Wagon coil $4.00
371	12.5¢ Pushcart coil $4.00
372	John J. Audubon $2.50
373	$10.75 Eagle booklet
	single $75.00
373A	Eagle booklet
	pane of 3 $150.00
374	5.9¢ Tricycle coil $4.00
375	Rural Electrification
	Administration $2.50
376	14¢ and 22¢ Penalty Mail
	sheet and coil $3.00
377	AMERIPEX '86 $2.50
378	9¢ Sylvanus Thayer $2.50
379	3.4¢ School Bus coil $4.00
380	11¢ Stutz Bearcat
	coil $4.00
381	Abigail Adams $2.50
382	4.9¢ Buckboard coil $4.00
383	8.3¢ Ambulance coil $4.00
384	Frederic Bartholdi $2.50
385	8¢ Henry Knox $2.50
386	Korean War
	Veterans $2.50
387	Social Security
	Act $2.50
388	Father Serra
	airmail $3.00
389	Veterans,
	World War I $2.50
390	6¢ Walter Lippmann $2.50
391	Horses $4.00
392	Public Education $2.50
393	Youth $3.50
394	Help End Hunger $2.50
395	21.1¢ Letters $3.00
396	Christmas,
	Poinsettias $2.50
397	Christmas,
	Madonna $2.50
398	18¢ Washington
	coil $3.00
	1986
399	Arkansas
	Statehood $3.00
400	25¢ Jack London $2.50
401	Stamp Collecting
	booklet $5.00
401E	Stamp booklet with
	missing colors $800.00
402	Love $2.50
403	Sojourner Truth $2.50
404	5¢ Hugo L. Black $2.50
405	Republic of Texas $3.00

406	$2 William J. Bryan	$6.00	**457**	Christmas, Madonna	$2.50	
407	Fish booklet	$6.00	**458**	Christmas, Ornaments	$2.50	
408	Public Hospitals	$2.50	**459**	Flag with Fireworks booklet	$2.50	

406 $2 William J. Bryan $6.00
407 Fish booklet $6.00
408 Public Hospitals $2.50
409 Duke Ellington $2.50
410 Presidents SS $30.00
411 Polar Explorers $5.00
412 17¢ Belva Ann Lockwood $2.50
413 1¢ Margaret Mitchell $2.50
414 Statue of Liberty $2.50
415 4¢ Father Flanagan $2.50
416 17¢ Dog Sled coil $4.00
417 56¢ John Harvard $3.00
418 Navajo Blankets $4.00
419 3¢ Dr. Paul Dudley White $2.50
420 $1 Bernard Revel $4.00
421 T.S. Eliot $2.50
422 Wood-Carved Figurines $4.00
423 Christmas, Village Scene $2.50
424 Christmas, Madonna $2.50
425 5.5¢ Star Route Truck coil $4.00
426 25¢ Bread Wagon coil $4.00

1987
427 8.5¢ Tow Truck coil $4.00
428 Michigan Statehood $3.00
429 Pan American Games $2.50
430 1987 Love $2.50
431 7.1¢ Tractor coil $4.00
432 14¢ Julia Ward Howe $2.50
433 Jean Baptiste Pointe Du Sable $2.50
434 Enrico Caruso $2.50
435 2¢ Mary Lyon $2.50
436 2¢ Reengraved Locomotive coil $4.00
437 Girl Scouts $3.00
438 10¢ Canal Boat coil $4.00
439 Special Occasions booklet $8.00
440 United Way $2.50
441 Flag with Fireworks $2.50
442 Flag coil with pre-phosphored paper $5.00
443 American Wildlife Series, (5 pages) $40.00
444 Delaware Statehood $3.00
445 U.S./Morocco Diplomatic Relations $2.50
446 William Faulkner $2.50
447 Lacemaking $5.00
448 10¢ Red Cloud $2.50
449 $5 Bret Harte $15.00
450 Pennsylvania Statehood $3.00
451 Constitution booklet $5.00
452 New Jersey Statehood $3.00
453 Signing of Constitution $2.50
454 Certified Public Accountants $2.50
455 17.5¢ Racing Car and 5¢ Milk Wagon coils $4.00
456 Locomotives booklet $8.00

457 Christmas, Madonna $2.50
458 Christmas, Ornaments $2.50
459 Flag with Fireworks booklet $2.50

1988
460 Georgia Statehood $3.50
461 Connecticut Statehood $3.50
462 1988 Winter Olympics $2.50
463 Australia Bicentennial $2.50
464 James Weldon Johnson $3.00
465 Cats $4.00
466 Massachusetts Statehood $3.50
467 Maryland Statehood $3.50
468 3¢ Conestoga Wagon coil $4.00
469 Knute Rockne $3.50
470 E sheet and coil $3.00
471 E booklet $8.00
472 E Penalty Mail coil $3.50
473 New Sweden airmail $3.50
474 Pheasant booklet $8.00
475 Jack London booklet (6) $6.00
476 Jack London booklet (10) $8.00
477 Flag with Clouds $2.50
478 Samuel Langley airmail $3.50
479 20¢ Penalty Mail coil $3.50
480 Flag over Yosemite coil $3.50
481 South Carolina Statehood $3.50
482 Owl/Grosbeak booklet $7.00
483 15¢ Buffalo Bill Cody $2.50
484 15¢ & 25¢ Penalty Mail coils $4.00
485 Francis Ouimet $2.50
486 45¢ Dr. Harvey Cushing $3.00

487 New Hampshire Statehood $3.50
488 Igor Sikorsky airmail $3.50
489 Virginia Statehood $3.50
490 10.1¢ Oil Wagon precancel coil $4.00
491 25¢ Love $2.50
492 Flag with Clouds booklet $8.00
493 16.7¢ Popcorn Wagon coil $4.00
494 15¢ Tugboat coil $4.00
495 13.2¢ Coal Car coil $4.00
496 New York Statehood $3.50
497 45¢ Love $3.00
498 8.4¢ Wheelchair coil $4.00
499 21¢ RR Mail Car coil $4.00
500 Summer Olympics $3.00
501 Classic Cars booklet $7.00
502 7.6¢ Carretta coil $4.00
503 Honeybee coil $2.50
504 Antarctic Explorers $4.00
505 5.3¢ Elevator coil $4.00
506 20.5¢ Fire Engine coil $4.00
507 Carousel Animals $3.50
508 $8.75 Eagle $20.00
509 Christmas, Traditional $2.50
510 Christmas, Contemporary $2.50
511 24.1¢ Tandem Bicycle coil $4.00
512 20¢ Cable Car coil $4.00
513 13¢ Police Patrol Wagon coil $4.00
514 65¢ General Hap Arnold $3.50
515 23¢ Mary Cassatt $2.50
516 21¢ Sitting Bull $2.50
517 Messages Booklet $4.00

*Numbers and pricing for 1988 issues subject to change.

Prices are courtesy of Charles D. Simmons, a stamp dealer specializing in Souvenir Pages.

Special Occasions Stamps Booklet

Diversity in Richness

...can Commemorative Panels are rich—rich in heritage, rich in
...on, rich in beauty. Special engraved reproductions and exquisite s...
...mbine to form a treasured philatelic collectible.
...h Panel is devoted to a separate commemorative stamp and is a wo...
...in itself, worthy of framing, exhibiting and sharing. A block of fo...
...issued, mint-condition stamps are mounted on an 8½ by 11¼ ″ par...
...vy, high-quality paper. The stamps' subject is portrayed in words a...
...es. Objects of true craftsmanship, American Commemorative Pan...
...coming increasingly popular with collectors.
...e the series began in 1972, thousands of stamp collectors have bec...
...r subscribers to USPS American Commemorative Panels. Because
...re printed in limited editions, the panels are available on an advanc...
...iption basis. For details, use the postage-paid request card followin...
...12 or write to:

Guide
...emorative Panel Program
...lic Sales Division
...States Postal Service
...gton, D.C. 20265-9993

American Commemorative Panels

The Postal Service offers American Commemorative Panels for each new commemorative stamp and special Christmas and Love stamp issued. The series began in 1972 with the Wildlife Commemorative Panel and will total 320 panels by the end of 1988. The panels feature mint stamps complemented by fine reproductions of steel line engravings and the stories behind the commemorated subjects.

1972
1	Wildlife	$15.00
2	Mail Order	$13.00
3	Osteopathic Medicine	$15.00
4	Tom Sawyer	$13.00
5	Pharmacy	$15.00
6	Christmas, Angels	$18.00
7	Christmas, Santa Claus	$18.00
7E	No. 7 with error date (1882)	$750.00
8	Stamp Collecting	$13.00

1973
9	Love	$16.00
10	Pamphleteers	$14.00
11	George Gershwin	$15.00
12	Posting of the Broadside	$14.00
13	Copernicus	$14.00
14	Postal People	$14.00
15	Harry S. Truman	$17.00
16	Post Rider	$14.00
17	Boston Tea Party	$42.00
18	Electronics	$14.00
19	Robinson Jeffers	$14.00
20	Lyndon B. Johnson	$17.00
21	Henry O. Tanner	$14.00
22	Willa Cather	$14.00
23	Drummer	$17.00
24	Angus Cattle	$14.00
25	Christmas, Madonna	$18.00
26	Christmas, Needlepoint Tree	$18.00

1974
27	VFW	$15.00
28	Robert Frost	$15.00
29	EXPO '74	$17.00
30	Horse Racing	$17.00
31	Skylab	$23.00
32	Universal Postal Union	$17.00
33	Mineral Heritage	$20.00
34	First Kentucky Settlement	$15.00
35	Continental Congress	$17.00
35A	No. 35 with corrected Logo	$150.00
36	Chautauqua	$15.00
37	Kansas Wheat	$15.00
38	Energy Conservation	$15.00
39	Sleepy Hollow	$15.00
40	Retarded Children	$15.00
41	Christmas, Currier & Ives	$22.00
42	Christmas, Angel Altarpiece	$22.00

1975
43	Benjamin West	$16.00
44	Pioneer	$25.00
45	Collective Bargaining	$16.00
46	Contributors to the Cause	$16.00
47	Mariner 10	$25.00
48	Lexington & Concord	$18.00
49	Paul Laurence Dunbar	$16.00
50	D. W. Griffith	$16.00
51	Bunker Hill	$18.00
52	Military Uniforms	$18.00
53	Apollo Soyuz	$25.00
54	World Peace Through Law	$16.00
54A	With August 15, 1975 date	$150.00
55	Women's Year	$16.00
56	Postal Service Bicentennial	$20.00
57	Banking and Commerce	$18.00
58	Christmas, Prang Card	$23.00
59	Christmas, Madonna	$23.00

1976
60	Spirit of '76	$25.00
61	Interphil 76	$24.00
62	State Flags	$50.00
63	Telephone	$18.00
64	Commercial Aviation	$25.00
65	Chemistry	$18.00
66	Benjamin Franklin	$20.00
67	Declaration of Independence	$20.00
68	Olympics	$22.00
69	Clara Maass	$19.00
70	Adolph Ochs	$19.00
70A	Same with Charter Logo	$25.00
71	Christmas, Winter Pastime	$25.00
72	Christmas, Nativity	$25.00
72A	Same with Charter Logo	$30.00

1977
73	Washington at Princeton	$30.00
73A	Same with Charter Logo	$30.00
74	Sound Recording	$45.00
74A	Same with Charter Logo	$45.00
75	Pueblo Pottery	$150.00
75A	Same with Charter Logo	$150.00
76	Solo Transatlantic Flight	$160.00
77	Colorado Statehood	$33.00
78	Butterflies	$36.00
79	Lafayette	$33.00
80	Skilled Hands	$33.00
81	Peace Bridge	$33.00
82	Battle of Oriskany	$33.00
83	Alta, CA, Civil Settlement	$33.00
84	Articles of Confederation	$33.00
85	Talking Pictures	$34.00

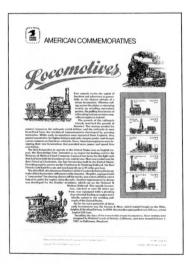

1986

255	Arkansas Statehood	$8.00
256	Stamp Collecting	$10.00
257	Love	$10.00
258	Sojourner Truth	$8.00
259	Republic of Texas	$8.00
260	Fish	$10.00
261	Public Hospitals	$8.00
262	Duke Ellington	$8.00
263	U.S. Presidents' Sheet #1	$10.00
264	U.S. Presidents' Sheet #2	$10.00
265	U.S. Presidents' Sheet #3	$10.00
266	U.S. Presidents' Sheet #4	$10.00
267	Polar Explorers	$9.00
268	Statue of Liberty	$10.00
269	Navajo Blankets	$9.00
270	T.S. Eliot	$8.00
271	Woodcarved Figurines	$9.00
272	Christmas, Madonna	$10.00
273	Christmas, Village Scene	$10.00

1987

274	Michigan Statehood	$8.00
275	Pan American Games	$8.00
276	Love	$8.00
277	Jean Baptiste Du Sable	$8.00
278	Enrico Caruso	$8.00
279	Girl Scouts	$8.00
280	Special Occasions	$8.00
281	United Way	$8.00
282	#1 American Wildlife	$10.00
283	#2 American Wildlife	$10.00
284	#3 American Wildlife	$10.00
285	#4 American Wildlife	$10.00
286	#5 American Wildlife	$10.00
287	Delaware Statehood	$8.00
288	Morocco/U.S. Diplomatic Relations	$8.00
289	William Faulkner	$8.00
290	Lacemakers	$8.00
291	Pennsylvania Statehood	$8.00
292	Constitution Booklet	$8.00
293	New Jersey Statehood	$8.00
294	Signing of the Constitution	$8.00
295	Certified Public Accountants	$8.00
296	Locomotives	$8.00
297	Christmas, Madonna	$10.00
298	Christmas, Ornaments	$9.00

1988*

299	Georgia Statehood	$8.00
300	Connecticut Statehood	$8.00
301	Winter Olympics	$10.00
302	Australia	$8.00
303	James Weldon Johnson	$8.00
304	Cats	$10.00
305	Massachusetts Statehood	$8.00
306	Maryland Statehood	$8.00
307	Knute Rockne	$10.00
308	New Sweden	$8.00
309	South Carolina Statehood	$8.00
310	Francis Ouimet	$8.00
311	New Hampshire Statehood	$8.00
312	Virginia Statehood	$8.00
313	Love	$8.00
314	New York Statehood	$8.00
315	Classic Cars	$10.00
316	Summer Olympics	$10.00
317	Antarctic Explorers	$8.00
318	Carousel Animals	$8.00
319	Christmas, Traditional	$10.00
320	Christmas, Contemporary	$9.00

*1988 issues subject to change.

Prices are courtesy of
the American Society of
Philatelic Pages and Panels,
an organization specializing
in Commemorative Panels.

NO POSTAGE
NECESSARY IF
MAILED IN THE
UNITED STATES

BUSINESS REPLY MAIL
First Class, Permit No. 73026, Washington, D.C.

OFFICIAL BUSINESS
Penalty for Private Use $300

United States Postal Service
Philatelic Sales Division
Washington, DC 20265-9980

Additional Information on Subscription Services

*You can expand your stamp collection and keep it updated
with philatelic products from the USPS. Check the box next
to the subscription services you'd like to learn more about.*

☐ *Standing Order Service*
☐ *Commemorative Stamp Club*
☐ *Souvenir Page Program*
☐ *American Commemorative Panels*

…And **Free** Offers!

*Let us know which complimentary offers you're interested
in receiving.*

☐ *Two tickets to WORLD STAMP EXPO '89*
☐ *A copy of the **Philatelic Catalog***

*Neatly print your name and address below, and drop this card
in the mail—no postage necessary.*

Information that you provide is protected and only disclosed in accordance
with the Privacy Act of 1974.

Mr./Mrs./Ms.

Street Address
(Include P.O. Box, Apt. No., R.D. Route, etc. where appropriate)

City   State   ZIP Code

Please detach at perforation.

Souvenir Cards

These cards were issued as souvenirs of the philatelic gatherings at which they were distributed by the United States Postal Service or its predecessor, the United States Post Office Department. They were not valid for postage.

The forerunner of the souvenir cards is the 1938 Philatelic Truck souvenir sheet which the Post Office Department issued and distributed in various cities visited by the Philatelic Truck. It depicts the White House, printed in blue on white paper. Issued with and without gum. Price with gum, *$95,* without gum, *$10.*

First values listed are for uncancelled cards; values in italics are for cards bearing USPS cancels. Values for cancelled cards prior to 1980 are not listed because they vary according to the type of cancel applied. Descriptions include the Scott Catalogue numbers for the U.S. and foreign stamp designs reproduced on the cards, as well as text in languages in addition to English. Prices are courtesy of Brookman Stamp Co. of Bedford, New Hampshire.

United States Post Office & United States Postal Service

1960, BARCELONA 1st International Philatelic Congress, Mar. 26-Apr. 5. Card of 1. #231. 350.00

1968 EFIMEX, International Philatelic Exhibition, Nov. 1-9, Mexico City. Card of 1. #292. Inscribed in Spanish. 3.00

1970 PHILYMPIA, London International Stamp Exhibition, Sept. 18-26. Card of 3. #548-550. 3.00

1971 EXFILIMA '71, 3rd Inter-American Philatelic Exhibition, Nov. 6-14, Lima, Peru. Card of 3, #1111 and 1126, Peru #360. Card inscribed in Spanish. 2.00

1972 BELGICA '72, Brussels International Philatelic Exhibition, June 24-July 9, Brussels, Belgium. Card of 3. #914, 1026 and 1104. Card inscribed in Flemish and French. 1.50

OLYMPIA PHILATELIC MUNCHEN '72, Aug. 18-Sept. 10, Munich, Germany. Card of 4. #1460-1462 and C85. Card inscribed in German. 2.00

EXFILBRA '72, 4th Inter-American Philatelic Exhibition, Aug. 26-Sept. 2, Rio de Janeiro, Brazil. Card of 3. #C14, Brazil #C18-C19. Card inscribed in Portuguese. 2.00

NATIONAL PHILATELIC FORUM VI, Aug. 28-30, Washington, D.C. Card of 4. #1396. 2.00

1973 IBRA '73 Internationale Briefmarken Ausstellung, May 11-20, Munich, Germany. Card of 1. #C13. 2.75

APEX '73, International Airmail Exhibition, July 4-7, Manchester, England. Card of 3, #C3a, Honduras #C12 and Newfoundland #C4. 2.50

POLSKA '73, Swiatowa Wystawe Filatelistyczna, Aug. 19-Sept. 2, Poznan, Poland. Card of 3. #1488 and Poland #1944-1945. Card inscribed in Polish. 2.75

POSTAL PEOPLE, Card of 10. #1489-1498. Distributed to Postal Service employees. Not available to public. $125.00 (est.)

1974 HOBBY, The Hobby Industry Association of America Convention and Trade Show, Feb. 3-6, Chicago, Illinois. Card of 4. #1456-1459. 3.50

INTERNABA, International Philatelic Exhibition, June 7-16, Basel, Switzerland. Card of 8. #1530-1537. Card inscribed in French, German and Italian. 3.50

STOCKHOLMIA '74, International Frimarksustailning, Sept. 21-29, Stockholm, Sweden. Card of 3. #836 and Sweden #300 and 765. Card inscribed in Swedish. 3.50

EXFILMEX '74 Philatelic Exposition Inter-Americana, Oct. 26-Nov. 3, Mexico City, Mexico. Card of 2. #1157 and Mexico #910. Card inscribed in Spanish. 3.50

1975 ESPANA '75, World Stamp Exhibition, Apr. 4-13, Madrid, Spain. Card of 3. #233 and 1271 and Spain #1312. Card inscribed in Spanish. 2.75

ARPHILA '75, June 6-16, Paris, France. Card of 3. #1187 and 1207 and France #1117. Card inscribed in French. 2.75

1976 WERABA '76, Third International Space Stamp Exhibition, Apr. 1-4, Zurich, Switzerland. Card of 2. #1434 and 1435 se-tenant. 5.00

BICENTENNIAL EXPOSITION on Science and Technology, May 30-Sept. 6, Kennedy Space Center, Fla. Card of 1. #C76. 4.00

COLORADO STATEHOOD CENTENNIAL, Aug. 1. Card of 3. #288, 743 and 1670. 4.50

HAFNIA '76, International Stamp Exhibition, Aug. 20-29, Copenhagen, Denmark. Card of 2. #5 and Denmark #2. Card inscribed in Danish. 4.00

ITALIA '76, International Philatelic Exhibition, Oct. 14-24, Milan, Italy. Card of 3. #1168 and Italy #578 and 601. Card inscribed in Italian. 4.00

NORDPOSTA '76, North German Stamp Exhibition, Oct 30-31, Hamburg, Germany. Card of 3. #689 and Germany #B366 and B417. Card inscribed in German. 4.00

1977 AMPHILEX '77, International Philatelic Exhibition, May 26-June 5, Amsterdam, Netherlands. Card of 3. #1027 and Netherlands #41 and 294. Card inscribed in Dutch. 4.00

SAN MARINO '77, International Philatelic Exhibition, Aug. 28-Sept. 4, San Marino. Card of 3. #1-2 and San Marino #1. Card inscribed in Italian. 4.00

1978 ROCPEX '76, International Philatelic Exhibition, Mar. 20-29, Taipei, Taiwan. Card of 6. #1706-1709 and Taiwan #1812 and 1816. Card inscribed in Chinese. 5.00

NAPOSTA '78, International Philatelic Exhibition, May 20-25, Frankfurt, Germany. Card of 3. # 555 and 563 and Germany #1216. Card inscribed in German. 4.00

1979 BRASILIANA '79, International Philatelic Exhibition, Sept. 15-23. Rio de Janeiro, Brazil. Card of 3. #C91-C92 (C92a) and Brazil #1295. Card inscribed in Portuguese. 7.50

JAPEX '79, International Philatelic Exhibition, Nov. 2-4, Tokyo, Japan. Card of 2. #1158 and Japan #1024. Card inscribed in Japanese. 7.50

1980 LONDON '80, International Philatelic Exposition, May 6-14, London, England. Card of 1. #329. 6.00 *30.00*

NORWEX '80, International Philatelic Exposition, June 13-22, Oslo, Norway. Card of 3. #620-621 and Norway #658. Card inscribed in Norwegian. 5.00 *7.50*

ESSEN '80, International Philatelic Exposition, Nov. 15-19, Essen, Germany. Card of 2. #1014 and Germany #723. Card inscribed in German. 5.00 *7.50*

1981 WIPA '81, International Philatelic Exhibition, May 22-31, Vienna, Austria. Card of 2. #1252 and Austria #789. 5.00 *7.50*

NSCM, National Stamp Collecting Month. October. Card of 2. #245 and 1918. 5.00 *7.50*

PHILATOKYO '81, International Philatelic Exhibition, Oct. 9-18, Tokyo, Japan. Card of 2. #1531 and Japan #800. Card inscribed in Japanese. 5.00 *7.50*

NORDPOSTA '81, North German Stamp Exhibition, Nov. 7-8, Hamburg, Germany. Card of 2. #923 and Germany #B538. Card inscribed in German. 5.00 *7.50*

1982 CANADA '82, International Philatelic Youth Exhibition, May 20-24, Toronto, Ontario, Canada. Card of 2. #116 and Canada #15. Card inscribed in French. 5.00 *6.50*

PHILEXFRANCE '82, International Philatelic Exposition, June 11-21, Paris, France. Card of 2. #1753 and France #1480. Card inscribed in French. 4.00 *6.50*

NSCM, National Stamp Collecting Month, Oct. Card of 1. #C3a. 5.50 *6.50*

ESPAMER '82, International Philatelic Exposition, Oct. 12-17, San Juan, Puerto Rico. Card of 3. #810, 1437 and 2024. Card inscribed in Spanish. 5.00 *6.50*

1983 Sweden/U.S. joint stamp issues, Mar. 24, Philadelphia, PA. Card of 3. #958 and 2036 and Sweden #1453. Card inscribed in Swedish. 4.75 *6.50*

GERMAN/U.S. JOINT STAMP ISSUES, Apr. 29, Germantown, PA. Card of 2. #2040 and Germany #1397. Card inscribed in German. 4.75 *6.50*

TEMBAL '83, International Philatelic Exposition, May 21-29, Basil, Switzerland. Card of 2. #C71 and Switzerland #3L1. Card inscribed in German. 4.75 *6.50*

BRASILIANA '83, International Philatelic Exhibition, July 29-Aug. 7, Rio de Janeiro, Brazil. Card of 2. #1 and Brazil #1. 4.75 *6.50*

BANGKOK '83, International Philatelic Exhibition, Aug. 4-13, Bangkok, Thailand. Card of 2. #210 and Thailand #1. Card inscribed in Thai. 4.75 *6.50*

International Philatelic Memento, 1983-84. Card of 1. #1387. 2.50 *4.50*

NSCM, National Stamp Collecting Month, October. Card of 1. #293. 4.00 *6.50*

1984 ESPANA '84, International Philatelic Exhibition, Apr. 27-May 6, Madrid, Spain. Card of 2. #223 and Spain #428. Card inscribed in Spanish. 4.50 *6.50*

HAMBURG '84, International Philatelic Exhibition, June 19-26, Hamburg, Germany. Card of 2. #C66 and Germany #669. Card inscribed in French and German. 4.50 *6.50*

CANADA/U.S. JOINT STAMP ISSUES, June 26, Massena, NY. Card of 2. #1131 and Canada #387. Card inscribed in French.   4.50 *5.50*

AUSIPEX '84, International Philatelic Exhibition, Sept. 21-30, Melbourne, Australia. Card of 2. #290 and Western Australia #1.   4.50 *5.50*

NSCM, National Stamp Collecting Month, October. Card of 1. #2104.   4.00 *5.00*

PHILAKOREA '84, Oct. 22-31, Seoul, Korea. Card of 2. #741 and Korea #994. Card inscribed in Korean.
4.50 *5.50*

1985 INTERNATIONAL PHILATELIC MEMENTO, 1985. Card of 1. #2.   4.50 *5.50*

OLYMPHILEX '85, International Philatelic Exhibition, Mar. 18-24, Lausanne, Switzerland. Card of 2. #C106 and Switzerland #746. Card inscribed in French.   4.50 *5.50*

ISRAPHIL '85, International Philatelic Exhibition, May 14-22, Tel Aviv, Israel. Card of 2. #566 and Israeli #33. Card inscribed in Hebrew.   4.50 *5.50*

ARGENTINA '85, International Philatelic Exhibition, July 5-14, Buenos Aires, Argentina. Card of 2. #1737 and Argentina #B27. Card inscribed in Spanish. 4.50 *5.50*

MOPHILA '85, International Philatelic Exhibition, Sept. 11-15, Hamburg, Germany. Card of 2. #296 and Germany #B595. Card inscribed in German. 4.50 *5.50*

ITALIA '85, International Philatelic Exhibition, Oct. 25-Nov. 3, Rome, Italy. #1107 and Italy #830. Card inscribed in Italian.   4.50 *5.50*

1986 MEMENTO '86, Statue of Liberty Centennial, Mar. 4. Card of 1. #C87.   3.00 *4.00*

STOCKHOLMIA '86, International Philatelic Exhibition, Aug. 28-Sept. 7, Stockholm, Sweden. Card of 2. #113 and Sweden #253. Card inscribed in Swedish.   4.50 *5.50*

1987 CAPEX '87, International Philatelic Exhibition, June 13-21, Toronto, Canada. Card of 2. #569 and Canada #883. Card inscribed in French.   4.00 *5.00*

HAFNIA '87, International Philatelic Exhibition, Oct. 16-25, Copehagen, Denmark. Card of 2. #299 and Denmark #B52. Inscribed in Danish.   4.00 *5.00*

EXPOSITION PHILATELIQUE, Nov. 13-17, Monte Carlo, Monaco. Card of 3. #2287 and 2300 and Monaco #1589. Card inscribed in French.   4.00 *5.00*

1988 FINLANDIA '88, June 1-12, Helsinki, Finland. Card of 2. #836 and Finland's 1988 New Sweden issue. Card inscribed in Finnish.   4.00 *5.00*

 Helsinki, Finland
1-12 June, 1988

Finland recently issued this stamp in commemoration of the 350th anniversary of its first settlement in America.
Suomi julkaisi äskettäin tämän postimerkin Amerikan ensimmäisen suomalaissiirtokunnan 350-vuotisjuhlan kunniaksi.

The United States issued this stamp in 1938 to note the 300th anniversary of Finnish and Swedish settlement in America.
Yhdysvallat julkaisi tämän postimerkin 1938 Amerikan suomalais-ja ruotsalaisasutuksen 300-vuotisjuhlan vuoksi.

FINLANDIA 88, the largest philatelic exhibition ever held in Finland, celebrates the 350th anniversary of the first post office established in Finland.
Suomen postilaitoksen perustamisen 350-vuotisjuhlien yhteydessä järjestetään FINLANDIA 88, joka on suurin Suomessa järjestetty postimerkkinäyttely.

The U.S. Postal Service is pleased to issue this souvenir card in honor of FINLANDIA 88.
USA:n postilaitos julkaisee tämän näyttelykortin FINLANDIA 88-näyttelyn kunniaksi.

© USPS 1988

315

Subject Index

IMPORTANT NOTE: This Index covers all issues from the 1893 Columbian Exposition issues (#230) through 1988. Listings in italic typeface refer to Definitive or Regular issues. The numbers listed next to the stamp description are the Scott numbers, and the numbers in parenthesis are the numbers of the pages on which the stamps are illustrated.

316

319

322

323

328